THE MENDIPS

THE MENDIPS

A. W. COYSH E. J. MASON
V. WAITE

ROBERT HALE AND COMPANY
63 Old Brompton Road, London S.W.7

First published (*in the* Regional Series) *March, 1954*
Reprinted June, 1954
Reprinted November, 1956
Second edition, 1962
Third edition October, 1971

ISBN 0 7091 2244 6

MADE AND PRINTED IN GREAT BRITAIN BY
WILLIAM CLOWES AND SONS, LIMITED
LONDON, BECCLES AND COLCHESTER

ACKNOWLEDGMENTS

To the many people who in various ways have given valuable and unstinted help in obtaining information and material for this book the authors wish to record their indebtedness. Special thanks are due to the following individuals and organisations: the Axbridge Caving Club, H. E. Balch, J. H. Harwood of the National Coal Board, Bristol Exploration Club, Butler and Tanner Ltd., C. E. Burnell, the Cave Diving Group, Christopher Chapman, C. R. Clinker, Edward Cockey and Sons Ltd., R. N. Cove, Canon S. J. Christelow, J. Dewar of British Railways, J. W. Duck, Islwyn Evans of the National Coal Board, Gough's Caves, R. E. F. Heal of Banwell, Eric Hobbis, Hugh Hobhouse of Oakhill, The Lord Hylton, Sir Geoffrey Hippisley-Cox, Mrs Dorrien Mason, the Bristol Waterworks Company, John Norman, A. M. Quick, the Rev. Santo Read, Mrs Dorothy Rowlands, Bert Russell, the Rev. K. C. Scott, J. W. Singer and Sons Ltd., E. W. Sharpe, Dom Alphege Shebbeare of Downside Abbey, Mary Snelson, Allan Stockdale, Dr Mary Somers, M. Unwin, C. Victor White, the late J. W. Walker, F.R.C.S., Wookey Hole Caves Ltd.

CONTENTS

ILLUSTRATIONS

LINE ILLUSTRATIONS

ACKNOWLEDGMENTS

The line illustrations, with the exception of Wookey Hole Cave drawn by J. D. Hanwell, are by Gunnel Beech and the sketch map of the area was drawn by A. E. Taylor. Illustrations Nos. 10 and 21 are reproduced from photographs taken by Reece Winstone, Bristol; No. 24 is by permission of the National Coal Board; the remaining illustrations are reproduced from photographs taken by D. A. Coase.

CHAPTER I

"ON MENDIP"

MOST people have a feeling for places. They visit a place once, like it, and return again and again—for holidays in the same rocky cove; to fish for trout on the same stretch of river; to climb the same rock faces. And with the years the sentiment grows, until place seems to belong to person, and person to place. That is how I have come to feel about the Mendips. I have known these hills for nearly forty years under most conditions and at all seasons—in rain and in snow, in summer sunshine and autumn mist.

As a small boy I was taken by my parents by the little railway from Bristol which swung round through Yatton and Congresbury to Burrington. And there, with my elder brother, I explored the tiny valleys of the twin streams which flow down the face of Black Down. As a schoolboy I scrambled through the small swallet entrance to the newly discovered Read's Cavern and slithered in dungarees over wet clay slopes to the boulder-strewn floor below. I well remember the look of horror on the faces of my experienced caving guides when I committed sacrilege by catching my head against a small curtain of stalactite, which shattered and fell tinkling to the rocks beneath. In my early twenties I searched for fossils in Mendip quarries and on coal-tips. I cycled along the by-roads and free-wheeled down the long two-mile hill into Wells when the flats below were enveloped in a sea of rolling white mist from which Glastonbury Tor stood out as a mysterious island. I have leaned on the gates of Mendip farms and listened to the slow, shrewd words of the farmers. Today these hills have an irresistible attraction for me—an attraction which has grown slowly as I have come to know them. My respect for the people who live and work there has grown too. And I am not alone in that: if you start a conversation with a farmer or farm-worker in one of the nearby lowland villages it will not be long before he refers to what his neighbours do "on Mendip". It is a phrase which often implies much more than a mere geographical location—a deep respect for those who live and work where nature demands a stubborn toughness and where success is hard won.

Many times I have travelled by plane from Bristol Airport to the Channel Islands. The route takes you above the Mendip plateau, and for the first time I saw the whole long line of hills stretching from the Wiltshire border, near Frome, to the headland of Brean Down pointing out into the Bristol Channel towards the last outpost of Mendip—the island of Steep Holm. From the air you realise clearly for the first time that there are really three contrasting types of Mendip country. To the west beyond the main Bristol to Bridgwater road the hills break up into a number of smaller ridges—Sandford Hill, Banwell Hill, Bleadon Hill, Wavering Down with Crook's Peak, and Brean Down. Then there is the wide tableland of the Central Mendips which extends from the Bridgwater road to the Wells road—upland country with a bare, bleak landscape of rolling olive-green fields bordered by grey loose-stone walls. Occasional clusters of windswept firs or beeches huddle together in the hollows and a few gaunt chimneys of derelict mines bear witness to a former prosperity. Its remoteness and level surface give this Mendip land a strange desolation. It is a place of rapidly changing moods: when the sun shines the sky is full of larks and the wind whistles crisply through the bracken with a note of almost sardonic cheerfulness; but on wet days the blinding rain drives down mercilessly and sullen mists blot out the landscape.

The Mendip country east of the Bristol to Wells road is different again, for here the plateau tapers and sinks gradually down in confused undulations to the town of Frome. It is softer country, with a field pattern that differs less in character from the farmlands of the valleys, except that enclosures are still often bounded by stone walls, though pithead gear and occasional tips of waste mark the presence of coal mines on the northern side.

The great traffic arteries which bring holiday-makers each summer from the Midlands and North of England to the South Coast and to Devon and Cornwall cross over the Mendip Hills, yet for every traveller who pauses to see something of the real character of the country, hundreds of thousands pass by with no more than a glance from a train or car window. The main roads fan out from Bristol to Bridgwater and Wells; the chief rail route, known as the "Somerset and Dorset", once ran from Bath through Radstock to Shepton Mallet. And many visitors stop just short of the Mendips at Weston-super-Mare. To begin this book it may be useful to take these routes in turn and to examine the country they pass through.

When you leave Bristol by the Bridgwater road, the Mendips are first seen from Lulsgate Bottom, disappearing and reappearing as the road dips and rises until you reach the top of Redhill where the full line of the hills comes into view. Ahead lies the single sandstone ridge of Black Down, a smooth outline of heather moor where the peaty soil is covered with ling, heath, rough grass, and whortleberry. To the west are the ridges of Banwell, Bleadon, and Brean Down.

At the bottom of Redhill you pass close to Cowslip Green, a pleasant house a few hundred yards along a turning to the left. For many years it was the home of Hannah More, whose work in the Mendips had a profound effect on the farmers and labourers, and the miners for lead and calamine, for whose children she established day schools in many of the villages. Her influence is gratefully recalled to this day. This is the valley of the Blagdon Yeo (there are several rivers called Yeo in Somerset), though you are not likely to notice the river as you pass over Perry Bridge. It is a small, sluggish stream, for most of the water has been impounded in the Yeo Reservoir, two miles away. At Langford, the main road crosses a branch of the old Great Western Railway. This branch links the main line at Yatton with Congresbury, Wrington, Burrington, and Blagdon, but it is now nearly fifty years since it was in regular use.

The slopes of Dolebury Warren which now lie ahead can be seen across the parkland of Langford Court. They are well wooded, as are many of the northern parts of Mendip, and in one place the trees sweep from the very crest of the hill to the flat fields below. Among the trees there once stood Mendip Lodge which was built towards the end of the eighteenth century by Dr Whalley, an eccentric clergyman, and was visited during his lifetime by Mrs Siddons, Hannah More, de Quincey and many other notabilities. Whalley had married the wealthy heiress of Langford Court before he begun to build the cottage that was later to become Mendip Lodge. "This little *maison de plaisance*", wrote the editor of his *Journals and Correspondence*, "was added to from time to time till it grew into a mansion, and in the meanwhile the mountain site on which it was built became clothed with firs and deciduous trees. This was the first experiment which had been made of planting upon the Mendips, and ill were the general auguries of success, but the thousands of acres which now adorn the slopes of the hills owe their existence to this beginning." Most of the fine wood planted in Dr Whalley's time was felled and sold during the timber-hungry years of the 1914–18 war, but the slopes are still well covered with overgrown laurel and rhododendron bushes and occasional deciduous trees.

From the village of Churchill, near the western end of Dolebury

Warren, the road begins to rise across a low pass which takes it between the western ridges of the Mendips and the main massif, and by the roadside you can see the steeply inclined strata of the grey mountain limestone which forms the main part of the hills. But the climb is short: at a little over 300 feet the land flattens as the road passes through Sidcot, where there is a well-known Quaker co-educational boarding-school which can be traced back to an earlier school established here in 1699. To the west, under the lee of Wavering Down, lies the tower of Winscombe church; to the east the steep slopes of Shute Shelve Hill show the typical limestone scenery of Mendip where the grey rock comes close to the surface and the shallow soil is covered with short turf and stunted hawthorn bushes. In summer passing motorists park on the grassy verges of this unfenced stretch of road for a picnic meal and to admire the view across the plain below.

Anyone with an hour or so to spare can walk from Shute Shelve over Wavering Down to Crook's Peak, with one of the finest views in Somerset. After passing through a small wood the track follows a grey stone wall past a lonely farmhouse, and then an easy climb gives fine views on either side. The path then drops down over the ridge and rounds the flank of Crook's Peak. A short scramble over the last rocky ledge of the hill brings you to the summit. To the north there are the green uplands and wooded valleys towards Clevedon; to the east the bulk of Black Down rises above the curving range of the Mendips; to the west there is the glitter of the Channel bending into Bridgwater Bay; and over the water in the distance the dark outlines of the Welsh mountains stand out against the horizon. Out of the great flat moorland plain, cross-ruled by the silver streaks of rhines lined with willows, Brent Knoll rises up like the island it once was, and farther south the Quantocks push their way into the sea, with Dunkery Beacon showing a darker purple behind them. The lower line of the Poldens and the Blackdown Hills sweeps round to Glastonbury Tor and the Vale of Avalon, the traditional cradle of Christianity in Britain.

The motorist who is prepared to lengthen the journey to Bridgwater by three or four miles may take an alternative route after leaving Churchill, turning left about a mile beyond the village where there is a signpost to Cheddar. The roadside fields as far as Shipham are rough and hummocky where the grass has grown over old mineral workings.

The village of Shipham is set in so quiet a hollow in the hills that it is difficult to believe that little more than one hundred and fifty years ago it had the reputation of being the toughest of all the mining villages . . . "the people savage and depraved almost even beyond Cheddar, brutal in their natures, and ferocious in their manners". The lead mining and digging for calamine have long since ceased on Mendip; today the chief occupation, after farming, is probably quarrying. You are soon aware of this, for a mile beyond Shipham there are large limestone quarries on either side of the road producing lime and road metal. The clatter of the machines fills the air and they throw out a fine dust which in dry spells during the summer settles on the trees and hedges of the valley, turning them a pale grey, so that from a distance they look as though they are covered with hoar-frost. Here the road drops steeply to the Cheddar Valley, where the red soil of the gentle southern slopes is cultivated intensively, producing early strawberries, especially for North Country and Midland markets. In the month of June you can buy Cheddar strawberries in chip baskets from roadside stalls which are set up during the short picking season. As you descend the hill many of the larger strawberry fields lie away to the West, with Cheddar Reservoir beyond them. To reach the Bridgwater road again you turn right through the narrow street of Axbridge.

But if you have never seen Cheddar Gorge, it lies only a mile to the east. In summer it is easier to walk than to take a car, for the approach roads are often congested with holiday traffic; in any case the cliffs rise so abruptly that it is quite impossible to see them properly from a saloon car. I like Cheddar best in the spring, before the crowds come. The little shops and cafés are freshly painted and have an expectant air, and the jackdaws chatter and scream as they carry building materials for their nests on the rock ledges.

The first flowers are coming into bloom in spring and early summer, and the vegetation which grows from the joints and crevices of the rock —yew, ivy, ash and whitebeam—is freshly green. In June, red valerian flowers freely. Unfortunately, the famous Cheddar pink (*Dianthus glaucus*), which was first recorded here in 1696, is now very rare, but it still grows with other flowering plants on some of the more inaccessible limestone ledges, and nowhere else in England, except perhaps in the gardens of some of those visitors who have taken plants away. Many of the wild flowers of the cliffs drop their seeds on the banks and screes below, where they grow and flourish, especially the yellow Welsh poppy and the ox-eye daisy. There are many caves at Cheddar; two of the larger and more spectacular groups have been lit by electricity and are open to visitors.

The second main traffic artery across the Mendips lies some ten miles east of the Bridgwater Road and connects Bristol with Wells. There is also a branch road to Shepton Mallet. These roads cross the plateau from Farrington Gurney, which lies to the north of the Mendips and serves both hill and valley land. The village has a blacksmith's shop, builders' yards, and a weekly market which centres on a fine old house built of mellow red sandstone which stands at the crossroads near the foot of Rush Hill, half hidden in summer by two large acacia trees. On Mondays, farmers from all over the district gather round the cattle and sheep pens, or bargain with the owners of the stalls where buckets and rubber boots, hand tools, seeds, and veterinary sundries are sold. In the old courtyard behind the house are the cages for poultry, and one of the back doors leads to the auctioneer's office.

Rush Hill winds up from Farrington Gurney to plateau country just over 500 feet above sea-level, and here the scenery begins to change. There are fewer large trees and fewer hedges. Many of the fields are separated by grey stone walls built of mountain or lias limestone, and there is hardly a building to be seen until you drop down into the village of Chewton Mendip with its superb Perpendicular church tower. The road climbs again still higher and continues in a dead straight line for several miles until it reaches the southern slopes of the Mendips and descends in a long, curving hill for some two miles into the city of Wells.

On the plateau, half a mile beyond Green Ore, an avenue of beech trees fringes the road on the eastern side and, in summer, long-distance motor coaches slow down so that the drivers may point out an unusual monument to their passengers. On a well-made stone wall four slender concrete pillars support a slab on which a she-wolf stands suckling two human babes. On the slab are the words GAETANO CELESTRA. Towards the end of the last world war a number of Italian prisoners were interned in Penlee Camp between Wells and Wookey, now used by a firm making parts for television sets. Some of these prisoners were sent to surrounding farms as agricultural workers—among them Gaetano Celestra, a mason and builder by trade, who was billeted on a farm where he fed the pigs and made himself generally useful. One day he pulled out a 50-lire note and showed the farmer an engraving of Romulus and Remus on the back, asking if he might use his spare time to make a model based on this engraving. Thinking he meant a small ornament of some kind the farmer readily agreed. A few days later he was surprised to see in his outhouse a large wire frame on which Celestra was plastering soft concrete with his hands—shaping and smoothing it to form the statue now seen by the roadside. This was erected at Hill Grove in 1945 when the Italians were no longer restricted to farm work. Celestra, as a mason, had been given the job of repairing the boundary wall and of rebuilding it at one point where it had been entirely destroyed by a small bomb. Here he was allowed to mount his hollow statue. The cavity has since provided a home for several families of blue-tits; I have several times watched a parent bird, bringing food to its young, pass in and out of the wolf's mouth. And one year it was used by a swarm of bees as a hive.

When the time came for the repatriation of Italian prisoners, Celestra opted to stay in Britain, for although born of Italian parents he had lived all his life in North Africa until he joined the army. Later he lived in Chewton Mendip and worked on contract, rebuilding and repairing many of the old stone walls.

A very pleasant detour from the Wells road gives an excellent impression of the Mendip plateau. Take the first turning to the right after leaving Chewton Mendip, towards the village of Priddy. The road climbs past the woods of Eaker Hill to over 900 feet, where it crosses obliquely the route of an old Roman road before passing over the slight ridge of North Hill. This is an area rich in archæological remains. To the north lie three hut circles, to the south are Ashen Hill Barrows, Priddy Nine Barrows, and the caverns of East Water and Swildon's Hole.

On the right are the kennels of the Mendip Farmers' Hunt, which operates over the whole of the Central Mendips from East Harptree to Dinder Wood and from Priddy Pool to Chilcompton, and also over some of the lower farmlands to the north.

Most of these plateau roads have wide grass verges. At one time they were probably grass droves between stone walls along which sheep and cattle were driven from place to place. Today only the centre strip is metalled, and the flat verges are ideal for parking a car on a summer day. They abound with wild flowers. Early in the season white ribbons of flowering cow-parsley almost obscure the boundary walls, and occasional hawthorn bushes are heavy with blossom. In early July there is an invasion of colour: sometimes a patch of red poppies, sometimes a strip purple with mallow or bright yellow with buttercups, and on the grey walls vivid patches of yellow stonecrop or brave clumps of herb-robert with bright red stems. Later follow heavy-scented meadow-sweet, yarrow, knapweed and—unfortunately for the farmer—yellow ragwort. All the same, I hope these verges will never be sprayed with modern weed-killers. It would destroy one of the loveliest features of these upland by-roads.

The little patches of deciduous woodland are well worth a visit if you are interested in wild flowers, for there you may well see the blue gromwell, a relatively rare plant which flowers more freely on Mendip than anywhere else in the country. In November and December, when the last leaves have fallen from the few roadside hedges, the bare branches are festooned with the smoky-grey "wool" of old man's-beard or traveller's joy—a plant which flourishes on these shallow limestone soils.

The first road on the left after passing the Mendip kennels, leads to the village of Priddy, which is fully described elsewhere. Here you are in the heart of Mendip. On a day when visibility is poor the return to the main road is best made by travelling almost due east past Hunters Lodge Inn. But if the day is fine and clear, pass through the village and take the narrow road to the south, for on the brow of the hill, above the village of Westbury, magnificent views of Somerset and of the distant hills of Dorset lie ahead. Below the road and railway keep close to the hills above the old marshlands, and away to the left the rocks of Ebbor Gorge (National Trust) show above a patch of hillside woodland. It is, in fact, possible to drive along this narrow track past Ebbor Farm and the Paper Mill at Wookey Hole to Wells.

An alternative route across the Mendips from Farrington Gurney leads to Shepton Mallet, swinging left from the main Wells Road at the top of Rush Hill. Here a double row of beech trees marks the western boundary of Ston Easton Park, which was laid out by John Hippisley-Coxe in the second half of the eighteenth century, though the fine Georgian house is unfortunately not visible from the road. Beyond the village of Ston Easton the road crosses the main Bath to Wells road at Old Down Inn, now painted conspicuously in cream and green, and a useful landmark on a misty night. Its appearance is deceptive, for at first glance it looks to be a relatively new building. It is, in fact, an old coaching house where the Commissioners of the Wells Turnpike Trust sometimes met. In 1774 it was possible to travel from Bath to Old Down Inn by post-chaise for a sum of ten shillings and sixpence.

Beyond Old Down the road passes through limestone country which has been extensively quarried for many years. In fact, the villages of Gurney Slade and Binegar owe their very existence to the quarries. The workmen's cottages are simply built of stone and the garden walls are draped with ivy and cotoneaster. At one time many of the men who worked during the summer in the quarries would spend the winter working in the famous brewery at Oakhill, less than two miles away. But today quarrying employs fewer than it did formerly, partly because it is not possible to push on with road making and repairing schemes as rapidly as some would wish, partly because the work in the quarries is now more highly mechanised. From Gurney Slade the road climbs over Beacon Hill, by-passes Shepton Mallet, and joins the ancient Fosseway at Cannard's Grave.

Apart from the main roads which cross the Mendips there was, until its closure in 1960 under the Beeching plan, a through rail route from the Midlands to the South which, between the Somerset city of Bath and the Dorset coast, was known as the Somerset and Dorset Railway, or affectionately as the "Slow and Dirty" or "Slow and Doubtful", though once defended by an engine-driver I spoke to as the "Sweet and Delightful". It was inevitably slow at times between Bath and Shepton Mallet, for the gradients on either side of the Mendips average 1 in 50. A single engine took some eight passenger coaches along this stretch, but longer trains, including the famous "Pines Express", added a pilot engine, and freight trains used bank engines. The Somerset and Dorset maintained its identity after nationalisation and will obviously be remembered as such, for it can be described in no other way. It did not fall naturally into any one part of the Regional system of British Railways. It was operated by Southern Region; commercially the northern part which crossed the Mendips was linked with the Western Region and staffed by Western Region men, and it used some old L.M.S. engines which were specially built to operate on the line, and also old L.M.S. brake-vans on the freight trains which enabled the guard to couple and uncouple the bank engines with a long iron hook while the train was in motion.

From Bath the line tunnels through Combe Down to Midford and then follows the valley of the Wellow Brook to Radstock along the route once taken by an old horse-drawn tramway which brought coal from the Somerset Coalfield to a canal at Midford linked with the Kennet and Avon Canal. Some coal mines with their pithead gear and tips of waste could be seen from the carriage windows as the train slowed down when approaching Radstock—Writhlington Colliery to the left and Braysdown Colliery to the right.

From Radstock the trains began a long, slow climb along the slopes of Norton Hill below Norton Hill Colliery, then an up-to-date and flourishing mine, before reaching the station of Midsomer Norton South. It was joined by a mineral line from the colliery, which provided the chief freight carried on the Somerset and Dorset line—coal for industrial use in the southern counties. Over much of the Somerset coalfield the coal measures are covered by Jurassic strata, and in the railway cuttings nearby, where they are not too overgrown with vegetation, you can occasionally see horizontal beds of lias limestones and clays.

At Chilcompton the steepest part of the climb was over and the train gained speed a little. It crossed the main road from Bristol to Shepton Mallet at Marchant's Hill, near Old Down Inn, and wound its way past deep quarries of grey mountain limestone to Binegar Station. Here passengers and staff were warned of the approach of "a passenger train booked to stop" by an old brass handbell inscribed S.C.R. which was normally kept in the signal-box. This dated back to the period before 1862 when the Somerset Central Railway was amalgamated with the Dorset Central Railway. On the left-hand side of the line at Binegar a large shed with a gently curved roof on stone piers, rather like a very solid Dutch barn, stood in the station siding. It was not often used, but at one time it was the terminus of a private railway from Oakhill Brewery which brought the famous Oakhill Stout to Binegar for distribution all over the country.

Beyond Binegar the line climbs again to Masbury Halt (spelt Maesbury on Ordnance Survey maps). The banker engine used on this incline was allowed to return on the same line—a rare occurrence in railway practice. A key in the Binegar signal-box locked the signal levers and was handed to the driver of the engine before he left the station. This ensured that the signals were against all down trains on the line until the key was returned and the line cleared.

Before the days of motor coaches and regular bus services, the halt at Maesbury was a busy one, especially on Bank Holidays, when people came to picnic on Maesbury "Ring", and hikers set out to tramp over the hills to Wells. The earthworks on the hill above are sometimes referred to locally as the "Ring", sometimes as the "Castle". The builder of the stationmaster's house at Maesbury evidently thought they represented the remains of a real castle, for he carved a castle in outline on one of the facing stones. In the 1939–45 war the station waiting-room was fitted out as a little Nonconformist chapel with chairs and a harmonium by a lady who leased it on Sundays for a nominal rent, and regular services were held there. Today the archaeologists and sightseers who visit Maesbury Castle travel by car along the old Roman road from Green Ore.

Beyond Maesbury the descent of the southern slopes of Mendip begins and the train rattled down at considerable speed past a series of old limestone quarries and across plateau country of grey-walled farmlands to Shepton Mallet. Just before reaching Shepton Mallet station it passed across a fine viaduct of several arches some eighty feet above the main road. For the original viaduct the engineers used limestone from the Jurassic beds of the quarries on each side of the valley. After some years the increased volume of traffic forced the directors of the Somerset and Dorset Railway to build a second track. All the existing bridges had to be widened and at Shepton Mallet it was decided to build up a second series of arches against the original viaduct without actually joining the two. The building was pressed forward at top speed and the second line was completed in November, 1892. All went well for fifty-three years, and then, in 1945, the railway engineers began to be worried by a slight movement between the two sections of the viaduct. At first this was not considered serious, until it was found impossible to arrest the movement. It was then decided to close this newer section of the viaduct to all traffic. The decision was taken only just in time: at 11 o'clock on a bitter February night in 1946 people living nearby heard weird noises. Families living in four of the houses very close to the arches hurriedly moved out, some of them clad only in their night clothes. Then stones started falling, and finally, with a series of mighty crashes, about 500 tons of masonry hurtled down into the road. The later viaduct had collapsed, leaving the railway line and sleepers festooned across the gap.

During the preceding month there had been heavy rain and cold nights, so that this hastily built second line of arches became waterlogged and literally disintegrated from top to bottom under the action of the frost. Fortunately the original single-line viaduct remained intact and a service was maintained while a firm of Bristol engineers faced the difficulties of rebuilding a second line. The reconstruction was completed by the first week in August, in time to take the Bank Holiday traffic—a remarkable feat in six months. As a result of this experience other old bridges on the line were examined and several which showed signs of overhasty building were reinforced by injecting liquid cement.

There is no doubt, then, that travellers crossing the Mendips can see a great deal that is of interest *en route*. Many thousands reach the coast at Weston-super-Mare each year without the need to cross the hills, but they are nevertheless in sight of the last rocky outposts of Mendip from the promenade—the peninsula of Brean Down and the island of Steep Holm in the Bristol Channel. Steep Holm is not easily (or cheaply) reached, but anyone who cares to cross the ferry over the River Axe near Uphill can wander over the 180 acres of Brean Down at will.

This peninsula is composed of highly inclined beds of mountain limestone which dip to the north, giving rise to a precipitous scarp face on the south and gentle slopes to Weston Bay. The highest point, little over 200 feet above sea-level, lies towards the western end, and from it there are fine views across the Berrow Flats to the south, where silt is still being deposited to form new land at a surprisingly rapid rate.

At one time Brean Down very nearly sheltered a major Atlantic port. In 1841 Captain Evans (later to become Admiral Evans and Conservator of the River Mersey) gave evidence before a Select Committee of the House of Commons on West Indian Mails. "There is no part of the kingdom in my opinion," he said, "so well suited for a Packet Station as Brean Down in the Bristol Channel." Twenty years later John Coode published a report on a Brean Down Harbour Scheme, in which he wrote favourably of the nature of the bottom on the northern side of Brean Down for construction and anchorage, the depth of water, facility of approach, and the shelter provided by the "Down" from southerly and south-westerly winds. Early in 1889 the Directors of the Harbour Construction Company Ltd. turned their attention to the promotion of the Brean Down Harbour and Railway Act, which passed through Parliament and received the Royal Assent on August 26th in the same year. It authorised the newly constituted Brean Down Harbour and Railway Company to raise £348,000 by shares, and £116,000 by borrowing, to construct a deep-sea harbour on the northern side of the Brean Down and about five miles of railway to link it with the main Bristol to Exeter Great Western Railway line just south of the Axe. It is interesting to examine some of the arguments so confidently put forward in the Company prospectus:

> "Brean Down occupies the finest situation in the country for a Trans-Atlantic Port. The saving in time by the Brean Down route between America and London would be nearly one whole day as compared with Liverpool. . . . The track for vessels being in a direct line to New York would avoid the circuitous and sometimes dangerous detour by the Irish Channel, and the serious delay often caused by the bar at the mouth of the River Mersey. The distance from London to Brean Down is only 140 miles, as compared with 200 miles from London to Liverpool, thus shortening the railway journey by at least one hour."
>
> "The Brean Down route to America will therefore be shorter both by land and sea than the existing route by Liverpool, and . . . will inevitably attract a large proportion of the American traffic. It is confidently anticipated that the Government must avail themselves of this Port when completed for the despatch of the Mails to America."
>
> "Brean Down Harbour will also furnish an excellent landing place for cattle and other livestock from the South of Ireland."

The great importance of saving time was stressed since

> "during a long journey many cattle die through being battened down during bad weather; many, on the other hand, die from undue exposure. At Brean, cattle could be turned out to grass immediately on arrival."
>
> "The largest vessels afloat could enter the harbour at any time or tide, and no pilot would be required."
>
> "The proximity to the Welsh Coal Fields (Cardiff and Newport being within 17 miles by sea of Brean Down) will afford ample facilities for a cheap and expeditious supply of the best steam coal for the steamers using the harbour."
>
> "The shipping trade of the Bristol Channel has grown to an enormous extent, and is now at least one-fifth of that of the whole of England."

The first stone of this harbour was actually laid on the northern side of the peninsula by Lady Wilmot in 1864. The War Office also became interested in Brean Down at about this time and a fort was built with seven 7-inch guns at the western end. The harbour scheme ran into financial difficulties and progress was slow. On December 9th, 1872, a great storm carried away the stone pier and the project was finally abandoned. The fort, however, remained intact until, in 1900, a soldier, when returning from a trip to Burnham, fired a shot into one of the magazines and a large part of the building was destroyed in the explosion. During the 1939–45 war, parts of the fort were reconstructed and emplacements were made for two 6-inch naval guns. Brean Down has a further historical interest: it was here in 1897 that Marconi carried out one of the earliest experiments in wireless telegraphy when signals were successfully transmitted across the nine-mile stretch of the Bristol Channel to Lavernock in South Wales.

Brean Down is the home of ravens and peregrine falcons, and for nearly forty years was maintained by the Royal Society for the Protection of Birds as a bird sanctuary. For some years Brean Down was the subject of rivalry between two neighbouring local authorities. Weston-super-Mare now owns the old fort together with four acres of land at the western end. Axbridge Rural District Council, wishing to avoid developments on the Down and to protect it for bird lovers and members of the general public purchased the remainder. In 1951, as a Festival of Britain gesture, the Council offered Brean Down to the National Trust and the offer was accepted.

The Mendips, then, are full of fascination and interest. But how did these hills originate? Their geological history can be reconstructed from the evidence offered by rock exposures, many of which are described in detail in a valuable little book by Professor S. H. Reynolds—*A Geological Excursion Handbook for the Bristol District.*

Essentially they consist of a core of old folded rocks exposed at the western end and overlain by a thin layer of newer rocks in the east. The oldest rocks, which are Silurian, outcrop in a narrow belt about three miles long between Beacon Hill and Downhead quarry. They include the only example of volcanic rock in the Mendip area. This core of Silurian rocks is surrounded by the Old Red Sandstone which was laid down in land-locked shallow water as a series of reddish sandstones and pebbly conglomerates. These rocks now form the highest land of Mendip—Black Down, North Hill, Pen Hill and Beacon Hill. Very slowly and for a long period there was gradual depression of the earth's crust over the whole of the area. After the Old Red Sandstone comes the Carboniferous or Mountain Limestone, which was formed mainly in relatively shallow, clear water from the remains of marine creatures which can often be seen as fossils in the grey limestones which form the ridges of the Western Mendips—Uphill, Bleadon Hill, Banwell Hill, Wavering Down, Brean Down and the island of Steep Holm in the Bristol Channel. In the Eastern Mendips the Mountain Limestone is only exposed in detached inliers where erosion has removed the covering of newer rocks, as in Vallis Vale, Nunney Combe, Whatley Bottom, and Wadbury Valley, or where there are deep quarries. The little inlier of Old Red Sandstone and Mountain Limestone at Spring Gardens, a mile north of Frome, is not only the eastern end of the Mendips but the most easterly exposure of these rocks in the south of Britain.

During the Carboniferous Period the sea became shallower and shallower, until the time came when it was no more than a vast swamp. This is marked by the change from limestone to the Millstone Grit and finally to the Coal Measures, a series of sandstones and shales in which coal seams represent the fossilised remains of swamp vegetation. Subsidence was still taking place, for these rocks accumulated to a thickness of several thousand feet. They are exposed on the northern flanks of the Eastern Mendips in the Midsomer Norton–Radstock area. During the whole period of depression and deposition from the formation of the Old Red Sandstone to the formation of the Coal Measures it has been estimated that sediments over 10,000 feet in thickness were laid down in the Mendip area under water that was probably never more than 1,000 feet deep.

The Carboniferous Period was followed by a period of intense earth

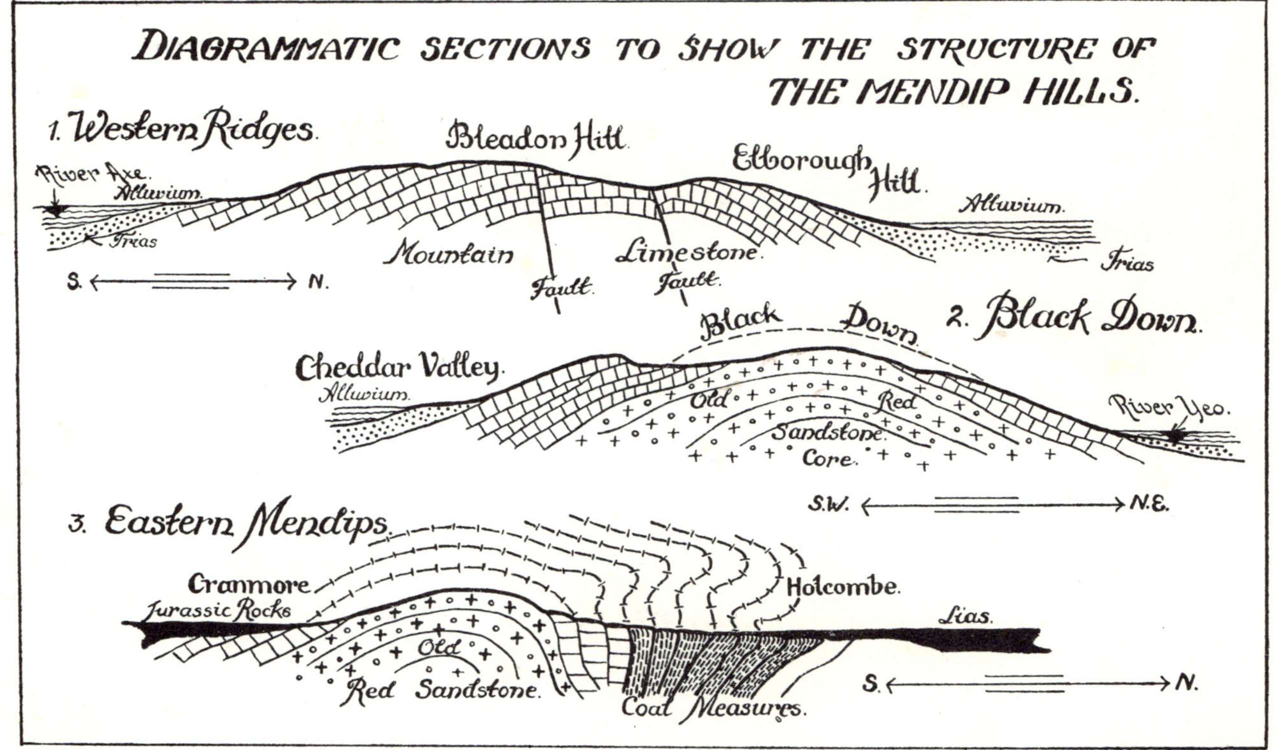

Diagrammatic sections to show the structure of the Mendip Hills

Rome returns to Mendip

movement, and the strata were subjected to pressures from the south which folded them into solid waves with crests and troughs trending mainly in a west-to-east direction. In the Western Mendips the folding is relatively simple; it takes the form of a single arch or anticline, broken in places by cracks or faults in the earth's crust. In the Central Mendips the folding gave rise to a much more complicated disposition of the rocks. Sometimes the pressures caused the folds to break and older strata were thrust over younger rocks. The Old Red Sandstone has been thrust above the Mountain Limestone at Pen Hill, for example. In the Eastern Mendips the rocks are sometimes overturned and faulted as though the solid wave were breaking (Section 3). Inverted limestone strata can be seen in the quarries at Vobster, and the distortion and shattering of the rocks caused by these violent movements makes the tracing of coal seams in the Somerset mines a major problem. This was the period, too, when hot gases rose through fissures in the limestone to give the veins of metallic ore, especially lead ore, which were mined from time to time from the period of the Roman occupation until the end of the nineteenth century.

This period of earth movement was followed by a quiescent period when the hills were exposed for long periods to weathering. The Mendips probably formed a long, rocky island ridge in an inland lake or sea fringed by smaller islands near the southern shore. The climate was arid and the sea received the sediment from desert dust storms which was deposited as the red marls which we now call the Trias. Stones and boulders of Old Red Sandstone and Mountain Limestone accumulated along the shores and creeks and were cemented together by material deposited from the water to form the red and grey rocks known as the Dolomitic Conglomerate—widely used as a building stone. A period of subsidence followed and the Mendip ridge was submerged. The Jurassic rocks were laid down under the water as a series of clays, shales, and limestones, covering the older rocks almost everywhere. In Vallis Vale the Jurassic rocks can be seen lying horizontally on the upturned, eroded edges of highly inclined beds of Mountain Limestone. Around Radstock the thin limestones of the Lias—the oldest of the Jurassic rocks—have been worked in many shallow quarries to provide a local building stone, and most of the houses and cottages in Radstock, Midsomer Norton, Paulton, and the other coal-mining villages have been built with this stone.

After the Jurassic and probably even younger rocks had been laid down over the Mendips came a long period of elevation during which

The Wall and Ditch of Maesbury Camp

they were exposed to the denuding action of a shallow sea. The best description I know of this process is by Dr C. Lloyd Morgan:

> "As the oozy bottom was slowly raised to the surface it was played upon by waves, which could readily erode the soft layers of recently deposited and little-consolidated material. We may picture a battle of contending forces. Those of upheaval were striving by steady uplift to raise the sea-bottom into dry land. Those of marine denudation lashed with their waves the oozy deposits as they came to the surface. Layer after layer were swept away by the breakers. . . . It is not improbable that over the Mendips marine denudation, during the process of upheaval, held its own until the hard core of the old range was laid bare."

In the Western Mendips the covering of younger rocks has gone, revealing a topography essentially similar to that which existed before the red Triassic rocks were laid down, even to the islands in the Trias sea which now show as a line of limestone hills—Nyland, Lodge Hill, Lyatt Hill, Dulcote Hill, Church Hill, Knowle Hill, and Friar's Oven. In the east a thin covering of the newer rocks remains.

All the hard rocks of the Mendip area have been used for building or for making roads. The Old Red Sandstone was used to build the tower of Blagdon Church, for example; many other churches are built of Mountain Limestone. So are most of the stone walls which serve as field fences. I have often seen gateposts of Pennant Sandstone from the Coal Measures and of Dolomitic Conglomerate from the Trias. Many of the gravestones in Mendip churchyards and the stone flags which form the floors in Mendip farms are also of Pennant Sandstone. The Jurassic rocks include the famous Doulting Stone which built Wells Cathedral, and the Lias limestones are used wherever there are outcrops. But most of the quarrying on Mendip has been, and still is, in the Mountain Limestone. Today it is used mainly for road metal. In general most of the quarries do not disfigure the countryside, though some of them are very large indeed—Highcroft Quarry, near Binegar, Waterlip Quarry, Vobster quarries, and Asham Quarry are examples.

Some years ago the proposed extension of one particular quarry at Dulcote Hill, near Wells, caused a public outcry. A number of inhabitants of Wells, and other lovers of the city, feared that quarrying would destroy this local landmark which forms part of the backcloth against which Wells Cathedral and the Bishop's Palace are seen from the west. A large quarry with an output of 100,000 tons of rock a year had already bitten deep into the southern slopes of the hill and the Ministry of Town and Country Planning had agreed that its serrated crest might be lowered 100 feet by further quarrying. When a public enquiry was held in November, 1948, thirty-seven people raised objections, and argued that there were scores of other places where similar limestone could be obtained from the Mendips without endangering amenities. Finally the Ministry agreed that quarrying should continue, but laid down that the western extremity of Dulcote Hill must be preserved intact.

A year later objections were also raised to a proposal to divert a footpath over Milton Hill, which lies to the west of Wells, in order that Underwood Quarry, owned by the Somerset County Council, might be extended. This path offers a direct route from Wells to Wookey Hole, following the ridge to Arthur's Point, so named because from this vantage point King Arthur is supposed to have planned the death of the famous Witch of Wookey. It was not the first time that there had been trouble over this footpath. In 1895 citizens of Wells, armed with pitchforks and scythes, and led by the town band, marched along this right of way and swept away barriers that had been erected by the then landowner.

Such protests are healthy, for they reflect a sentiment that arises from something more than mere economic pressure and self-interest. The people of Mendip love their countryside as they love their homes. Let us hope that they will always fight to preserve it from desecration. It is encouraging to know that the interest and beauty of the Mendips are now officially recognised. In the Somerset Development Plan the whole range from Brean Down to Frome was scheduled as an area of great landscape value.

CHAPTER II

MENDIP IN THE STONE AGE

TODAY we can stand on the top of Mendip, or on Brean Down where the range dips into the sea, and look across the Bristol Channel to the mountains of Wales and Monmouthshire. Yet there was a time, perhaps 20,000 years ago, when there was no Bristol Channel, but in its place a wide valley. The climate was cold, for the mountains were capped with ice, the southern edge of the great ice cap. In spite of the harsh climate, men and animals roamed the plain and the hills. The animals were very different from those found in England today and were much more adapted to the cold climates. Some, like the reindeer, we would recognise, but others, such as the mammoth, have long since disappeared. The men were great hunters, trapping huge creatures like the mammoth and killing them with nothing more than the weapons they had shaped out of flint or chert. These materials were so greatly valued for the making of implements that men often brought them from a long distance. Today the ploughed fields yield quite a harvest of flint fragments, many of them belonging to this remote period, which is popularly known as the Old Stone Age.

During the eighteenth century many eminent thinkers were puzzled by discoveries in this country of bones of ancient animals, such as the lion, elephant, rhinoceros, and hyæna. They believed that the world and its animals were created very much as they knew them and it was impossible to imagine lions and elephants anywhere but in their native Africa. Not realising that these finds represented extinct species, they tried to explain their occurrence so far from their present habitats, and this led to the most fantastic theories. During the last half of the eighteenth century and the beginning of the nineteenth century the most popular explanation was that the animals had been washed from their tropical homes by the waters of the Great Flood, to be deposited in the caves and crevices of our land as the waters subsided. This was known as the "Deluge Theory" and one of its supporters was Dr Alexander Catcott, Vicar of Temple Church, Bristol, whose manuscripts and diaries have contributed much to our knowledge of Mendip in the eighteenth century.

One of the most outstanding investigators of the nineteenth century was a geologist, the Rev. William Buckland, who later became Dean of Westminster. Although he still thought that certain deposits were the result of the Deluge, he did not agree that the bones found in them were the remains of carcases brought by the Flood from afar. He noticed that certain bones from a cave in Kirkdale, Yorkshire, had been gnawed. He identified the teeth marks with the hyæna, and to confirm his discovery he kept a modern hyæna in captivity and studied its gnaw marks on meat bones. Thus he established that the animals had actually lived in this country and had been eaten by hyænas. Buckland coined the word "antediluvian" to describe those cave deposits which he thought had been laid down before the Flood.

In a letter of February 15th, 1823, to Lady Mary Cole of Penrice, Gower, Buckland wrote:

> ". . . & passing through Wells I heard tidings of human Bones at Wokey [*sic*] Hole, which I went to examine and discovered lying in its inmost Recesses with them a fragment of rude unbaked Pottery—they are from 2 individuals (1 young & changing the teeth) and sconced in a Place barely above the flood level of a River that runs through the Cave—these also are not antediluvian but still very old. Leaving Wells in a chaise with a strange Gentleman, he told me of another Cave with Bones near Axbridge, of which I did not have time to stop to make further enquiries as I was nearly buried in snow."

In the same year Buckland published *Reliquiæ Diluvianæ*, and from the description given in it, there seems to be little doubt, that the place in Wookey Hole was the beach on the opposite side of the Witch Chamber, leading to what is now known as Charon's Chamber. Mr H. E. Balch and also members of the Cave Diving Group have since dug there, but without success. From more recent evidence, it would appear that the bones belonged to Roman times. The rough appearance of the pottery made Buckland think it was unbaked, but this could hardly have been the case, since there is no unbaked pottery known in Britain, even from New Stone Age times, when pottery was first used.

Needless to say, Buckland had many opponents, one being Granville Penn, whose theory was that the rocks had dissolved in the Flood waters and that the caves themselves had actually formed as bubbles blown by the gas from decaying carcases as the rocks solidified. The pressure of escaping gas formed the passages leading to the surface. This theory was not entirely original, since the dissolving of the rocks by the Flood waters was a suggestion which John Woodward had put forward in 1695. He also argued that the layers of different kinds of rocks found in cliffs and quarries had been formed by the varying weights of different particles as they settled.

Buckland's views are illustrated by his work at Aveline's Hole, a cave in Burrington Combe, on the opposite side of the road to the Rock of Ages and a little higher up the Combe. It was discovered quite accidentally in January 1797 by two men who were trying to dig out a rabbit. In the cave were found about fifty human skeletons, which were later identified as belonging to the end of the Old Stone Age. Buckland lost no time in visiting the cave and removing many of the bones, which he announced were "post-diluvial".

The work of Buckland and his contemporaries inspired a Mr Beard of Banwell to take a keen interest in the search for ancient animal remains in the Mendip caves, so much so that locally he was known as the "Professor". He followed in Buckland's footsteps by digging in Aveline's Hole, but his greatest work was in connection with the caves at Banwell, which he began to excavate in 1824.

One of these caves was discovered in the eighteenth century by miners in search of ore. Since it had no particular interest for the miners, they abandoned it, but the story of its discovery lingered on for a long time. This story was one with which Beard had been well acquainted for many years, and, with his ever-increasing interest in bone caves, he sought out one of the miners, John Webb, who showed him the position of the cave. Once more John Webb dug the shaft he had helped to dig many years before and opened up a cave, which became known as the "stalactite cave". The Bishop of Bath and Wells decided to open the cave to the public to assist the new Charity School at Banwell, and this meant that an easier access must be made. A fissure running towards the cave was opened up and about twenty feet from the surface it entered a cavern, but much to the workmen's surprise, it was a different cave from the one they were seeking. This chamber was almost full of earth and rock debris, which Mr Beard was delighted to find contained an enormous quantity of prehistoric animal bones. These included the huge cave bear, cave lion, reindeer, wolf, hyæna, bison, mammoth, and woolly rhinoceros. Beard removed the best specimens and the remainder he built up against the walls of the cave, not as loose heaps, but arranged in neat piles, the long bones being placed in layers, and often panelled off into squares by borders of long bones. Well-built walls of bones were built up in this fashion.

Today the Banwell Bone Cave, after a century and a quarter, has lost little of the character it must have had in Beard's day. The cave is

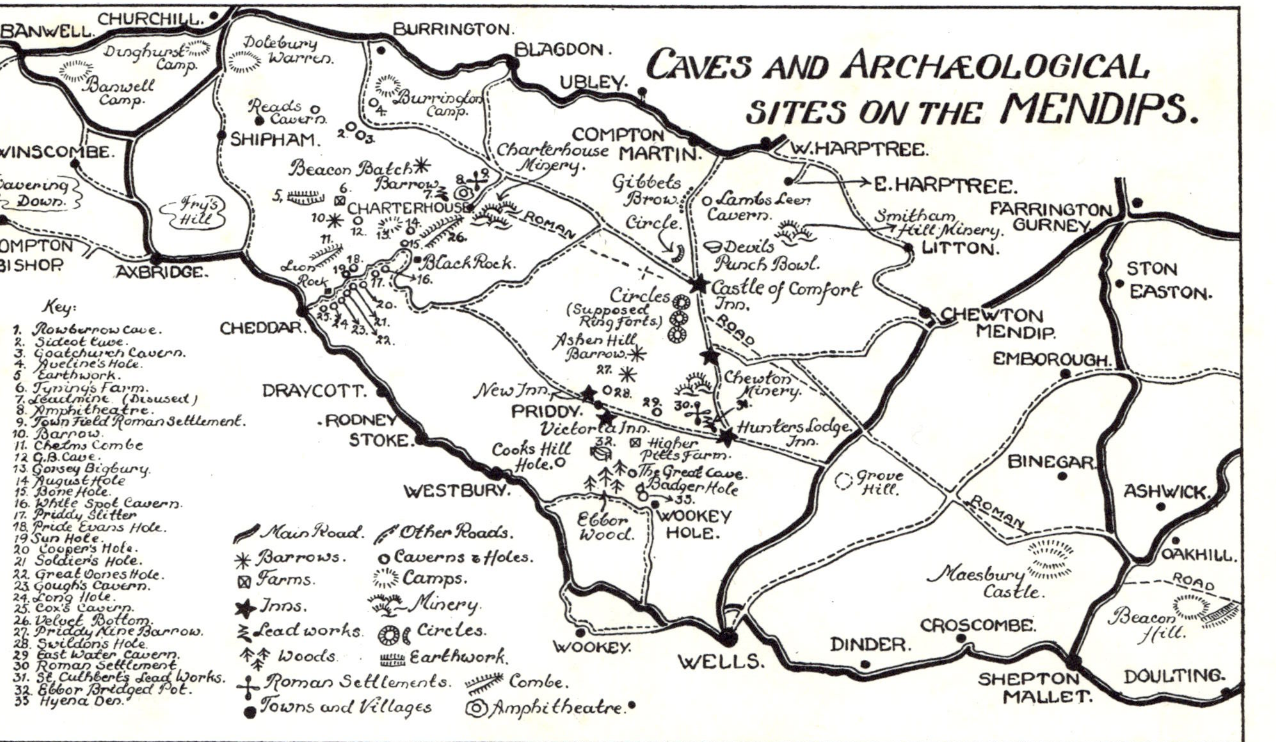

Caves and archaeological sites on the Mendips

approached by a narrow path between tall foliage in the grounds of the house appropriately known as "The Caves". Within a few yards of the path there are artificial grottos on either side of the courtyard, for at the time of the excavations it was the fashion to lay out romantic grounds with sham castles and caves and also to gloat over romantic aspects of prehistory, particularly Druidical rites. The grotto nearest the path is probably the most complete, for within a little stone recess there has been set up an oval stone table, while over the entrance a rectangular marble plaque still bears the following inscription:

> HERE WHERE ONCE DRUIDS TROD, IN TIMES OF YORE
> AND STAIN'D THEIR ALTARS WITH A VICTIM'S GORE
> HERE, NOW, THE CHRISTIAN RANSOMED FROM ABOVE
> ADORES A GOD OF MERCY AND OF LOVE.

There was, no doubt, a plaque on the opposite grotto, but this has long since disappeared.

The path ends at a wooden door which has a painted inscription. Inside, stone steps, carved in the rock and decorated at the side with natural bizarre-shaped pieces of limestone, lead down into the cave. There, as if left yesterday, are Beard's walls of bones and the undisturbed part of the floor which he left to show bones in position, and only a year or so ago old tools stood in the corner. There are few nineteenth-century archæological sites which retain so completely the background of the pioneer excavator.

At Park Farm, Banwell, lives a niece of Beard and the proud possessor of his most cherished portrait, the frame of which is decorated with bones from the Banwell Bone Cave.

Before Beard's death another cave excavator came to Mendip. His name was Sir William Boyd Dawkins, and he was to be one of the pioneers of cave excavation. His work was concentrated chiefly in the cave known as Hyæna Den, in the valley of the Axe, just below the entrance of the Great Cave of Wookey Hole. The cutting of a canal in 1852 led to the discovery of the Hyæna Den, which until then had been sealed with earth. The workmen found that this earth contained bones which they began selling. Sir William Boyd Dawkins, who was studying under the Vicar of Wookey, intervened and seven years later he started the systematic excavation of the cave, completing it in 1863. During the course of his work it became obvious that it had once been inhabited by hyænas, and so Sir William decided to give it the name by which it is known to this day.

As well as the remains of mammoth, rhinoceros, lion, bear, reindeer, hyæna, and other animals, the Hyæna Den contained bone and flint tools as well as charcoal from the fires of the old cave dwellers. By careful excavation, Boyd Dawkins and his assistants were able to establish that there had been various layers, each deposited at different periods, and showed that tools and hearths lay in the same deposits as extinct animals. From this evidence he concluded that man must have lived at the same time as these early animals. Similar deductions were being made at Brixham Cave and Kent's Cavern in Devon, and with them the Hyæna Den must share the credit of proving that man was the contemporary of extinct species such as the mammoth and woolly rhinoceros.

Many writers have referred to the Palæolithic discoveries at Wookey Hole, often confusing the remains from the Hyæna Den, and the later discoveries at Badger Hole, with those from the Great Cave, which although rich in Iron Age and Romano-British material, has produced nothing belonging to the Old Stone Age men. This is probably because all three caves are in the village of Wookey Hole, which is named after the Great Cave and not to be confused with Wookey, a village nearly two miles away.

Sir William Boyd Dawkins gave the name of "Aveline's Hole" to the Burrington Combe cave as a tribute to his teacher. Boyd Dawkins did, in fact, dig in the cave from 1860 to 1864, but had nothing of the success of Buckland, or indeed of Beard who had also dug there. The cave was finally excavated by the Bristol University Spelæological Society from 1914 onwards, although completion of the work was delayed by the 1914–18 war.

In the footsteps of Sir William Boyd Dawkins came H. E. Balch, who, in addition to his explorations of the subterranean streams of Mendip, was an indefatigable cave excavator in search of remains of the men and animals of the Stone Ages. A pupil of Sir William Boyd Dawkins he used to dig even in his old age in the Badger Hole, which is over the Hyæna Den, the old site of Boyd Dawkins, for whom he had a deep regard. Below the Badger Hole the river emerges from the Great Cave of Wookey Hole, where he excavated the dry passages and found numerous remains of occupation during the Iron Age and Roman times.

So much for the excavators of Mendip, but what do their discoveries tell us? Our earliest evidence of man's activities on Mendip is based on the study of the numerous stone tools and weapons. Like similar implements elsewhere, they are classified according to types originally studied in Europe. There are four areas in Mendip where our Old Stone Age ancestors chiefly settled. Each of these areas is a ravine in the limestone, where caves naturally come to the surface and provided shelter, not only for Old Stone Age men, but for people of various periods. Perhaps the first modern-type men to live in Mendip settled in the Hyæna Den and Badger Hole in the ravine of the River Axe which leads up to the Great Cave of Wookey Hole. It is a blind valley, blocked by a wall of rock, beyond which lies the Great Cave itself. These people left their flint implements in the Hyæna Den, but not their bones. In recent years fragments of skulls of two three-year-old children of this race have been found in the nearby Badger Hole, together with more of their implements. Their methods of fashioning their tools and weapons we call the Aurignacian culture. It seems probable that a flourishing little community lived in the Wookey Hole valley in these early times and, with nothing more than their flint weapons, hunted the great mammoth and woolly rhinoceros.

The climate was gradually becoming warmer and drier, and encouraged by the better conditions, a new race of people brought an advanced culture to Britain. They lived in the Wookey Hole valley, at Uphill, at Soldier's Hole in Cheddar Gorge, and possibly in Ebbor Gorge. This is the second ravine of Mendip where Old Stone Age men lived, and it is perhaps the loveliest and certainly the most unspoilt of all. It was presented in 1967 to the National Trust as a nature reserve.

The community who lived in Cheddar Gorge at the end of the Old Stone Age were more fortunate than most of their contemporaries. At this time the weather had become somewhat colder again and the Gorge must have given shelter from the bitter winds blowing across from the ice cap on the other side of the valley which was to become the Bristol Channel. The caves provided ready-made homes, with a never-failing water-supply, secure against hostile tribes and the wild beasts which still roamed the Mendip hills. Now the wild horse, reindeer, and red deer had replaced the mammoth and woolly rhinoceros, and perhaps the hunters used the Gorge as a natural trap: we can imagine them driving the herds across the plateau and over the edge of the great cliffs. We can imagine, too, the rejoicing of their families as they bore off the fresh meat to their caves and the ever-present threat of hunger retreated for a while.

In 1903 the bones of a member of this community were found in Gough's Caves. At this time Mr Gough was concerned about the flood water which, after heavy rains, prevented visitors from entering the cave, and gave orders to his workmen to dig out a fissure off the main passages to serve as a drain. While they were digging a trench, they came upon a human skull and a number of bones. This was the famous

Cheddar Man, whose reconstructed skeleton now stands in a glass case among objects in Gough's Museum. It was by mere chance that the bones of this young man of twenty-three years of age were preserved. Once it was thought he was drowned, perhaps by the flooding of the cave, but the bones are now believed to be the relics of normal burial. Not far away was a curiously pierced and decorated piece of antler. At one time this and similar objects were believed to be ceremonial wands and were called "bâtons de commandement", but it is now thought likely that they were used for straightening the shafts of arrows. Cheddar Man was only about 5 feet 4½ inches in height and slender in build. He was long-headed, with well-marked eyebrow ridges, and his leg bones show the slight flattening which we associate with people who squat rather than sit. Subsequent excavations by Mr R. F. Parry tell us more about these people and their way of life. Fragments of skulls of five more individuals were found, four of them ranging in age from twenty-five to three. There could have been little chance of living to a ripe old age in those days. It has been suggested that some of the limb bones may have been split for marrow, and this would imply that the Cheddar community were sometimes cannibals.

Other finds included another and more perfect "shaft-straightener", an ivory rod, and such an enormous number of flint implements that we can only conclude that Gough's Caves was a flint implement factory for a large community. A well-established trade route must have existed between Wiltshire and Mendip so that this vast quantity of flint could be brought to Cheddar Gorge. Even more extensive trading took place, however, for in 1950, while excavating close to the site of Cheddar Man, a large piece of Baltic amber was found. The flints and bone objects found at Cheddar, and indeed the human remains themselves, all point to the Magdalenian and Creswellian cultures.

A kindred people lived in Aveline's Hole in Burrington Combe, to the north of Mendip, the fourth ravine we are considering. Here the softness of the valleys which sweep up towards Black Down, with their close turf, gorse, and bracken, breaks up the rock formation of its main gorge. It is perhaps at its best in the autumn, when the yellow sunlight combines with the russet colour of the ferns to produce a softness unknown to Cheddar. There is a feminity about the Combe which has no place in the masculine ruggedness of Cheddar Gorge. The people of Aveline's Hole, like their contemporaries in other places, were fond of personal ornaments. These were worn by men and women alike and were made by piercing sea shells and animal teeth for threading with gut into necklaces and bracelets. About sixty pierced shells were found there. A large number of flint implements were discovered, but perhaps the most outstanding discovery was that of a very fine harpoon of stag antler, belonging to the latest phase of the Old Stone Age. It was typical of harpoons of that period found in the South of France and may have been imported from there, particularly as the craftsmen of that area were using stag antler instead of the superior reindeer antler because the reindeer had moved farther north, following the receding ice cap. It was fortunate that some plaster casts were made of the harpoon, since in 1940 the original was lost when the museum of the Bristol University Spelæological Society was destroyed during an air raid on Bristol. Although only one of the skulls removed from Aveline's Hole by Buckland could be traced, the Society's excavations provided plenty of skeletal remains for examination and it can be assumed that they were similar to Buckland's finds. These bones were destroyed at the same time as the harpoon, but records of them remain. It is usual to find that human skulls of this period were long-headed, and indeed many of the Aveline's Hole skulls are similar to Cheddar Man, but some of the fragments seem to indicate broad-headed people, the earliest evidence of a broad-headed race in this country.

About 9000 B.C. changes in climate marked the end of the Old Stone Age, for the cold-loving animals followed the receding ice field to the north and with them went the last of their hunters. The land became wetter because of the melting ice, while about 6000 B.C. the sea at last separated Britain from Europe. Forests with trees not unlike those we know today crept in from the south. Areas nearer the Equator, which had been good prairie land while our own country had formed part of the frozen north, were becoming dry and barren. Into the forests came other hunters; this time hunters of the small game which had invaded the new land. These were the hunters and fishers of the Middle Stone Age or Mesolithic Period. Their stone implements were smaller than those of the Old Stone Age men to suit the small game they had to hunt; in fact many were so small that they are called microliths.

Evidence of Mesolithic life in Mendip is doubtful, for although microliths have been found, many of them seem to have been associated with remains of later date. In any case, if Mesolithic man had been well represented on Mendip, then surely he would have lived in some of the caves, leaving there definite evidence of his occupation.

At the beginning of the New Stone Age or Neolithic Period, about 2500 B.C., a new people came from the Continent, people who for the first time brought agriculture to this island. Although there is no evidence that Neolithic Man ever cultivated the surface of Mendip, the hills have produced round-bottomed Neolithic bowls and polished axes. The most complete bowls are from Chelm's Combe near Cheddar, and from Rowberrow Cave on the north-west side of Black Down.

A very fine stone axe was unearthed at Bridged Pot Shelter in Ebbor Rocks. This rock shelter, which is on the east side of Ebbor Gorge, can be reached either from the big scree slope or from a narrow path where the sides of the gorge come close together. At first it appears to have two entrances, one above the other, but as we draw closer we see that it is a single cavity with a narrow bridge of rock linking the sides. In the material lying on the bridge the excavators found one of the most perfect New Stone Age axes to be discovered on Mendip. It was not of flint, which is the usual material, but of a green stone and highly polished. Excavated by Mr Balch and his companions in 1926, the axe is now in the Wells Museum, like many of the Mendip relics. Another polished New Stone Age axe in Wells Museum is of flint and was found in Dinder Wood, little more than two miles east of Wells, and yet another was found at Soldier's Hole in Cheddar Gorge. This rock shelter is on the same side of the Gorge as the show caves of Gough's and Cox's, but entails a climb from the road to a height of something like 150 feet. The deposits also produced some pieces of pottery which appear to have belonged to New Stone Age vessels. There were also other flints, some of the same period, but others of much earlier periods.

About two inches of the narrow or butt end of a polished stone axe was picked up on the surface at Nordrach-on-Mendip, not far from Charterhouse. This specimen is now in the possession of Mr Sykes of Clevedon, while a small fragment of another was found in 1951, not far from St Cuthbert's old smelting works at Priddy.

As well as pottery and stone axes, New Stone Age man himself has been found on Mendip. The remains of four or five skeletons were found not far from the rock shelter in Chelm's Combe. A small tomb, about a yard square, had been formed in a rock crevice and was no more than a yard from floor to roof. The people buried in this tomb were a long-headed race, a characteristic of New Stone Age people. The tomb is now quarried away, and even at the time of the excavation some of the bones had been disturbed by quarrying operations and were collected from the loose rock or scree in front of the chamber. The most complete skull was that of a man who must have been about forty years of age when he died, while one of the pieces of skull picked up from the scree was that of a woman, thought to have been about seventy-five years of age at death. This was quite a good life span for people of New Stone Age times. She suffered considerably from arthritis in the knees and back. They were not all adults buried there, for the tomb contained the bones of a child, probably a girl about six or seven years old. Leg bones from the tomb showed a slight flattening and there were certain features of the knee bones which tell us that these people squatted on the ground instead of sitting as we do today. These features are typical of many bones of prehistoric times, although from those studied we learn that the ladies did not suffer from these characteristics to the same extent as the men. Perhaps, like the housewife of today, they had little time to sit down.

Mendip is not well represented by the communal tombs or long barrows of the New Stone Age. Those that exist have been badly disturbed, either by ploughing or bad excavation in the past. Approaching the main mass of the Mendip Hills, one long barrow can be seen on the right-hand side of the Bristol–Wells road as it descends into Chewton Mendip. It was excavated many years ago before the introduction of modern techniques, with the result that the early excavators have cut it completely into two parts.

In 1909 the Rev. J. D. C. Wickham excavated a long barrow in Giant's Ground, two miles south of Radstock. The name is derived from the folklore of burial mounds, since long barrows were often thought to be the burial places of giants. According to the excavator, the remains of several people were found only 2 feet below the surface. Since the amount of earth and stones forming these mounds was usually considerable, the barrow must have been much disturbed, perhaps by ploughing. The stone burial chambers were evidently partly complete. With the bones were three flint implements, including two arrowheads, shaped like a laurel leaf, as was usual for arrowheads in New Stone Age times.

At Fromefield, Frome, in 1820, five skeletons were found in what was apparently the remains of a long barrow. Many long barrows have, in the past, been reduced to a few stones, all that is left of the original chambers. The Wimblestone near the Star Inn, not far from Shipham, is possibly an example. Another is near Nempnett Thrubwell and bears the charming name of Fairy Toot, since, so the tale goes, it was believed to be the abode of fairies, whose mirth and merrymaking could be heard coming from the mound. Today there is very little evidence of its existence.

Chapter III

METAL COMES TO MENDIP

ABOUT 1800 B.C. a new race of men came to Britain, bringing with them the first knowledge of the use of metal. In contrast to the New Stone Age farmers, these were a round-headed people, so sturdy and warlike that they are popularly known as the "Bill Sikes" type, although archæologists refer to them as the "Beaker Folk" because of the beaker-shaped drinking-cups which they brought with them. They were a warrior race who imposed themselves upon the peaceful population and lived off tributes of grain and cattle.

In some places sherds of pottery of the Beaker Folk have been found side by side with New Stone Age pottery, showing the impact of the Beaker culture on the earlier people. This is well borne out by the discovery in 1951, by Dr and Mrs Norris, of a typical Neolithic long-headed man who had been buried with a Beaker vessel of the Early Bronze Age in a shelter in Ebbor Rocks. The man's skull leaves no doubt about his New Stone Age origin, while the large sherd which once formed part of the beaker indicates that the pot was of the type known as a "bell beaker", the purest form of early Bronze Age types.

The Beaker Folk are famous for their great stone circles of Stonehenge, Avebury, and Stanton Drew. Stanton Drew is only a few miles north of the Mendip area. There are no such impressive circles on Mendip, but it has its "henge" monument of Gorsey Bigbury, one of the many earthen circles in Britain. This earthwork is in a field belonging to Lower Farm, Charterhouse, about halfway between Tyning's Farm and the Charterhouse cross-roads and at the northern end of Long Wood, which leads down to the valley at the head of Cheddar Gorge. Today these banks have nothing like their original height and in fact do not exceed 4 feet 6 inches at their highest point. Thousands of years of frost and rain and the efforts of generations of farmers have so levelled them that they are not easily located. Apparently these earthworks were not used for defensive purposes because the ditch is inside the banks. Probably the ditch was a boundary to separate the central and perhaps sacred area from those watching the performance or ceremony from the banks and it may have been thought to keep within

Animal bones in Banwell Cave

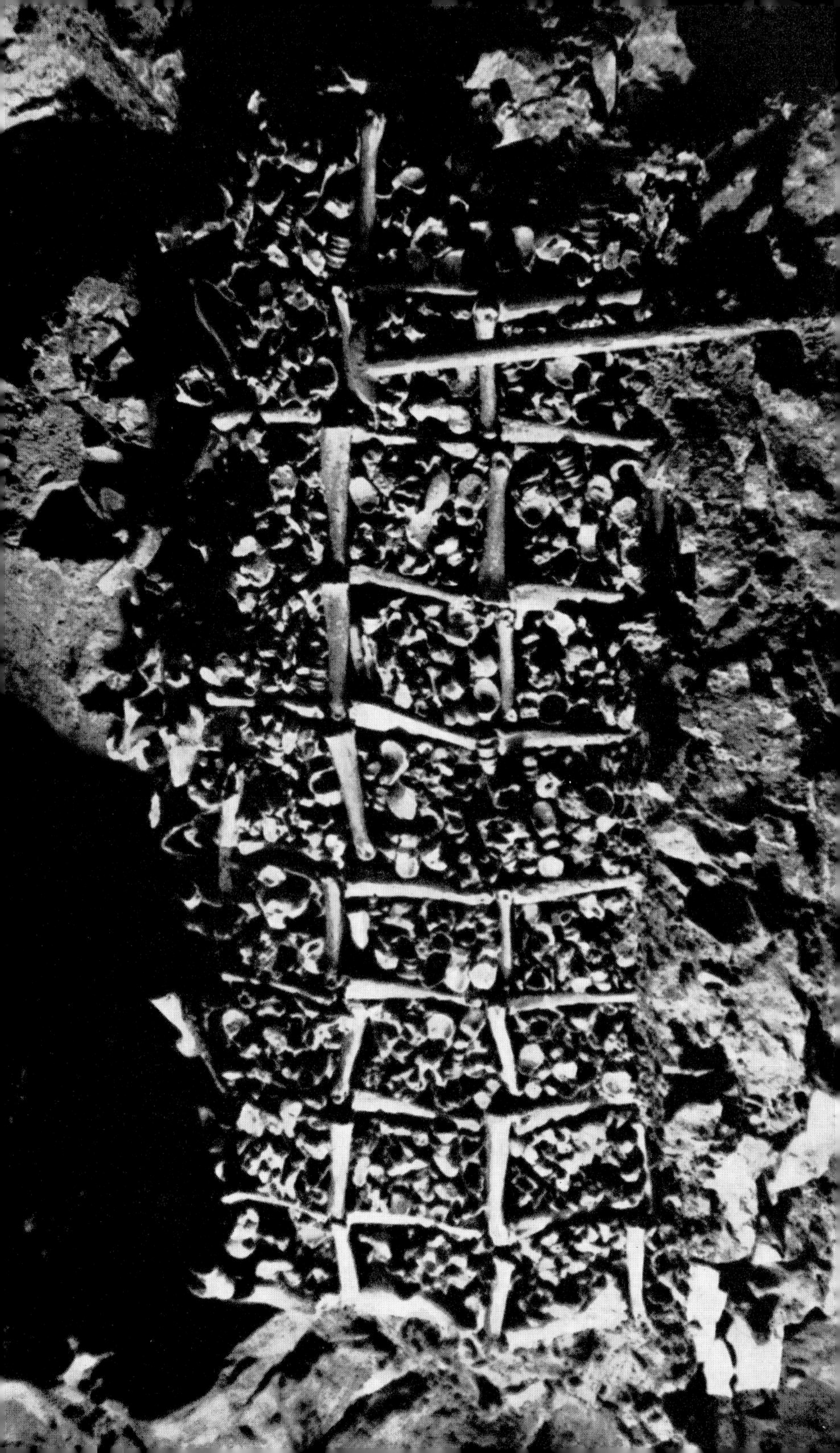

the circle the magical forces or harmful spirits released during certain ceremonies. We cannot be sure of the purpose of these ditches, nor indeed of the purpose of these "henges" themselves, but it is difficult to believe that they could have been used for anything but religious ceremonies. Although some human bones have been found in the ditch, there is no evidence that the earthworks were primarily intended as a burial ground. The most complete skeleton was found in association with four bone needles, a flint knife, part of a beaker, a bone scoop and a small arrowhead of the usual Bronze Age type. It was made of flint chipped into a triangle with two notches made in the base to form a central tang with the projecting sides as barbs. A similar barbed and tanged flint arrowhead was found in the forest plantation near St Cuthbert's works and a number of others were picked up in nearby ploughland.

Unlike the New Stone Age farmers, the Beaker Folk did not go in for mass burials, but buried their dead in a huddled position alone with a beaker, which may have contained the traditional beer of the warriors to cheer him on his cold and lonely journey to the afterworld. The mounds which covered these single burials were much smaller than the impressive long barrows of the New Stone Age and as they are circular they are called round barrows. This fact is easily remembered, as by a useful coincidence Bronze Age people were usually round-headed and were buried in round barrows, while the Neolithic farmers in this part of the world were long-headed and buried in long barrows.

The Beaker Folk left their distinctive pots in many of the Mendip barrows. In 1922 the Bristol University Spelæological Society found portions of an early beaker in a cist under a small barrow not far from Burrington Combe. These beakers are not confined to barrows. Parts of them have been found in Rowberrow Cave, Sun Hole at Cheddar, Chelm's Combe Rock Shelter, Gorsey Bigbury, and possibly at Bridged Pot Shelter, Ebbor Rocks. In 1936 heavy gales exposed the remains of a small pit on the beach below highwater mark on the south side of Brean Down. The pit contained an unworked flint flake, some charcoal, and pieces of a beaker.

Not all the barrows on Mendip were the work of the Beaker Folk. Many were built by their successors during the middle and late phases of the Bronze Age. About 1700 B.C. a new race of warriors reached the shores of Wessex and there established themselves as overlords of the Beaker Folk in the same way as the Beaker people had once imposed their rule on the Neolithic farmers. Unlike the Beaker Folk, these newcomers cremated their dead. Most of these barrows in the Mendip area

Burrington Combe

are of the type known as bowl barrows because their shape is something like an inverted bowl. There are one or two variants, such as a barrow close to the railway track between Doulting and West Cranmore of a type known as a bell barrow, again because of its shape. The burnt bones of the dead were placed in a cist, in a shallow pit, or on the surface of the ground before the building of the mound, together with such weapons and ornaments as they thought the deceased might need after death.

These people brought with them from Europe miniature vessels which are interesting because there are still doubts about their use. Many of them are pierced with holes and so would be useless for holding food or drink. Several of the barrows in the Priddy area were excavated by the Reverend Skinner of Camerton about 1815. In one of the barrows, thought by Mr H. E. Balch to be the second mound from the eastern end of the Ashen Hill group, Skinner found a cremation burial in a pit about one foot deep and covered with a stone slab. With the burial was a bronze ring, part of a bronze weapon, five red amber beads, no doubt intended as part of a necklace, and a miniature pottery vessel. It was like one found in a barrow at Manton in Wiltshire and is known as a "grape-cup". The outer surface is covered with grape-like projections or knobs and in this country they are restricted entirely to Wessex. In the northern barrow at Tyning's Farm, part way between Shipham and Charterhouse, were found three pygmy vessels, all copies of the more common and larger food vessels of typical British origin. Another vessel about 2 inches high was found at East Harptree, near the Castle of Comfort Inn. On Black Down, the highest land in Mendip, where there is a concentration of barrows, one mound produced a pygmy vessel of unusual shape, for although it was flat-bottomed its general form was egg-shaped, with the sides curving inwards towards the top to leave a small opening. In all cases these pygmy vessels were found with cremation burials and the burnt bones themselves were contained in a large urn.

Amber like that found by Skinner in the Priddy barrow was much in demand during the Bronze Age by the richer members of the community. It is still uncertain whether it was brought direct from the Baltic or whether these people relied on amber which is to be found washed up on Yorkshire beaches. Whether or not they imported amber, they certainly carried on an extensive foreign trade. They brought gold and bronze from Ireland, jewellery from Europe, and blue faience beads from Egypt. Rutter in his *Delineations of Somerset*, writing of the Priddy Nine Barrows and the Ashen Hill Barrows, says:

"Some of these barrows were opened in 1825 . . . and were found generally to contain a small circular hole, eighteen inches wide, and the same in depth, filled with burnt bones: in one of these holes, however, were contained a few beads, exactly similar to those found with most of the Egyptian mummies."

Like the long barrows and the earthen circles, the round barrows are only a fraction of their original size, having been worn down by countless feet, cattle, and ploughing, to say nothing of the devastating work of the rabbits, which can be seen running in and out of their tunnels in the sides of many of the mounds on Ashen Hill, Priddy. The barrows we can see today are probably only a proportion of the original number, as many are so worn away that they no longer show above the surface. Even so, the burial mounds of the Bronze Age peoples have certainly added a feature to the contours of Mendip. The famous group known as Priddy Nine Barrows and the adjoining Ashen Hill Barrows form a landmark on the skyline which can be recognised for many miles, but they are perhaps best seen when we enter the village of Priddy from the direction of Cheddar. Priddy seems to have caught a feeling of antiquity and remoteness from these ancient hills, so that it is in keeping with the lonely tumps on the hilltop behind it.

The end of the Bronze Age came with the introduction of iron by new invaders who arrived in Britain about 400 or 350 B.C., and the period from their arrival until the coming of the Romans we call the Early Iron Age. There were several waves of these invaders, and the two phases we call Iron Age A and B reached Mendip. The remnants of Iron Age A are not so common as those of Iron Age B in the Mendips, and indeed one would have been surprised if the earliest waves of invasion had made much impact on these remote hills. However, sherds of what appears to be Iron Age A pottery have been found, while Mr Balch recognised in the Great Cave of Wookey Hole a pot which might well have been of this period.

On the whole Mendip was very much the territory of the Iron Age B people, and they left here not only their weapons, ornaments, and pottery, but their great hill forts which they may have built as a protection against the warlike Iron Age C people or the Belgæ, who were spreading from the south-east of Britain. The most impressive of these hill forts on Mendip is Dolebury Camp at Churchill, forming part of Dolebury Warren, one of Mendip's well-known rabbit breeding grounds. This hill fort can be easily reached by a short climb from the road at Churchill Rocks, but for those who like walking and want to get the "feel" of Mendip, the best approach is over the bracken-covered heights above. Although the walk is well worth while, because it shows us Dolebury Camp as a part of Mendip, the ramparts appear more impressive from the other side, from Rowberrow or from the main Bristol road before coming to Churchill Rocks, or most of all, from Shipham. Here the huge banks seem to hang precariously over the side of the hill, as if threatening to crash down at any moment.

When we climb the ramparts or walk round the immense area they enclose, we realise why the local people used to call Dolebury Camp, "The City", but there is no evidence that any of these hill forts were used as permanent settlements. They seem to have been places of refuge when an enemy raid threatened, not only for the people, but for the herds of cattle on which their livelihood depended. When we take into account the disintegrating effect of 2,000 years of Mendip weather, we realise how much grander these defences must have been when they were first built. The ditch was not intended to hold water, but it was a formidable obstacle for the enemy, who would have to try to climb the defences against a hail of heavy stones from above.

On the opposite side of Churchill Rocks are the remains of Dinghurst Camp, which has suffered considerably from quarrying. Burrington Camp can be reached by climbing Burrington Combe above Aveline's Hole. It is not on the highest part of the hill, but occupies the slope above Burrington Village. The view from the camp is well worth the climb. An impressive Iron Age hill fort is Maesbury Camp, or Maesbury Castle, a little more than two miles north of Shepton Mallet. It crowns the top of the hill and since, like Dolebury Camp, it more or less follows the contours, Maesbury is within the class of fortifications known as "contour" camps. The other class of Iron Age hill forts are the "promontory" camps such as Blacker's Hill Camp near Downside Abbey. Such camps depend to a far greater degree on natural slopes for their defence. Their builders chose a natural promontory where banks and ditches would only be necessary on one or two sides. At Blacker's Hill Camp there are no fortifications on the two sides guarded by a ravine, while the other two sides are protected by defences, built at camp level. Other Mendip hill forts include those round the Mells area, such as Kingsdown between Radstock and Frome and Tedbury Camp.

The Iron Age is thought by many to have been on the whole a peaceful period, but the number of these hill forts shows that there were times when the fear of invasion hung over the people. Surely nothing but the presence of danger would have forced these comparatively cultured people to settle in the main chamber of Read's Cavern. The cave is now entered by a small hole not far from the track which leads from Burrington Combe to Dolebury Camp. To the large main chamber with its apex roof they even brought parts of their chariot, a two-wheeled cart of which only the bronze nave hoops remain. These bands encircled the projecting wooden hubs of the wheels to prevent them from splitting and are like the "bonds" of the modern wheelwright. Among the iron objects from Read's Cavern was a pair of iron slave anklets, although such things are usually associated with the Belgic territories of south-east England.

With the exception of a broken spearhead, the other discoveries at Read's Cavern were of a domestic nature, as, for example, the four latch lifters or Celtic keys. These were simply bent pieces of iron which were passed through a hole in a door to lift the latch at the back. It was perhaps not a very burglar-proof system, but a great improvement on the open cave entrance. No doubt attempts were made by the occupants to level up the floor to make the main chamber as comfortable as possible. A false flooring of wattle and daub had originally covered the entrance to a lower chamber and the iron binding of the edge of a shovel was found. Pieces of iron knives were still attached in their bone handles, while two brooches of the safety-pin type, bracelets, and rings show that, in spite of their uncomfortable dwelling, the people still liked their ornaments. The fate of some of them was certainly unexpected. Over their hearth at the entrance, the cave roof had fallen, trapping them beneath and obliterating all evidence of their existence, until the excavators in 1919 cleared the entrance and built up the story of its ill-fated inhabitants.

The Great Cave of Wookey Hole, now a show cave, must have been an "ideal home" compared with many caverns. It was spacious and airy, with outlets from the upper passages to carry off the smoke from the fires. There was plenty of living space a long way from the cave entrance, and here the temperature would be constant summer and winter. The cave was not too damp and the river provided a never-failing supply of running water within the cave itself, so that one would not have to brave wild beasts and hostile men in order to fill one's pitcher. As for the entrance, this was easily defended, for the approach was then a difficult scramble up from the river. No wonder then that Wookey Hole was inhabited for several centuries in Iron Age and Romano-British times and even years later was probably the home of a poor recluse whose memory has become perpetuated as the "Witch of Wookey".

The dry passages and chambers of the Great Cave were excavated towards the beginning of this century by Mr H. E. Balch, and he found a considerable amount of pottery and other articles of the Early Iron Age and Romano-British times, including decorated pottery similar to that from Glastonbury and Read's Cave. There were also some rather fragmentary human bones. Even after the Roman conquest, the native population still continued to live in the cave. They were probably the descendants of the original Iron Age people, since there are certain features about their bones which are not unlike those of the Somerset marsh villages. As well as pottery and human bones, the objects which Mr Balch discovered included a latch lifter similar to those found in Read's Cavern some years later, part of an iron saw with the teeth set in the opposite direction to those in use today, some gouges, a double-edged chisel, the metal hoof-plate of an ox, combs, spindle whorls, and personal ornaments.

When Mr Balch completed his excavations it was thought that little more could be found in the Great Cave. Nobody suspected that the river itself held human bones in a far better state of preservation, until 1946, when members of the Cave Diving Group stumbled upon skulls, as they charted the submerged river system between the First and Second Chambers. No sooner had the divers passed under the submerged arch than their underwater lights showed three skulls, some human bones and a pottery vessel, all partly buried in the soft sand of the river bed. The pot proved to be a bowl of the late first or early second century A.D., while the human bones found with it were assumed to be of the same date.

In 1947 a special archæological section of the Cave Diving Group was formed, with myself as archæological adviser, to deal with the material from the river. This meant that I had to train as a diver, so that I could examine the remains in their original position and help remove them. After some preliminary training in open water, I was ready for my first dive in Wookey Hole.

As the last public party left the cave, we carried the heavy equipment into the First Chamber. The rubber suits were tight-fitting and it took three assistants to force me into mine. The lead-weighted boots were pulled on, and I soon realised the literal meaning of the phrase "to feel like lead". There was more weight to come, for next the harness, which carried the oxygen and the carbon dioxide absorbant, was hoisted over my shoulders and strapped to the enormous buckles. Then, as if that were not enough, heavy lead weights were placed in the various pockets of the harness. Like some ungainly monster I was led to the water's edge, where the assistants screwed on the pipe leading from the mask to the oxygen supply, pushed the gag of the oxygen feed in my mouth, put a clip on my nose, and finally snapped into position the window of my face-piece. As I opened the valve of my oxygen supply and heard it hiss into the breathing-bag on my shoulders, I saw the log keeper enter the time on a form. His job was to record details of the operation and the times I entered and left the water, so that he could check when my oxygen supply ran low.

When I had done my oxygen-breathing drill to fill my lungs with oxygen and the shore line was fixed to my harness, I entered the water, my boots ploughing into the mud slope. When the surface of the water reached my face-piece the assistants on the shore held me back by the rope until they were satisfied that there were no bubbles of oxygen escaping from any of the joints in the breathing apparatus. I was then allowed to go deeper into the river. The water surface crept up the outside of my face-piece, above it the lights of the cave and below the green of the river, until the surface closed over my head. My fellow-diver switched on the underwater light he was carrying. Everything was green, while around my feet the mud formed a cloud which hung round my boots like a great green fungus. Flecks moved over the bed of the river, like a shoal of small fish. They were due to the reflection of the moving surface of the water. As I looked up, a drop of water from the roof of the chamber fell on the surface and it was strange to see the ring of ripples from beneath. The rope to the shore curved up to the surface and seemed to end suddenly as if cut by a knife. Outside the fluffy-looking mud cloud around my feet, the river bed was covered with ridges made by the flow of water, like sand ripples left on the shore by the ebbing tide. Everything looked bigger and nearer.

As we moved upstream to search for relics, I found that my weight no longer troubled me, but the force of the stream made me lean forwards against the water and I had to push my way along sideways. Presently the beam of the underwater light fell on a large pelvic bone, which turned out to be that of a horse. With our fingers we began to search the surrounding mud, putting everything which seemed to be a bone or piece of pottery into the specially constructed underwater carrier. My companion noted the position of these remains on an underwater writing pad as we worked. The disturbed mud began to rise and envelope us and our light. My companion gradually faded into the haze until only the white of his breathing-bag was visible and the light of the lamp dimmed to a yellow. We became colder and colder and before long had to turn to shore. The mud cloud was only local and we emerged from it instantly. The beam of the lamp assumed its usual intensity and shot along the rope to the shore. Suddenly the upper half of my window was flooded with a glare of shore lights and I could see the water line lapping my face-piece. My first diving operation at Wookey Hole was over.

During many diving operations we have brought out of the river, from various points between the river exit and the Third Chamber, no less than seventeen skulls, together with numerous other bones. Some of the skulls had characteristics showing that they were members of one family or closely akin. The bones were of people of both sexes, rather short in stature, being from about 5 feet 0¼ inches to 5 feet 7 inches. There was one child, about four or five years of age, while the ages of the adults ranged from about twenty-two years to forty years. They appeared to have been living in Romano-British times, but it is quite possible that they were descendants of the Early Iron Age people, particularly as the excavation of the dry passages shows no break in the occupation of the cave. Several pottery vessels and two lead ewers of the Romano-British period were found near the skulls and provide evidence for their dating.

We do not know how these skeletons came to be in the river, but there are several possibilities. It has been suggested that these people may have been victims of sacrificial rites with some connection with the "Witch" stalagmite, but since nearly all the bones were found upstream, it is difficult to imagine any association with the "Witch". Sacrifices may have taken place, of course, in the Third Chamber, but none of the bones show any signs of violence. The river may have been just a convenient way of disposing of the bodies of those who had died in a natural way. The skeletons may have been thrown into the river by a later generation, tidying up the cave for their own occupation, and indeed rodent teeth marks on certain of the bones may indicate that they had been buried or lain on dry land for a time. It is possible that the river occupied only part of its present bed and that the bodies were originally buried in the dry portion, to be disturbed when the water level was artificially raised by a dam for use at the paper mill. With the assistance of the Cave Diving Group I hope to find the answer to this problem by further operations at Wookey Hole.

There is probably no other cave in Britain which has figured in so many legends and writings. Clement of Alexandria, when writing at the beginning of the third century A.D., refers to a cave in Britain, at the side of a mountain, where a sound like the clashing of cymbals was heard when the wind blew into it. The Great Cave of Wookey Hole is known for occasional queer noises, including some like the clashing of cymbals. It is now known that these noises are connected with the flood levels of the river, and their cause is one of the things it is hoped the diving operations will bring to light.

The next definite account is one written by Willaim of Worcester, referring to his visit about 1470. He tells us that:

> "Below the parish at Wookey-hole, about half a mile from Wells, there is a certain narrow entrance [into the rock] where at the beginning is an image of a man who goes by the name of the porter, and it is the duty of the people who desire to enter the hall of Woky to ask permission of the porter, and they carry in their hands torches, which are called in English 'shevys of reed-sedge', for the purpose of lighting up the hall. The hall is about as large as Westminster Hall, and there hangs from the vaulted roof wonderful pendula of stone. . . .
>
> "There is a kitchen in a chamber near the entrance to the hall of an immense breadth, and roofed in stone. There is also a chamber called an ost, for the purpose of drying barley grain to make beer, &c., and the figure of a woman is there clad, and holding in her girdle a spinning distaff."

The next account known of Wookey Hole appeared in *Britannia*, written by the historian Camden in 1586. Referring to the Mendip hills, he wrote:

> "There is a cave or den far within the ground, wherein are to be seen certain pits and riverets. The place they call Ochie-Hole, whereof the inhabitants feign no fewer tales, nor devise less dotages, than the Italians did of their Sibyl's cave in the mountain Apenninus. The name no doubt grew of Ogo, a British word that betokeneth a den."

It is a pity that Camden did not think these tales worth repeating, as it is just possible that we may have met the Witch of Wookey in them for the first time. William of Worcester certainly did not mention any story of the Witch, but he does refer to "the figure of a woman", but this is a homely figure, quite unlike the sinister witch.

In 1612 Michael Drayton included in his *Polyolbion* a map on which Wookey Hole or "Ochie Hoole" is shown with a woman sitting at the entrance. It is possible that this figure represents a witch or the stone figure mentioned by William of Worcester, but it may well have no connection with either, since there is a human figure shown for nearly every place on the map.

The most detailed account of the cave in the seventeenth century was written in 1694 by Mr Rogers.

> "... we found the Cave very hollow, and so dark, that the Candles there scarce burning so bright, though there were 24, as two doth ordinary in the Night in one of our largest Rooms; we thought certainly we had come into the Confines of the Infernal Regions, or some such dismal Place, and began to be affraid to visit it, viz., *That although we entered in frolicksome and merry, yet we might return out of it Sad and Pensive, and never more to be seen to Laugh whilst we lived in the World* ..."
>
> "... A little farther on the right hand is another piece of the Rock that bears some resemblance of a Bell, and on the left hand a Vessel, which they term a But, in which the Beer of an old Sorceress (Cousin to the famous *Circe*, Lady Governess of this dismal Cave), used to be worked in; 'tis a hollow Cistern of a considerable depth always filled with Water, and now and then flowing over, to which the drops of Water which continually trickle down from the top of the Rock add every moment fresh supplies; hard by stands another Vessel of hers, in which they say, she made her Mault, they call it the *East Hurdle* 'tis likewise hollow, and of a pretty depth. Now appears unto your view the old Witch herself, heating of her furnace which seems black and sooty ..."

Apart from the fact that Rogers was no cave explorer by nature, two points of interest emerge from his description. For the first time "the figure of a woman" of William of Worcester appears as "the Witch", although the tradition of beer-making still remains. The custom of taking bottles of wine into "The Seller" or the Third Chamber accounts for the seventeenth-century wine bottles which the Cave Diving Group members have brought out of the river. We can compare this account with that of Celia Fiennes, who visited Wookey Hole three years later, in 1697. Unlike Rogers, she seems to have taken the visit in her stride.

> "Oaky Hole [Wookey Hole] is a large cavity under ground like Poole Hole in Darbyshire only this seemes to be a great hill above it; its full of great rocks and stones lying in it just as if they were hewen out of a quarry and laid down all in the ground; the wall and roofe is all a rocky stone, there is a lofty space they call the Hall and another the Parlour and another the Kitchen; the entrance of each one out of another is with greate stooping under rocks that hang down almost to touch the ground; beyond this is a Cistern allwayes full of water, it looks cleer to the bottom which is all full of stones as is the sides,

just like candy or like the branches they put in the boyling of copperace for the copperice or crust about it, this in the same manner so that the water congeales here into stone and does as it were bud or grow out one stone out of another; where ever this water drops it does not weare the rock in hollow as some other such subterranian caves does, but it hardens and does encrease the stone and that in a roundness as if it candy'd as it fell, which I am opinion it does, so it makes the rocks grow and meete each other in some places.

"They fancy many Resemblances in the rocks, as in one place an organ, and in another 2 little babys, and in another part a head which they call the Porters head, and another a shape like a dog; they phancy one of the rocks resembles a woman with a great belly which the country people call the Witch which made this cavity under ground for her enchantments; the rocks are glistering and shine like diamonds, and some you climbe over where one meetes with the congealed drops of water just like iceicles hanging down; some of the stone is white like alabaster and glisters like mettle; you walke for the most part in the large spaces called the Roomes on a sandy floore the roofe so lofty one can scarce discern the top and carry's a great eccho, soe that takeing up a great stone as much as a man can heave up to his head and letting it fall gives a report like a Cannon, which they frequently trye and call the Shooteing the Cannons; at the farther end you come to a water call'd the Well, its of a greate depth and compass tho' by the light of the candles you may discern the rock encompassing it as a wall round; these hollows are generally very cold and damp by reason of the waters distilling continually which is very cold as ice almost when I put my hand into the Cistern."

Some story about the Witch must have been well established at this time, as Celia Fiennes also refers to her, but there now appears to be some confusion between the Witch and Roger's "Daughter of the old Sorceress . . . like the Statue of a Woman that is great with Child". However, nobody seems to have set down the legend until about 1748, when Dr Harrington of Bath wrote a poem about it which was published in 1756 in *Euthemia or the Power of Harmony*. A version of the poem by Bishop Percy appeared in the *Reliques of Ancient English Poetry* and is as follows:

In ancient days, tradition showes,
A base and wicked elf arose,
The Witch of Wokey hight:
Oft have I heard the fearful tale
From Sue, and Roger of the vale,
On some long winter's night.

Deep in the dreary dismal cell,
Which seemed and was ycleped hell,
This blear-eyed hag did hide:
Nine wicked elves, as legends sayne,
She chose to form her guardian trayne,
And kennel near her side.

Here screeching owls oft made their nest,
While wolves its craggy sides possest,
Night howling through the rock:
No wholesome herb could there be found:
She blasted every plant around,
And blistered every flock.

Her haggard face was foul to see:
Her mouth unmeet a mouth to bee
Her eyne of deadly leer:
She nought devised but neighbour's ill,
She wreaked on all her wayward will,
And marred all goodly cheer.

All in her prime have poets sung,
No gaudy youth, gallant and young,
E'er blest her longing armes:
And hence arose her spight to vex,
And blast the youth of either sex,
By dint of hellish charms.

From Glaston came a lerned wight,
Full bent to marr her fell despight,
And well he did, I ween:
Sich mischief never had been known,
And, since his mickle lerninge shown,
Sich mischief n'er has been.

He chauntede out his godlie booke,
He crost the water, blest the brooke,
Then—pater noster done,
The ghastly hag he springled o'er:
When lo! where stood a hag before,
Now stood a ghastly stone.

Full well 'tis known adown the dale,
Tho' passing strange indeed the tale,
And doubtful may appear,
I'm bold to say, there's never a one,
That has not seen the witch in stone,
With all her household gear.

But tho' this lerned clerke did well:
With grieved heart, alas! I tell
She left her curse behind:
That Wokey nymphs forsaken quite,
Tho' sense and beauty both unite,
Should find no leman kind.

For lo! even, as the fiend did say,
The sex have found it to this day,
That men are wondrous scant:
Here's beauty, wit, and sense combined,
With all that's good and virtuous join'd,
Yet hardly one gallant.

Shall then sich maids unpitied moane?
They might as well, like her, be stone,
As thus forsaken dwell.
Since Glaston now can boast no clerks:
Come down from Oxenford, ye sparks,
And oh! revoke the spell.

Yet stay, nor thus despond, ye fair
Virtue's the god's peculiar care:
I hear the gracious voice:
Your sex shall soon be blest again,
We only wait to find sich men,
As best deserve your choice.

CHAPTER IV

LEAD MINING

ALL around the central area of Mendip are patches of "gruffy ground", land covered with circular hollows. The local people will tell you that these are the work of the "old men". In fact, wherever you go in this area you will hear of the "old men". "But who are these old men?" you may ask. "Why, the old lead miners," will be the reply. These lead miners have long left Mendip, but traces of their filled-in mining shafts or "gruffs" are still to be seen in the "gruffy grounds".

When did lead mining start on Mendip? It was at Charterhouse that the earliest known ingot or "pig" of lead was made, long before the time of the "old men". Today it is in the British Museum, for it is the earliest evidence of lead smelting, not only on Mendip but in the whole of Britain. There are other Roman lead mines in Britain, but they have not been able to produce a "pig" of lead which can be dated to A.D. 49, six years after the Claudian invasion. The fact that at Charterhouse there was a thriving lead-mining industry so soon after this invasion infers that its origins may have been earlier, and lead might well have been worked on Mendip before the Romans arrived there. At the marsh village at Glastonbury, which probably came to an end during the first century of our era, excavators found no less than thirty-two leaden objects, and the material, no doubt, came from the Mendips. However, under Roman rule the mining of lead was "nationalised".

The "pig" of lead in the British Museum is believed to have been found in 1853, while ploughing a field near Blagdon. It was certainly made at Charterhouse and was in all probability found there, since the mining area is in the parish of Blagdon. It found its way to a lead-shot factory owned by a Mr Williams of Bristol, where it was traced by those realising its historic importance. Mr Williams had preserved it and eventually presented it to the British Museum.

Although this lead "pig" escaped the furnace, this was not always the case, for three others discovered at Charterhouse in 1822 found their way to a plumber in Cheddar, who melted them down. Perhaps they form part of some domestic water-supply installation in that area, where householders can look at their lead pipes with interest and wonder if they are made of Roman lead.

Besides producing the earliest known "pig" in Britain, Mendip claims the heaviest Roman "pig" recorded in the country. It was found in Charterhouse in 1873 and weighed 223 lb. The usual weight of lead "pigs" varies, but it is usually between 150 lb and 200 lb. Although these "pigs" were all found in the Charterhouse area, others, probably from Mendip, have been found farther afield, even as far as the mouth of the Somme, showing that Mendip had an export trade in lead even in Roman times. Tacitus, the Roman historian, considered that Britain's mineral wealth was one of the incentives for the Claudian invasion. The Roman mines on Mendip were probably worked by slaves and prisoners of war. They are thought to have been entirely surface workings, for there is no evidence that Romans or their predecessors sunk any shafts. Further "pigs" have been found at Green Ore.

There is little to be seen at Charterhouse of the flourishing industry that must have been there in Roman times. The Roman settlement appears to have been principally in the area immediately north of the cross-roads at Charterhouse. Most of the evidence was found in Town Field and Upper and Lower Rains Batch, which adjoin the west of the road leading to Paywell Farm. Town Field is the second field north of the cross-roads and adjoins a lane on its north side. A red-roofed house stands within its own enclosure in the north-west corner of the field. The first archæological excavations to be carried out at Charterhouse in 1818 were by Sir Richard Colt Hoare and the Rev. John Skinner, who was then rector at Camerton. Subsequently Skinner made further visits to Charterhouse and carried out more excavations. Although he tells us that he found numerous pieces of pottery, glass, and coins, all indicating Roman occupation, we have no accurate list or measurements showing the position of the finds. There is no doubt, however, that Charterhouse was a Roman mining settlement. In the latter half of the last century a mining firm decided to resmelt much of the rubbish left behind by Roman miners and in doing so retrieved many bronze brooches, which can be seen today in the Bristol and Taunton museums. Many of these brooches are decorated in coloured enamel, a British tradition which the native craftsmen retained after the introduction of the Roman form of art. One of these brooches is of the type known as "dragonesque" and is in the Bristol Museum. It shows the curvilinear design of the old Celtic craftsmen and has some resemblance to a double-headed dragon. It is not so common as the usual type of Romano-British brooch, which is something like an ornate safety-pin and is typical of the remainder of the Charterhouse collection.

Although such a fine collection of brooches and other personal ornaments have been found in the district, a great deal remains to be known about the buildings of the settlement. Unfortunately no large-scale excavation has been carried out and so much of our knowledge has come from chance finds, such as foundations and box-tiles which have been uncovered from time to time by farmers and the smelting firm. Even then, the descriptions of these finds are so vague that they are of little value.

To the north-west of the Charterhouse cross-roads and on the slope of the hill to the west of the Town Field can be seen the oval earthwork known as the Amphitheatre. Although there are now three gaps leading into the flat enclosure, probably only the two which are directly opposite are original entrances. The earthwork may have had some connection with the Roman settlement at Charterhouse not far away, but it is not very big and if it had been used as a sports arena, there would have not been space for lavish spectacles. It may have been used as a meeting-place. The Bristol University Spelæological Society did some digging on this earthwork in 1938 and found a quantity of Roman pottery, but pottery is often found in this district and cannot be taken as any strong evidence that the site belongs to the Roman period. The pottery found was of both types of Roman pottery. The coarse ware, made in Britain, was obviously for everyday use, while the superior red pottery, with a high red glaze, known as Samian ware was imported from the Continent. The Amphitheatre itself is interesting, but the climb up the hillside past the earthwork is worth while for the view alone. To the south-west, the southern side of Cheddar Gorge cuts the skyline like giant steps, while between the top of the gorge and Charterhouse is Long Wood, under which is G.B. cave. At the bottom of the hill and adjoining the red-roofed house is Town Field, while on the opposite side of the road can be seen the slag heaps of the lead smelters of the last century. Beyond them on the far skyline rise the Bronze Age burial mounds known as Ashen Hill and Priddy Nine Barrows. In the opposite direction that dark peaty soil is Black Down, the highest land in Mendip, crowned by other Bronze Age barrows and known as Beacon Batch.

Between Town Field and the Amphitheatre a buried urn was found in 1846 with about 900 coins of the third century A.D. There were, of course, no banks in those days and many a hoard buried for safety was never recovered. This hoard, which had lain intact for about sixteen

A view of Priddy Nine Barrows

hundred years, has since been lost, but luckily not all the hoards found on Mendip shared the same fate. In East Harptree church there is a lead vessel, together with coins of the fourth century A.D., some of the great collection of nearly 1,500 coins found with the vessel not far from the place where the chimney of the old East Harptree resmelting works still stands. Not only did the vessel hold coins, but also a ring and silver ingots.

There have been many arguments about the existence of a Roman road for the transport of lead from the Charterhouse mines to Uphill on the Mendip seaboard, whence it might be shipped to Gaul. The existence of such a road is far from established, because there has been little excavation and that little has been done at isolated points between the Castle of Comfort Inn, near Priddy, and Green Ore. Although the existence of a road was proved in this area and the line of a road recognised by surface indications at other points, beyond Banwell there is no evidence that it went on to Uphill. The position of Uphill would have been suitable for a port, and in fact it has been used as one since Roman times; but as a port for continental trade it would have meant a long and difficult journey round Land's End. It is much more likely that a sea crossing would be kept to a minimum and a longer land route and more direct sea journey from the south coast is much more feasible. In fact, the Hampshire coast was the terminus of an established sea route for Continental visitors long before the Romans came to Britain. It may be that Uphill was used for sending lead over to the Welsh coast, but the evidence for its use as a port seems to depend upon a road which is merely conjecture in the Uphill area. That Roman coins have been found there means little, because Roman coins are fairly common in this country.

Although there is a great deal of uncertainty about this road from Charterhouse to Uphill, Mendip is not without its Roman roads. There is the Fosse, that interminable Roman road that divided Roman Britain diagonally from north-east to south-west. The sector between Bath and Ilchester comes up over Mendip from Radstock, and after passing through Stratton-on-the-Fosse, it rises over Beacon Hill, where you can stand and see its straight course below as a track between lines of trees. It leaves the southern side of Mendip a little east of Shepton Mallet, passing through the road junction known as Cannard's Grave.

It is possible that Charterhouse was not the only Roman lead-mining settlement on the Mendips. In 1950, during the cutting of turf in a field near the ruins of St Cuthbert's Lead Works at Priddy, a quantity of coarse and Samian pottery was found scattered over a wide area. An

The ruins of St. Cuthbert's lead works

examination of an air photograph of the field showed what appeared to be a small square inside a much larger one. These markings were due to a difference in vegetation. Both squares were then pegged out on the ground and in 1951 I directed excavations in the region of the inner square by the Bristol Exploration Club assisted by students of the Bristol Folk House. Within an hour traces of a rough masonry wall were discovered. Eventually the excavators uncovered a corner of a square enclosure, evidently the foundations of a dwelling. The walls were made of rough stones and about nine linear yards have been uncovered. Everywhere were parts of broken Roman pots, but what was more important, pieces of rough lead were found on various parts of the site. It looks as if this was yet another lead-mining settlement. Certainly whoever lived there had time for other pursuits, for the finds included two gaming-counters, one of bone and the other of stone, and lead and pottery spindle whorls.

There is a long gap between the time of the Roman occupation and the first recorded evidence of mine working on Mendip in the twelfth century, but this is due to the lack of records rather than any cessation of mining, for lead was certainly in demand.

From the twelfth century onwards, the lead mines and the Church are very much connected, since the Church owned extensive lands on Mendip and indeed in all parts of the country. The earliest written information about Mendip lead mining is in 1189, between Richard I, who had just become King, and the Bishop of Bath, allowing the future Bishops to dig for lead on their Mendip lands. Apart from being a source of income to the Church from the sale of lead, the mines played a great part in the construction and repair of churches.

Later we find the mining area divided into four lordships, each belonging to a Lord Royal. They certainly existed in the sixteenth century, as Leland, the historian, referred to them in 1543.

Each of the Lords Royal had his own court, before which were brought all mining disputes within his territory for lead mining had its own laws. These laws were common to all the lead-mining areas in Britain, although there were local modifications, according to the custom of the district. Some Mendip people will tell you that the laws can still be enforced, but it is doubtful whether many of them would be accepted today. What court, for instance, would today allow a man's hut and tools to be burnt over his head as a punishment for stealing another miner's equipment? Yet such was the old penalty on Mendip, although the thief must have been released from the burning hut alive, because banishment from Mendip followed this sentence. The offender would have fared no better in Derbyshire, where after repeated thefts he might find his hand knifed to the windlass of his mine and have the choice of either dying there or finding the courage to cut his hand free.

It is not known when the lead-mining laws were first introduced, but they were certainly recorded by the sixteenth century. Like many ancient laws, they are probably a collection of customs introduced from time to time. Any man could become a miner within any of the lordships or liberties, provided he obtained a licence from the Lord or his mining agent. Neither the Lord nor his mining agent, the lead reeve, could refuse and the miner could then dig on the common and enclosed waste land in the liberty wherever he liked, so long as he did not interfere with any other man's working, complied with the mining laws, and surrendered a proportion, generally, a tithe or tenth, to the Lord. Having dug a hole to waist height, he would then stand in it and throw the digging tool or hack in both directions in line with the vein of lead ore. The places where it fell became the extent of his claim. This practice seems to have been varied by local custom. So that there should not be any unfair advantage, there was a recognised way of throwing the hack, and because digging tools vary in weight, a special tool was kept for the purpose called a law hack. The excavation was called a "gruff" or "groove", and although no gruffs are dug in Mendip today, the farmers still call their land scarred by these workings "gruffy ground", while place-names such as Green Ore and Hillgrove or Hillesgruff, as it used to be called, still show Mendip's mining associations. Most of the old shafts or gruffs have collapsed, although a few are still to be seen, while many workings were mere depressions.

One of the most extensive areas of "gruffy ground" is in Lamb Bottom, near Gibbet's Brow, which lies about halfway along the road from Compton Martin to the Castle of Comfort Inn. The name "Gibbet's Brow" is a relic of the times when gibbets stood at vantage points along the highway as a warning to evildoers. Just before the hill and before the entrance to an old quarry on the east side of the road is Lamb Bottom. "Bottom" is the usual name for a valley in this part of the country, while small gorges are known as combes. As far as you can see along the north side of the valley, there are small depressions, the remains of numerous "gruffs". At the other end of the valley can be seen the chimney of the nineteenth-century smelting works at Smitham Hill.

Today the "gruffy grounds" are quiet, but in their heyday of the seventeenth century the thud of the hacks and the creaking of the winches, as the elm buckets full of ore were drawn up, must have been familiar sounds. We learn something of conditions in the lead mines from the Rev. Joseph Glanvil, writing in 1668. He was the vicar of Frome and writes:

> ". . . The *Groove* is 4 foot long, 2½ foot broad, till they meet a stone, when they carry it as they can. The *Groove* is supported by Timber of a Divers bigness, as the place gives leave. A piece of an Armes bigness will support 10 tun of Earth. . . . If they cannot cut the Rock, they use Fire to aneale it, laying on Wood and Coale, and the Fire so contriv'd, that they leave the Mine before the Operation begins, and find it dangerous to enter again, before it be quite clear'd of the Smoak; which hath killed some. . . . They convey out their Materials in *Elme*-buckets drawn by Ropes. The Buckets hold about a Gallon. Their Ladders are of Ropes. . . . They beat the Oar with an iron flat piece; cleanse it in Water from the dirt; sift it through a Wire-sive. The Oar tends to the bottom, and the Refuse lies at top."

Each "gruff" was worked by solitary miners or their families, who sold their ore direct. Each miner had to take his ore to the smelting buildings owned by the Lord Royal. This was to ensure the deduction of the lot lead, the share claimed by the Lord. Besides, the smelting had to be carried out where water was plentiful for washing the ore, and there were very few places in the mining areas of Mendip where there was enough water for this purpose and where this water would not endanger drinking supplies. For Glanvil goes on to say:

> "There is a *flight* in the smoak, which falling upon the Grass, poysons those Cattel that eat of it. They find the taste of it upon their lips to be sweet, when the smoak chances to fly in their Faces. Brought home, and laid in their houses, it kills Rats and Mice. If this flight mix with the water, in which the Oar is wash't, and be carried away into a streame, it hath poisoned such Cattel, as have drunk of it after a Current of 3 miles. What of this *flight* falls upon the sand, they gather up to melt in a Slagg-hearth, and make Shot and Sheet-lead of it."

Naturally, there would be disputes between the miners, perhaps about the boundaries of a "gruff", or with the lead reeve, an officer appointed by the miners whose duty it was to control the mining area on behalf of the Lord Royal, to weigh the ore and deduct the Lord's share. The lead reeve sometimes robbed both the Lord and the miners. Although there is evidence concerning a number of mining disputes, it would be wrong to judge all the miners entirely on these records, for the names of the hundreds of honest, hardworking men appeared in these records no more often than they do in newspapers today. Sometimes the troubles came from outside the mining community. On more than one occasion, the miners were attacked by armed bands, who robbed them of their ore. These ruffians were sometimes well-organised gangs in the pay of certain "gentlemen" of Mendip. Such a gang, led by "Ferdinand Hipsley of Stoneaston, gentleman, and Edward Hipsley of Chewton, gentleman", raided the mines of John Allen of Blagdon in 1609.

Until the end of the lead mining on Mendip, the miners continued to use their old methods, but one new practice was introduced about 1684, the use of gunpowder instead of fire for splitting rocks. However, the use of gunpowder could not solve the general difficulties that occurred in the lead-mining industry at the end of the seventeenth century. The veins which ran close to the surface and so were easily followed had been worked out and the expense and effort of draining the deeper levels of flood water was too great to allow any profit to be made from the ore.

In 1825 a final blow was given to the already dying industry when the duty on imported lead was greatly lowered, and about 1850 lead mining on Mendip had practically finished. However, with the decline of the lead mines another industry rose to prosperity on Mendip, that of calamine mining.

On entering Shipham it is hard to believe that, with the neighbouring village of Rowberrow, it was once an industrial centre, but if you have learned to look for "gruffy ground", you will soon notice it on the very edge of the village. Many of the people who lived there were miners digging for calamine, which was mixed with copper to make brass and was also used for the production of zinc. Today the lanes are peaceful and the secluded scene of Rowberrow Bottom, with the conifers of the new Mendip Forest spreading into the valley like a huge carpet, is a far cry from the days of the unruly and poverty-stricken miners who lived in the district in the latter part of the eighteenth century and early nineteenth century.

Calamine was worked at Burrington, Wrington, and Winscombe, but none of these workings were so lasting as those at Rowberrow and Shipham. There were a large number of brass works in and around Bristol, so that there was a ready market for the Mendip ore. In 1684 Mr Giles Pooley, of Wrington, wrote to Sir Robert

Southwell, President of the Royal Society, about the Mendip calamine workings:

> "The Method they take for finding out a Vein is by digging a Trench as deep as till they come to the Rocks where they expect it lies, across the place where they hope for a Course; which Trench they generally dig from North to South, or near upon that Point, the Courses usually lying from East to West, or at Six a Clock, as their Term is. Though this is not constant neither; for sometimes the Courses, Seams or Rakes as they call them, lie at Nine a Clock, and sometimes are perpendicular, which they call the High time of the Day, or Twelve a Clock; and these Courses they esteem the best."

Although lead mining was very much on the decline before calamine working had reached its zenith, by the time that calamine mining was declining in its turn, the resmelting of the old lead slag heaps had started up in Mendip and many of the Shipham miners could find employment at the resmelting works at Charterhouse. The old path they used to take is still called the "slaggers' path" and can still be followed from Shipham, across Black Down, and continues by the lane past the Amphitheatre and Town Field to Blackmoor Bottom, where the Charterhouse resmelting works stood.

The ruins of these and other resmelting works are still to be seen. Their condition is not entirely the result of natural deterioration. Damage was done in removing the smelting plant, some walls have been demolished because of their dangerous state, while much of what remained has been taken off as building material. Next to the ruins are the heaps of bright black slag, the residue of lead smelting, and much of it has been resmelted several times. The long brick and stone tunnels which form a conspicuous part of the ruins are not entrances to mines, for the buildings were not pit-head works, but merely used for resmelting the old slag. Much of the lead was volatile and would go up in smoke. To save as much of this lead as possible, the smoke was passed through these long tunnels or flues before it reached the chimney, and in this way much of the lead could be recovered.

The most extensive of the ruins are those of St Cuthbert's Lead Works to the north-west of the cross-roads at Hunter's Lodge Inn at Priddy. The works closed down in 1908 and were the last to disappear. To approach the ruins, perhaps the most interesting route is to leave the road at Waldegrave Pool, a favourite spot for visitors at week-ends, and to walk along the grass-covered dam. This brings us to a track along which the old mineral tramway used to run to St. Cuthbert's. On the slope of the hill above the track are half-hidden horizontal flues of the old Chewton lead works, and at right angles to these an exceptionally long flue, with its roof broken in many places, can be followed up the hillside to the base of the chimney which once stood there. These flues are all that are left of the old Chewton lead works. The track continues past a pool surrounded by reeds where swallows collect before migrating. In the autumn large numbers of them start up from the reeds in a great cloud and wheel over the water. It is in this pool, too, that divers train for cave diving. The water was artificially trapped for use in the washing of lead at St Cuthbert's. There is little to guide the casual visitor, but there are still one or two Mendip men who can point out the carpenter's shop and other parts of the works—Bert Russell, for instance. Words like "buddles", "launders", and "slimes" * come easily to his lips, for he helped his father work there. He still keeps pieces of galena or lead ore in nooks and crannies in his garden walls, but the day of the lead smelter has gone, and so one day will go the ruins of St Cuthbert's.

Much of the debris resmelted in the old works was taken from a ravine adjoining St Cuthbert's. On the far side an artificial watercourse is made by a wooden conduit or "launder" across a stream, which disappears into a pit. This pit is known as Plantation Swallet and the inflowing stream eventually helps to swell the River Axe, which emerges at Wookey Hole. Together with the fall in the price of lead, this swallet was a contributory factor in the final closing of the old lead works. At lead-smelting works water is essential for the cleaning of the ore, and because most of the Mendip water goes underground, there are only certain places where surface streams can be found in the lead-mining areas. The valley leading from Waldegrave Pool down to St Cuthbert's is one of them, so that we should expect to find smelting works there. As we might also expect, there was keen competition between the Chewton Minery and the owner of the Priddy Minery, which was later to become the property of the St Cuthbert's Lead Smelting Company. The trouble started because the owners of the Chewton Minery trapped all the water in the upper part of the valley and prevented it from flowing on to the Priddy works. In 1860 the owner of the Priddy works successfully took the matter to court. However, his troubles did not end there, for suddenly he found himself the central figure in another court case. This time he was accused of water pollution. The waste water, which was passing from the works into Plantation Swallet, was contaminated with lead and this polluted the River Axe, which formed the drinking supply at Wookey Hole.

* Smelting refuse.

The mining company lost the case. It was then that the works were taken over by the St Cuthbert's Lead Smelting Company. They were obliged to adopt extravagant methods of smelting which would avoid pollution of the water, but none of them were really successful. For a long time the works were closed. They reopened for a short time, but the water difficulty and other troubles still existed and in 1908 they finally closed.

There is less to see of the resmelting works at Charterhouse. What is left of the buildings is fast becoming overgrown by woodland. The parallel horizontal flues are still to be seen, as well as the reservoir and the heaps of slag. Old launders still carry water down the Blackmoor Valley. This valley and Velvet Bottom were originally one valley, but are now separated by the road which joins Charterhouse and Priddy. A number of well-formed circular depressions can be seen in the Blackmoor Valley where it adjoins this road. These parallel rows of circular depressions were the buddles, the tanks where the ore was washed and graded. This valley contains what are probably the most perfect buddle depressions to be seen on Mendip.

The last of the resmelting works still to possess a chimney is that which stands on Smitham Hill near East Harptree. This chimney can be seen when looking up Lamb Bottom from Gibbet's Brow. It is also a good landmark when approaching the northern escarpment of the Mendips from the country around Chew Stoke. Again, it can be seen from above the amphitheatre at Charterhouse. But apart from the chimney, the old works has little to show except its reservoir, ore debris, and the straight-cut water channels nearby. Today young conifers are growing up round the deserted chimney and snakes slither into the reservoir on the approach of the visitor.

Besides the "gruffy grounds", the place-names, and the ruins of the old smelting works, there are other reminders of the lead-mining days, and these are the old mining inns. Those who visit Priddy for the first time are impressed by the number of these inns. Three serve the small scattered village. Adjoining the green itself is the New Inn, a grey stone building with a neat grey stone wall in front. Was there ever a time when this inn, with its massive blackened beams, worn flagstones, and great open chimney, was actually the "New Inn", bright and raw-looking and even a bit newfangled in the eyes of the "old men"? Just along the road to Wookey Hole is the Victoria Inn, and on the road near St Cuthbert's works is the Hunter's Lodge. A name to cheer the tired, wet miner must have been the Castle of Comfort, at the junction of the roads leading to the old mining areas of Priddy, Harptree, and

Chewton Mendip. There are several "Miner's Arms" on Mendip, one at Shipham and one, near the Castle of Comfort.

They all belong to a time when good trade was to be had from the lead workers, and then words such as "grooves", "hacks", and "rakes" were common terms around their firesides. They were the scene of many a brawl between rival miners. They were often the places for deals in stolen lead and sometimes the hide-outs of desperate outcasts from the mines. Now farm workers quietly drink their beer and cider and are only occasionally disturbed by a new generation from the underworld, the cavers of Mendip.

Chapter V

CAVING

At week-ends numbers of men and women appear on Mendip wearing mud-stained overalls and miners' helmets and carrying coils of ropes and rope ladders. They are explorers of the intricate cave systems which lie beneath the surface of the hills. The show-caves of Cheddar and Wookey Hole are well known, but most of the Mendip caves are inaccessible to the casual visitor: their exploration means crawling over rocks, wading underground streams, climbing rope ladders, sometimes clambering down waterfalls and wriggling at full length along tiny passages. Cavers, as these explorers are called, are part of the life of Mendip. They invade the lonely farm with pickaxe and sledge-hammer and enthral the farmer with visions of vast unknown caverns beneath his land, if only they can remove a few score of tons of earth and boulders. Their nailed boots ring on the stone floors of the Mendip pubs, as they discuss a promising new passage or seek out the farm-worker who remembers a sheep falling down a fissure many years ago.

Caving was established on Mendip as a recognised sport about fifty years ago by Mr H. E. Balch and Mr Ernest A. Baker, who eventually founded the Mendip Nature Research Committee, an off-shoot of the Wells Natural History Society. The number of clubs has increased with the growing interest and at least three of them have their own field headquarters in the area, to provide a place for members to sleep, eat, and store their tackle within a reasonable distance of the Mendip caves.

The first trip of any newcomer to a caving club will probably be Goatchurch Cavern in the Lower Twin Brook Valley in Burrington Combe, since it provides a fair sample of mud and tight passages without ladder descents. A narrow path leads up to both entrances and beside the larger of them can be seen a notice board with instructions for calling out the Mendip Rescue Organisation in case of accidents in the cave. Just inside, the remains of an iron handrail follows beside some steps cut in the stone floor and gradually descends into the interior. These were provided when an iron gate was erected some seventy years ago by Mr Gibson of Langford, a former Lord of the Manor. The main way is down through a cleft at the far end of the entrance chamber and known as the Giant's Steps, a succession of projecting boulders. At the bottom a narrow passage turns abruptly to the left. The walls are parallel, but slope at an angle which makes it impossible to stand upright. A hollow depression in the floor is the result of an excavation which produced pieces of a mammoth's tusk, together with a few fragments o bear. Usually there are one or two bats here hanging down like black inverted tulips. A series of small clefts leads downwards to a chamber strewn with large boulders, known as the "Boulder Chamber". A sloping hole in the floor and a slide over a flat slab of rock known as "The Coffin Lid" leads to the Water Chamber, so named because of the small stream there. The exploration of the cave ends in a passage almost round in section, except for the flat floor. Cavers call it the "Drain Pipe". So small that the only way to get along is to lie flat and work along with elbows and toes, the "Drain Pipe" is a little less than forty feet in length; and there is a slight projection in the floor part way along which wedges the caver with too much in his pockets, I know only too well. Passages like these prove that the best clothing for exploring caves is the one-piece boiler suit. Eventually you emerge into a small chamber, vowing that never again will you go through that passage, but this is the end of the cave and if you want to see daylight again there is no alternative.

On the opposite side of the Twin Valley is Sidcot Hole, named after its discoverers, the boys of Sidcot School. It is much smaller than Goatchurch Cave and it is known for its exceedingly tight passages.

Although the majority of cavers take up caving as a sport, many of these sportsmen soon turn to some more serious aspect of caving. The obvious question they ask is "How were these systems formed?" and for the answer they have to turn to geology and hydrology. The Mendip caves are found in Carboniferous Limestone, a rock which is dissolved by the small amount of carbonic acid present in rain water. The rain, falling on the rock, gradually enlarges the small crevices and joints by dissolving the limestone. Then the water finds its way down the cavities as a stream and enlarges them by washing down pebbles and stones, sometimes undermining great boulders, which eventually crash down and shatter into small pieces, to be washed away. These streams are known as vadose water. Perhaps an even greater force in cave formation is that of phreatic water. In many instances the caves were formed when they lay beneath the water table. Fissures and cavities were entirely filled with slowly moving water under varying degrees of pressure, which gradually dissolved away the rock. Most caves were formed by a combination of these two types of water action.

Drops of water laden with a solution of the limestone form on the roofs, walls, and floors of the caves, leaving behind tiny crystals to accumulate into the stalagmites and stalactites which are such a spectacular feature of some caves. Stalactites are the formations which hang from the roof of the caves, and stalagmites are those which rise from the floor. It was once popularly supposed that an inch of stalagmite formed in a thousand years, but cave geologists have found that the rate of growth varies tremendously according to the dampness, air currents, temperature, and other factors.

Swildon's Hole, near Priddy Green, was one of the best stalagmite caves in Mendip but has been despoiled by too many visitors. It was discovered in 1901 by a group of explorers working under the leadership of Mr H. E. Balch. The cave derives its name from St Swithin's Priory, and this name is appropriate, as a stream runs through the cave and the explorer has little chance of keeping dry. He has the choice of following the stream down the Wet Way, or of crawling along the so-called Dry Way, which he soon finds is only relatively dry. A series of passages, occasionally opening out into a chamber with many curtains and columns of stalagmite, brings him to the Water Rift. Farther along, the Water Rift narrows down and is almost barred by curtains of stalagmite. Squeezing through a hole in the last of these curtains, the caver once found himself on the edge of a 35-foot waterfall. The normal means of descent was first by rope ladders, although nowadays these have been replaced by narrower and lighter ladders of wire and aluminium, which make for an easier and quicker journey through the first part of the cave. The explorer escaped the main force of the water, as a pipe threw the stream clear. There have been embarrassing accidents. Once, when I was leading a party, a caver's belt broke because of the weight of water and he had to make the descent of the twisting rope ladder clutching his trousers with one hand. At that time the waterfall was a more breath-taking experience, as provision had not then been made for throwing most of the water clear. The next obstacle is a 20-foot pot. The first man down has to climb through the water, but he can then pull the ladder out of the stream for the rest of the party. One day the 35-foot waterfall collapsed and in its place was a muddy incline. The waterfall which had been one of the splendours of Swildon's Hole had disappeared. The majority of cavers come to the end of their exploration at the Sump, where the water passes through a small submerged tunnel, and indeed until 1936 this was the end of the cave for everyone. In that year Graham Balcombe and Jack Sheppard, founders of the Cave Diving Group, passed the sump with home-made helmets. The way goes on for some 200 yards, when a second sump is reached, and beyond that there are two small chambers. Here the stream passes on through submerged passages and is thought to emerge at Cheddar. During 1941 and 1950 a new series of passages was discovered in this part of the cave by the Mendip Nature Research Committee, and further exploration has been done since.

Shortly after the discovery of Swildon's Hole, the same party forced an entrance into East Water Cavern. Here are few stalagmites and the black, sharp rocks tear the visitor's clothes and hands. At the entrance the caver descends a 20-foot shaft by climbing from rock to rock, at the bottom of which the system changes direction and the daylight is left behind. Many times have I entered the cave in daylight and left it when it was dark. For some reason it always seems easier to find the way into the cave than out again. At first the caver climbs over sharp rocks and crawls along muddy passages and eventually reaches the two Rift Chambers. Nearby a passage leads to the First Vertical. This is a shaft some 90 feet deep, but from a ledge 35 feet down the caver makes his way to the top of the Second Vertical. Then follows a ladder descent of some 35 feet and a steep descent of 25 feet to several muddy passages which run for some distance until they gradually narrow down. There is a stream here which is believed to flow to Wookey Hole. Yet another passage was found years ago, leading to a vertical rift with a ladder climb of 175 feet. The climb is strenuous and the approach extremely narrow. It is called the "Primrose Path", with the touch of the caver's sardonic humour typical in the naming of different parts of a cave.

The limestone area of Mendip is full of surface depressions which tell us of the honeycomb of caves yet undiscovered. These depressions are caused by the collapse of the roof of some underground cavity. When a stream flows into one of these depressions to disappear into an underground cave system, the depression is known as a "swallet", probably meaning the place where the stream is swallowed. The entrance is usually blocked by masses of fallen earth and boulders. As it is the ambition of most cavers to find a new cave, many of them spend a great deal of their time trying to remove the surface debris and so enter these unknown systems. Frequently these efforts end in disappointment, but sometimes the excavators do force an entrance, and in this way was found the cave system on Mendip, G. B. Cave, named after the two principal discoverers, F. Goddard and Dr C. Barker of the Bristol University Spelæological Society.

The chief feature of G.B. Cave is the Main Chamber. Here the greatest height is 120 feet, the length being about the same, while its breadth is 60 feet at its widest part. From a natural gallery part way up one side of the chamber, you can see both the drop to the floor and the height of the ceiling, where enormous stalactites hang like drapery. G.B. Cave is also known for the Devil's Elbow, a tight horizontal squeeze, so named because of its awkward bend. To get through it you have to lie flat with one arm outstretched and kick wildly with your feet. It takes a lot of energy to travel only a few feet through a place like the Devil's Elbow, but most cavers think it well worth while to reach the Main Chamber. On one occasion there was so much water passing through Devil's Elbow that a cave explorer acted as a stopper and had to force his body against the roof to let the water pass beneath him instead of drowning him. He says it was the only time he was frightened in a cave. Now another passage has been forced to avoid this awkward crawl.

The combined cave systems of Long Wood Swallet and August Hole are other examples of successful swallet digging. In Long Wood near Charterhouse there is a chain of swallets. The Sidcot School Spelæological Society began the work of clearing one of these swallets of earth and debris in 1944 and broke into the side of a shaft worn by water action. A way was cleared into a low bedding plane which many well-built cavers find the most difficult part of the system. A drop of about 10 feet now leads to a boulder slope forming the floor of the Rift Chamber. Passages lead to a drop of 33 feet, beyond which is the Great Chamber. The final exploration of the Main Chamber and the remainder of the system was the work of three caving clubs, including the Sidcot party. There were strong indications that somewhere in this system there was more to explore. In 1947 it was noticed that an accumulation of sediment within the cave had disappeared down a rift. After moving boulders a shaft was found leading to the extended system known as August Hole.

Often a cave passage ends in an inviting-looking archway, where the only obstacle is water reaching to the roof. Then the bolder spirits may turn to cave diving. After preliminary land drill, they train beneath safe water for five hours and may then be chosen to take part in the exploration of submerged passages. They may even be the first to enter an unexplored cavern far below the surface. The Cave Diving Group consists almost entirely of cave explorers, who specialise in exploring

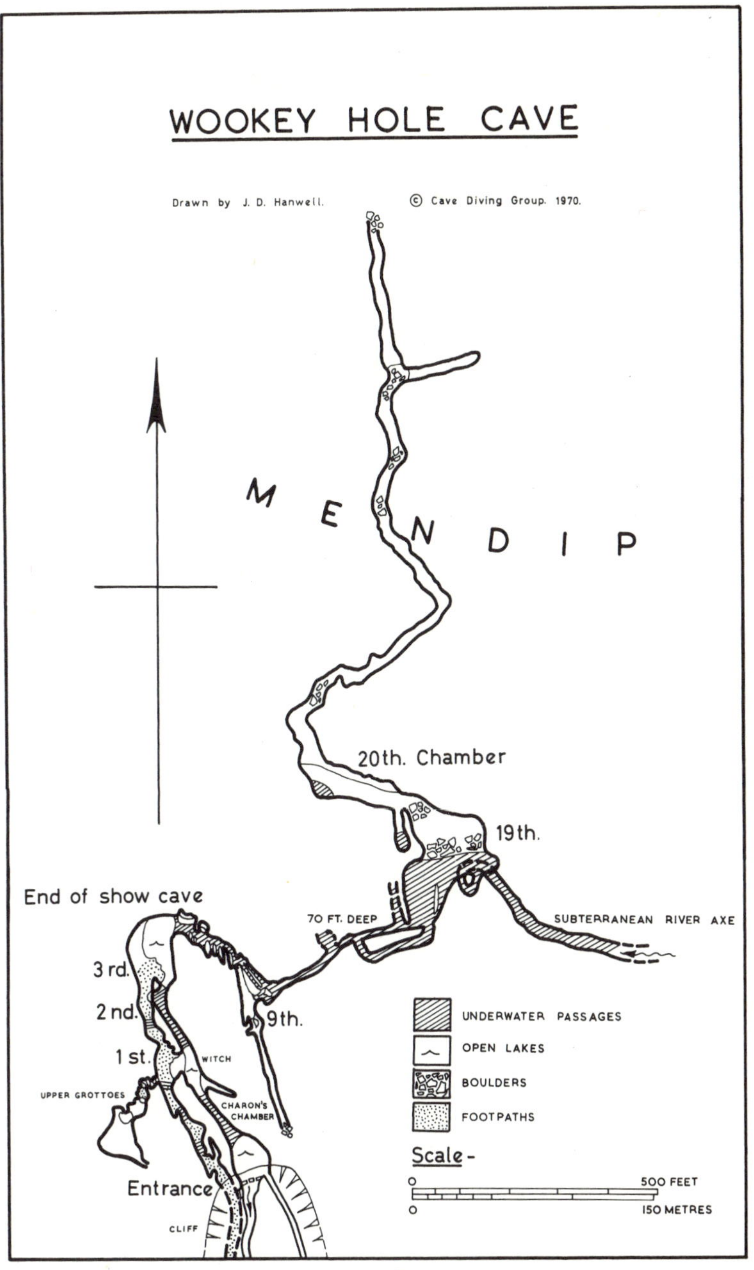

WOOKEY HOLE CAVE
Drawn by J. D. Hanwell.
© Cave Diving Group. 1970.
MENDIP
20th. Chamber
19th.
End of show cave
70 FT. DEEP
SUBTERRANEAN RIVER AXE
3 rd.
2 nd.
9th.
1 st.
WITCH
UPPER GROTTOES
CHARON'S CHAMBER
Entrance
CLIFF
UNDERWATER PASSAGES
OPEN LAKES
BOULDERS
FOOTPATHS
Scale -
0
500 FEET
0
150 METRES

Aveline's Hole, Burrington Combe

the submerged parts of caves. Sections of this group are to be found in several parts of Britain, but it is in the Great Cave of Wookey Hole that they have done some of their finest work. Here they had added no less than sixteen chambers to the previously known cave system. This does not include the Fourth Chamber, for before the River Axe was dammed to assist in the work of the paper mill, it was possible to enter this chamber without any diving equipment. Today the visitor to the Third Chamber can see only the diffused rays of an underwater light, which has been placed in the arch leading into the Fourth Chamber. It is from this point that the Cave Diving Group begin their explorations of the inner chambers.

The first diving attempts were made in 1935, when air-fed diving suits were used, but the suits were heavy and the air lines difficult to manage. Now members of the Group wear various types of suits, but the air-fed equipment has been abandoned. A number of the suits are like those worn by frogmen, but they have been adapted and heavy boots and weights have been added. Fins are generally worn when it is essential to travel above the river bed to avoid stirring up mud, and like frogmen, the explorers carry oxygen or air cylinders strapped to their suits. The diver carries a powerful underwater light, with a reel attached, wound with stout wire and marked with tallies every ten feet. One end of this wire is fixed to the shore or to a suitable rock or belay, so that the reel unwinds as the diver moves. By winding in the wire the diver can find his way back, or he can fix the line in position for guidance or measurement. This apparatus is known as "aflolaun". The letters stand for "apparatus for laying out lines and underwater navigation". Sometimes it also has a small flag to show which way the current is flowing, a compass, and a smaller reel with a marked line and a hollow ball. When the line is released, the ball floats up to the surface, so that the depth of water can be measured. Much of the diver's time is spent in surveying and he can draw under water on a special pad.

Certain of the chambers at Wookey Hole through which the divers have passed are completely filled with water, which means that the diver is unable to surface in an emergency and the only way out is under water. Not all the chambers are like this. Some have quite a big air space between the water surface and the rock ceiling and some, such as the Ninth Chamber, have dry ground. The diving has not been pure exploration. As well as surveying, a lot of experimental work had to be done, much of it abortive. Lines often have to be refixed or cleared of the silt which has covered them. Then, too, a lot of information has

Cave diver at Wookey Hole—emerging with an ancient skull

to be gathered about the structure and geology of the chambers. One of the greatest tasks of the explorers was the construction of an emergency platform above the water level in the Sixth Chamber.

In Wookey Hole, in 1949, the Cave Diving Group suffered their first fatality. On this occasion their guest diver was Gordon Marriott, who had been a frogman during the war and was now a demonstration diver. With the other divers he reached the Ninth Chamber, where he remained with one of the Group divers on dry ground, while two other members went on to the Eleventh Chamber. After exploring the last chamber, the two divers returned and rejoined the others in the Ninth Chamber. From there they entered the water one by one to return to base in the Third Chamber. Marriott did not arrive at the base and the Group divers immediately returned through the mud cloud which had been stirred up. They found Marriott about 25 feet from the ladder leading to the emergency platform. The oxygen in his breathing apparatus had run out, and after a long and unsuccessful attempt at artificial respiration on the platform, his body was brought back by the divers. At the inquest it was decided that death had been caused by lack of oxygen due to a faulty gauge and not because of any lack of organisation or precaution on the part of the Cave Diving Group.

Exploratory diving is not the only work carried out by the Group at Wookey Hole. Their underwater archæological work has been described in Chapter III.

Stoke Lane Swallet is another cave where the Cave Diving Group came into action. It was the general opinion that a large system would never be found on East Mendip. True, there was the stream passage of Stoke Lane Swallet, but although it was long and tortuous, it had no large and imposing chambers. In June 1947, the cave of Stoke Lane suddenly became news. Some pupils of Kings' School, Bruton, forced a new passage in the cave, only to find that further exploration was barred by a pool of water. As the water flowed through a submerged passage, it was clearly a job for the Cave Diving Group, and members passed under the short length of submerged rock into the passages beyond. Since then, explorers pass through the short stretch of water without diving apparatus, and although the submergence is only a matter of seconds, it is unpleasant, especially as the stream contains sewage. Once through the trap, the explorer passes through five large chambers with a great wealth of stalagmite. Surprisingly enough, in the final chamber human and animal bones were found, some of them stalagmited to the rock, scattered over a boulder slope. One human jaw had the teeth and part of the chin coated with stalagmite. Needless to say, this chamber became known as the "Bone Chamber". For a time the removal of these bones was one of my most difficult problems. Most of them were in a very fragile state. Plans were made to force another entrance into the Bone Chamber from the surface, but these have not yet matured. In the meantime, there was always the danger that explorers might damage the bones by accident and I decided to remove them through the submergence. With the co-operation of the Bristol Exploration Club and the Mendip Research Society, they were brought out through the water trap in waterproof containers. The age of these bones, which are of "modern" type, is not yet known, but when a new entrance has been forced, I hope to find out more about them by excavating in the Bone Chamber.

Besides digging in swallets for new caves and diving through submerged passages to reach new chambers, many cavers spend their time hunting through old books, scrutinising old records, and perhaps most profitably, questioning the oldest inhabitants of Mendip about stories of lost caves. In 1937 Andrew Lyons, then an old man of eighty-three, told members of the Mendip Nature Research Committee how he, in his youth, had rediscovered the lost cave of Lamb Leer, on the information of two old men in a Mendip inn.

Lamb Leer is one of several fine caves in the Priddy area and is near the road between the Castle of Comfort and Compton Martin. The story of the cave begins sometime in the seventeenth century, when lead miners broke into the cavern. They often came upon caves, but the enormous size of its principal chamber immediately attracted attention. Mr Beaumont of Ston Easton described the cave in some detail in 1681, and here is his account of his descent into the principal chamber, which is entered from a passage in one of its rock walls about 75 feet above the floor:

> "By the light of our Candles we could not fully discern the roof, floor, nor sides of it: I encouraged the Miners by offer of a double Salary to any that would go down in to it, they all refusing I fastned a cord about me, and ordered them to let me down gently after the Rocks, but being down about two Fathom I found the Rocks to bear away from me, so that I could touch nothing to guide myself by, and the rope began to turn round very fast, whereupon I ordered the Miners to let me down as quick as they could, and upon the descent of 12 Fathom I came to the bottom, where untying my cord I went about to search the Cavern."

Beaumont also says that the cave was in a hill called "Lamb", which accounts for the first part of the name. In the previous century the locality was known as Lambdon. As for the origin of "Leer", Beaumont, when writing in the *Philosophical Transactions* of 1676, mentions "Leiry places (as they call it) that is cavernous". Dr Catcott in 1763 wrote of a great Leer called Beamont's [*sic*] Hole, and the historian Collinson in 1791 referred to it as "Lamb Leare". Today the cave is often called "Lamb Lair", but cavers are trying to revive its original name.

It is hard to understand how a cave of the size of Lamb Leer could be lost for 200 years, but the entrance shaft made by the miners in Beaumont's time was very narrow and eventually fell in. Since the whole of the area round the cave is pitted with the remains of filled-in mine shafts or "gruffs", the position of the cave is not easily found, even today. In 1873 a mining company took a lease of land which they thought might be suitable for the revival of lead mining and in it was the area known as Lamb Bottom. One of the members of this company was a Colonel Bolton, who knew the story of Lamb Leer and who set about finding it. His interest may have been mercenary, as Beaumont mentioned that the cave contained some "good Lead-Ore".

Success came in 1880. Andrew Lyons got into conversation with two old men at the local inn and managed to lead the conversation round to Lamb Leer. They told him that at Lamb Bottom and not far from the road was a hole, and at the bottom, the devil was supposed to live. Lyons found the hole blocked part way down and he and his two mates began to clear it out. They came to an old mining passage or "level" at a depth of 60 feet, but it ended in solid rock. They managed to get some ore from it, but as there was no sign of a cave they decided to abandon the working. Later in the day one of them found that he had left some tools in the level. Lyons made two journeys down the shaft to bring back the tools, and as he gathered up the last of them, the light on his hat went out. He had some difficulty in keeping it alight and looked about him to find a draught coming from a small crack. With the help of his friends he broke through the thin rock wall, and there below them was the lost cave. This discovery was soon followed up. Under the direction of the agent of the Waldegrave Estate, the shaft was made more secure and an easier path made at the bottom. Wooden ladders were erected in the shaft and visitors were allowed to view the cave. Taking a revolver with him to signal to the hauling party, Lyons had the privilege of being the first man to be lowered into the Great Chamber from the lip of the connecting passage.

Among the people who explored the cave towards the end of the nineteenth century was Mr H. E. Balch of Wells, the pioneer of modern cave exploration on Mendip, but once more the entrance fell into disrepair, the shaft became a rubbish tip and Lamb Leer but a story. The twentieth-century cave explorers were not content to let it remain so, and in 1934 members of the Mendip Nature Research Committee entered the cave again, not without considerable difficulty. The cave is now kept locked and is held on licence by three clubs. The trap-door can be seen in the bottom of a depression about 60 feet from the road at Gibbets Brow. The Great Chamber of the cave, which is its most spectacular feature, lies under the land on the opposite side of the road to the entrance shaft. This chamber is shaped something like a huge bell and is 110 feet at its highest point and 90 feet wide. Between the entrance shaft and the Great Chamber lies the Beehive Chamber, containing some very beautiful stalagmites, among them the Beehive Stalagmite, so called because of its shape. Beyond the Great Chamber is the last of the three main chambers of the cave, the Cave of Falling Water, which derives its name from the water which trickles down the steep wall of stalagmite.

There are two lost caves in Burrington Combe. Rutter in his *Delineations of Somersetshire*, after describing Aveline's Hole, mentions that "About half a mile distant, another of these curious places of sepulture was discovered, which was calculated to contain not less than one hundred skeletons". No trace has ever been found of the cave or the skeletons. In a now disused quarry, nearly opposite the Rock of Ages, some quarrymen found a pit in 1875. One of the men, Plumley, volunteered to be lowered into the shaft. During the descent he became alarmed and called out to the hauling party to pull him up, and in the ascent his back was broken. It is believed that the pit was never descended to its full depth. After Plumley's death it was partly filled by a tree and quarry debris and completely closed in 1924.

Another cave closed in recent years is Coral Cave on Wavering Down. It was entered through a slot in a small buff of rock on the side of the hill, and as the entrance was practically invisible to anyone running down the hill, it was always a potential danger. Finally, after an accident, the hole was blocked. The slot led into the roof of a large chamber and the caver could make the 60-foot descent by rope ladder or by bosun's chair. The last method was often the most eventful. The "chair" was a short plank of wood suspended on a rope which passed through a pulley. One party lowered the "chair", while another paid out the lifeline, but not always at the same rate, so that the unfortunate passenger was sometimes dangled on the lifeline a few inches above the "chair". I once fell out of the "chair" and swung helplessly on the lifeline until hauled up.

All that remains of one Mendip cave is in the British Museum. In 1935 quarry-workers at Windsor Hill Quarry, adjoining Ham Wood, broke into a small cave containing some fine stalagmites. As the cave would have to be destroyed by quarrying, the stalagmites were removed and part of the cave reconstructed as a museum specimen.

Sometimes the cave explorer is fascinated by the tiny creatures he notices among the rocks and in the pools, and he learns that often the small animal life in a cave varies from that of the surface. Sight and colouring mean nothing in the perpetual blackness, so that cave conditions favour the survival of certain types of blind or colourless creatures. He may decide to make this his special interest and collect specimens of the small creatures he may find in caves. Large spiders, some of a special cave variety, haunt the entrances of many caves, chilling the blood of some cavers. Others eagerly hunt them down, and when I borrow a fellow-caver's matches, I am never sure whether the box will produce matches or a particularly repulsive spider.

The only representatives of the higher forms of life to be found in Mendip caves are bats, which like the even temperature. The darkness is no drawback to them, as they have very little sight, although one of the most interesting things about these small mammals is their extraordinary ability to avoid objects which they cannot see. Some cavers make a study of their habits and are trying to trace their movements from cave to cave by fixing marked rings to their forelimbs.

Many amateur photographers find a new outlet for their enthusiasm in cave photography. Much of the skill lies in the placing of the flash bulbs, which now replace the magnesium powder used in the earlier days. A fine stalagmite may be silhouetted against a rock wall or the length of a passage may be emphasised in this way. There are endless possibilities for the possessor of patience, imagination and a good camera.

Sooner or later the most ardent of sportsmen cannot fail to be impressed by the discovery of some bones or pottery in a cave, and some of them, like myself, may be sufficiently impressed to become cave archæologists. Then they leave the caves as the caver knows them and turn to the smaller caves and rock shelters, for prehistoric peoples had little use for the watery, inaccessible haunts of the cave explorer.

As cavers, people fall into two categories. Those whose first cave trip is their last, and those who are caught and held by the fascination of the underground. There are experiences which can be found only there: the ceaseless pounding of water on helmet and shoulders like a lead weight; the catch in your breath and the gasp for air, as you swing out of the fall like a drowned rat, with water pouring from boots and trouser legs; the velvety darkness when your light fails, a darkness so thick that you seem to feel resistance when you put your arm out; mud that is so clinging that your overalls drag in a solid mass; the intensity of the silence when you have been left behind to wait for your party; the noise that a drip of water makes when it breaks that silence; and, at the end of the trip, the unbelievable comfort of a hot bath and dry, clean clothes.

On Mendip was a caving crew,
Now mark well what I say,
On Mendip was a caving crew,
The toughest lads I ever knew.
I'll go no more a-caving
With that cave crew.

(Chorus)

A-caving, a-caving,
Since caving's been my ru-i-n.
I'll go no more a-caving
With that cave crew.

We met on the edge of the hole that night,
Now mark well what I say,
We met on the edge of the hole that night,
But that bloomin' crew they had no light.
I'll go no more a-caving
With that cave crew.

(Chorus)

Their ropes were frail, their rungs were thin,
Now mark well what I say,
Their ropes were frail, their rungs were thin,
You got part down and fell right in.
I'll go no more a-caving
With that cave crew.

(Chorus)

You climbed halfway and got quite hot,
Now mark well what I say,
You climbed halfway and got quite hot,
For then you knew they'd a granny knot.
I'll go no more a-caving,
With that cave crew.

(Chorus)

They propped a cave that wasn't safe,
Now mark well what I say,
They propped a cave that wasn't safe
And put their hope in luck and faith.
I'll go no more a-caving
With that cave crew.

(Chorus)

There came a day when they kicked that prop,
Now mark well what I say,
There came a day when they kicked that prop
And down came the roof and killed the lot.
I'll go no more a-caving
With that cave crew.

(Chorus)

(Cavers' Tavern Song)

Chapter VI

STEEP HOLM

In the Bristol Channel off Weston-super-Mare are two islands, Flat Holm and Steep Holm. You can recognise Flat Holm by its lighthouse and Steep Holm by its high, dark cliffs, capped with a green dome. As Brean Down, the Mendip hills run into the sea, to reappear some three and a half miles out as the rocky island of Steep Holm, a lump of Carboniferous Limestone a little more than half a mile long, less than a quarter of a mile across, and 256 feet at its highest point. Visitors are usually sharply divided in their opinions of the island. They see it either as a lonely, dreary place or fall under its peculiar fascination. Just what is this fascination is difficult to say. Perhaps it is because, unlike Flat Holm, Steep Holm is uninhabited and they may feel that this isolated rock is theirs, if only for a week-end. Perhaps it is because the difficulty of landing and taking off again lends a sense of danger and uncertainty and turns a commonplace motorboat trip into something approaching an adventure. Landing on the island in rough weather is a precarious business because of the small shelving beach of shingle, with half-buried stanchions, remnants of the war fortifications. In addition, the beach is bounded by formidable walls of rock and it is easy for a boat to drift against them in a strong wind. A number of years ago some birdwatchers were marooned there for several days and reduced to their last scrap of cheese before they were rescued. In spite of these hazards, scores of visitors land on the island in the spring and summer, for it is full of interest to ornithologists, historians, and naturalists.

Steep Holm has not always been deserted. Legend tells us that in the sixth century, Gildas, the West of England Briton, went to live on Steep Holm and there wrote his *De Excidio et Conquestu Britanniæ*. We do not know whether Gildas wrote his work on Steep Holm or even went there. The evidence is not very strong, since a thousand years had already elapsed before the event was recorded in *Collectanea* by Leland, the royal antiquary to Henry VIII. He based his information on that of an unknown writer.

After being defeated at Watchet in 918 the Danes fled to either Steep or Flat Holm, but apparently had the same difficulty in finding food on the island as people marooned there today, for many of them died of hunger and the remainder were forced to cross over to South Wales. Another story is that Githa, the mother of King Harold, went to Steep Holm in the year following the Battle of Hastings, in readiness for her departure to St Omer. There may be some truth in the stories of Gildas and the Danes, but the island cannot claim this royal visit, because we now know that there was an error in translating the Saxon Chronicle, which tells us that she stayed on Bradanreolice, the Saxon name for Flat Holm. Certainly Bradanreolice must have been a better resting place for Githa than the forbidding-looking rock which the Saxons called Steopanreolice.

The first real evidence of the island's occupation lies in certain references to the Priory of St Michael and in what little is left of the foundations. This priory was a very small religious house and stood on the top of the island at its eastern end, close to the junction of the present perimeter path round the top of the island and the path which leads down to the beach. The residents were not always beyond reproach, for two of its lay brothers were found guilty of larceny in 1243. From documents in Berkeley Castle it is known that the priory was in existence at the end of the twelfth century, and although there is no record of its founding, this was probably some time between 1100 and 1166. The priory could not have been large at any time, for judging from the foundations the building was a small one, and it is recorded that at some time in the thirteenth century the community consisted of a minimum of two Austin canons, the elder one being the Prior. The only Prior whose name has been recorded is one, William.

A sixteenth-century writer, John Smyth, states that the priory was rebuilt early in the fourteenth century by the third Lord Berkeley, but there is no evidence that either the buildings or the community were ever restored. Today there is practically nothing to be seen of the Priory. What little is left has become well covered and the roots of the privets have bitten deeply into its crumbling foundations. The War Office, oblivious of its existence, erected a Nissen hut over part of it, for so little remains to distinguish it from decaying walls of more recent date. It is with conditions such as these that the members of the Bristol Folk House Archæological Club are trying to expose the ruins and, with infinite patience, sort out the pieces of mediæval pottery from the mass of modern nails, bolts, and wire left behind by the Army. Before the island was fortified in 1867, one of the priory walls, about seven feet high, was still standing.

Much of the building was laid bare during the construction of the Garden Battery, one of the six batteries erected during 1867, and so named because it was reputed to have been built on the site of the garden of the priory. While clearing the ground, the foundations of the building were uncovered and, according to Knight, skeletons were found a few inches below the surface, packed closely together. Close to the human bones were the remains of deer, some brass rings (probably really bronze), a coin with the figure of an archer and many other coins, but the inscriptions could not be deciphered. The bones are said to have been taken to a show cave on the mainland, but there does not appear to be any record of this. Excavations were carried out in 1935, 1938, 1951 and in later years but very few human bones were found.

Knight does not mention that coffins were discovered with the skeletons, yet a thirteenth-century stone coffin-lid was found during the military works of 1867 and was built into the sidearm store attached to the Tombstone Battery. The inscription built in with it stated that it was found close by, but there is no record of the actual spot. Because of this doubt, excavations were begun in 1951 between the Tombstone Battery and the wall of the old cottage on the summit of the island, but although mediæval pottery was discovered, there were no signs of burials. One piece of pottery was of a type used during the eleventh century and to the middle of the twelfth century, so that it may have been used by the earliest of the priory residents.

Although all these people have lived on Steep Holm, it has had its lonely periods. It was apparently not inhabited in 1776, for Collinson in his *History and Antiquities of the County of Somerset* states that in that year a building was constructed on the island as a refuge for stranded fishermen, presumably because there were no inhabitants to give them shelter.

The island was sold in 1832 to Colonel Tynte, whose successors owned an estate on the mainland. Near the beach Colonel Tynte built a house which played a considerable part in the story of Steep Holm, for it was an inn for the greater part of its life. The pebble shore and the ruins of this house to the right of it can be seen from Weston-super-Mare on a clear day.

The following year the island was visited by the Rev. John Skinner of Camerton, one of the most enthusiastic local antiquarians of the nineteenth century. His chief interest was in the pieces of ancient pottery which were being turned up in a potato patch by an old man whom he called "the island's Alexander Selkirk". Skinner thought the pottery belonged to the priory. The old man possibly has some connection with the Harris family, for it must have been about 1832 that they leased the island from Colonel Tynte and ran the house by the beach as an inn. It was frequented by the pilots and skippers of sailing-ships and was a favourite haunt for the six or eight gunners when the garrison was established on the island in 1867. It also had its frequent visitors from the mainland, for the inn enjoyed certain advantages. The sailing-ships brought in not only their thirsty captains but contraband. Good rum and tobacco were smuggled on to the island, and some of it brought over to Uphill and sold secretly to contacts on the mainland. Cheap smuggled rum was not the only privilege of the inn. For over fifty years the innkeeper claimed that, since Steep Holm was not included in any parish, the inn was not subject to an excise licence and was free from the restrictions of other inns. His claim was finally contested and it was overruled in the courts in 1884. The inn was no longer a profitable business. It closed down and the Harris family left the island. Today Steep Holm is still outside parish boundaries, but for Parliamentary purposes only it has been included with Weston-super-Mare.

In 1867 there was great activity on Steep Holm, for it was then that the island was fortified. The six batteries known as the Garden, Split Rock, Rudder Rock, Summit, Laboratory and Tombstone batteries were erected, as well as the barracks, still the best building on the island. The stone-built battery positions have long since been abandoned, but the semicircular gun emplacements are still there and the stone-and-brick underground magazines.

When the Harris family left the island, the garrison still remained there. One member of the family took the name with her, for she had been christened Beatrice Steep Holm Annie Cooper Harris. Her brother, Frank Harris, at the age of seven threw a stone over the cliff near the winding path and threw himself off as well. He was fortunate, for when this passage was written he was living at Cardiff at the grand old age of eighty-three, but not without memories of the fall, a year in hospital, and a scar on the forehead.

As soon as the Harris family left, the island was let for a few years to a Mr W. L. Davies. His family ran the inn as a hotel to cater for day and holiday visitors, offering them fishing, shooting, and boating. A number of Belgian hares were imported to improve the shooting, but none of these seem to have survived. The Davies family were said to have grown certain crops and to have produced hay for cattle which they kept on the island. Today it is hard to believe the land could have been farmed. They owned several small craft, for fishing was a profitable business and three tons of fish a tide were not unknown, for besides line fishing nets were fixed on the long spit of shingle which stretches out from the beach for over 300 yards at low tide. The fish were mostly sprats and whiting, but other catches included cod, conger, and skate, and the Davies family found a ready market for their sea produce in Cardiff.

The garrison left Steep Holm in 1903, and in the previous year the inn building had already become a ruin. Since then the island has had other tenants. Tom Sleeman, later residing at Weston-super-Mare, spent twenty years on the island and for a great part of that time he lived alone, working his garden, keeping goats, and fishing. Tom Sleeman and the Harris family had many hair-raising experiences with goats, for the rocky sides of Steep Holm made them difficult to catch. The goats were kept both for milk and meat and were particularly useful for milk, as today the lack of any fresh milk is one of the minor hardships of camping on the island. Sometimes the animals would hide away along the ledges on the steep northern side and the only way to dispose of them was to shoot them, but this was not always easy and one particular billy-goat was hunted for twelve months, playing a game of outlaw on the difficult faces of the island.

In 1931 the island was let to the late Mr Harry Cox, who for many years kept it as a bird sanctuary, looking after it in conjunction with Brean Down. During the last war the Army were back again on Steep Holm and the bird life suffered in consequence, but now the wild birds are coming once more into their own.

One of my first visits to Steep Holm was in early spring. I went with an excavating party to start work on the priory and some birdwatchers and cave explorers came along with us. At the top of the beach was the Bristol boundary stone of pennant sandstone, dated 1897, to remind us that we were now in a "no man's land". This boundary was first fixed in 1373 in the reign of Edward III when Bristol received its charter as a county. As we scrambled up a rough concrete ramp to the path, we could see the tall ruins of the old inn whose tenants had found it so advantageous to be outside parochial authority. Then we began the slow climb with our packs up the zigzag path to the top of the island. We envied the Indian Army company who, during the last war, used mules to carry their burdens up from the beach. All this time we were surrounded by hundreds of screeching, whirling gulls, mostly herring gulls. They were annoyed at this invasion of the island at such a time, just when their young were hatching. The eggs were everywhere, on every ledge, in every clearing in the undergrowth, and right on the path, for there are usually no intruders for them to worry about.

Presently we reached two small brick huts where the path rises steeply to the left. These were the late Mr Cox's huts which he used when birdwatching on the island. Here we stopped for water. I scrambled down some rough steps and there, almost hidden by bushes, was a small pool of fresh water. Steep Holm could not have supported its various inhabitants without this well, fed by a rock spring, and believed never to go dry. When the garrison was on the island, the well was thought to be insufficient and they provided their own water supply by means of an underground tank behind the barracks. It was first constructed for the garrison of 1867. In 1940 it was considerably enlarged and kept filled by water brought by barge from South Wales, first in large numbers of four-gallon cans and later pumped to the tank by pipe from the barge the *Peter Piper*.

Behind the huts we found plants of the famous wild peony, which may have originally escaped from the priory garden. They are not easy to find, which is perhaps just as well, as there are little more than a dozen plants on the island. We looked at the plants, but did not of course disturb them. In fact, to remove a peony plant is one of the greatest sins which can be committed on the island, for it is the only place in Britain where it grows wild. It has been known on Steep Holm for 160 years, but was probably there long before but not noticed by the visiting naturalists.

Returning to the path, we toiled upwards through masses of sycamore and elder bushes, which gave us some relief from the attentions of the gulls. Indeed this is one of the few places on the island where small birds such as the hedgesparrow and the blackbird can get some cover from the gulls. Here and in the rafters of the barracks building can sometimes be found a homing pigeon, if they are lucky enough to reach shelter before being swooped upon by the peregrine falcons which nest on the northern side of the island. The peregrine falcons were driven away when the soldiers were on the island, but now it is uninhabited again they are coming back. Before the construction of the barracks, they say there were puffins on Steep Holm, but although an occasional puffin has been seen nearby, they have never since lived here. Quite a lot of species of birds have been recorded, but a great many of them are only passing visitors and do not breed on Steep Holm.

We emerged from the bushes, rounded another zigzag bend, and then climbed some steps to the Garden Battery, built on the garden of the priory. With the moon rising, we heard the island ghost story to the accompaniment of the gulls' cries. Ghostly footsteps on the gravel path were heard on such bright moonlight nights by several people who have stayed on the island. According to Tom Sleeman, who lived there for twenty years, much of the time by himself, there was one spot in the priory garden where a dog would not pass, particularly if there was a full moon. The footsteps, we were told, belong to the old monks of the priory.

Soon we came to the barracks, a strong building, which has survived nearly a hundred years of gales. Most of the windows were broken, weeds festooned the gutters, and the gulls had obviously roosted there. Still, the great main room provided reasonable shelter. In one of the two fireplaces we soon had a good fire going of wood salvaged from the decaying Nissen huts. Our occupation of the island had thoroughly alarmed the gulls and this meant no sleep for them tonight and little for us, for as we turned in our sleeping-bags on the hard floor, their screeching rose in a great crescendo, mingled with unearthly squawks and screams and sometimes a wild laughing note. The wind rose and howled through the broken windows, banging the doors and lifting the loose ironwork, but sleep came at last and all at once it was a fine morning. The wind had dropped and there was a strange sound above the harsh cries of the gulls, the song of a blackbird.

After breakfast we set out to see the rest of the island. Between the barracks and Rudder Rock was the territory of the greater and lesser blackbacked gulls, who came swooping out of the sky with raucous cries as we came near their eggs. These birds were bolder than the herring gulls, and when I lingered behind the others for a moment to look at a newly hatched chick, the mother dived down on me repeatedly, once skimming my head with her feet. Knight in his *Seaboard of Mendip* says that the gulls' eggs on the island used to be collected and sent to sugar refineries in Bristol. Most of the eggs are said to be found on the sides of the steep cliffs, but we came across these olive-coloured eggs, marked with brown flecks, everywhere, on the paths, on pieces of corrugated iron, in the old fireplaces in the deserted huts, and on the flat bases where stoves once stood.

The Steep Holm peony is not easy to find, but we certainly had no difficulty with the other famous Steep Holm plant, the alexander. These tall green plants, transformed in the autumn into dry sticks with heads of black berries, covered every open space. The plant is usually found on the Mediterranean coasts and on the Atlantic coast of Europe, and although known in this country, the environment on Steep Holm is more like that adopted by the plant in the Mediterranean areas. In Britain it generally seeks damp places, often rubbish tips. First recorded after a visit in 1562, it may have been originally cultivated as a pot-herb in the priory garden, and if so, the monks were responsible for introducing the most outstanding feature of the present vegetation, for the alexanders grew so thick and tall that we had difficulty in forcing our way through them. We were soon to find that one of the chief difficulties of digging on the priory site was due to their deep, thick roots and the dense privet bushes. This privet was another obstacle to our walk, and as we drew near some ruined cottages on the highest part of the island, the masses of privet bushes became almost impenetrable. There are over 250 varieties of plants on Steep Holm. For an island little more than half a mile long and less than a quarter of a mile across, this number is remarkable. Some of these plants are rare, but many of them are well known to the countryman, such as the common vetch, red campion, fool's parsley, wood sorrel, wood violet, cow parsnip, and scarlet pimpernel.

Presently we came to Rudder Rock, the western extremity of the island, and climbed down the concrete steps to the old military look-out. We could not see the Rock itself, but we had already seen it from the boat. It is the narrowest end of the island and has been pierced in several places by the sea to form natural arches. This peculiar formation has been likened to the rudder of a ship, with the island as the vessel itself. Above Rudder Rock, about 1899, a sloping target was constructed. Then the cruiser *Arrogant* steamed up and down the Channel, firing many rounds of shells from her 6-inch and 4·7-inch guns at a range of about 2,000 yards. The direct hits blew the bulk concrete of the target to pieces.

Past Rudder Rock the cliffs became high and sheer. Like most weathered limestone cliffs, they are dangerous to climb, as the rock is likely to break off in places. This danger has been greatly increased on Steep Holm, as an accumulation of rock debris has been dumped on some of the upper slopes by the military. The debris has become covered with small plants and at a casual glance is little different from the natural slopes of shallow earth on a solid rock foundation. I ventured a little way down one of these slopes to get a better view of the cormorants which we saw now for the first time. The rubble moved beneath my weight, sliding forwards towards the almost vertical slope, ending in the sheer cliffs below. I beat a hasty retreat. The cormorants nest on these northern cliffs and we first saw them flying, black against the sky, with necks stiffly extended. We climbed down the long flight of steps on the north side and saw them away on the ledges to the left, sitting up stiffly on their nests, like black stuffed toys. Somebody came up with a slow worm, a dainty creature, lying motionless in his hand. Snakes, lizards, toads, frogs, and newts are not found on Steep Holm. It is perhaps more remarkable that there are no rats or mice on the island since the mainland is so near and large stores were brought over when the troops were there. One of our party reported that they had found five shrivelled carcases of moles on the concrete floor of a Nissen hut near Rudder Rock. A dead mole was picked up in 1938, but it is possible that all of these had been brought from the mainland by gulls and that no moles live on the island. It is said that a small bat is sometimes seen round the barracks, but none appeared while we were there.

We were coming round to the eastern side of the island, trampling through the derelict Nissen huts, clattering over rusty sheets of corrugated iron. Now we approached Tombstone Battery. The sidearms store had been almost completely demolished, but we could still see part of the coffin-lid in the outside face of the remains of its western wall. Although partly destroyed during demolition, there was still enough left to show its moulded edge and the engraved fleury cross, but the 1867 inscription had disappeared completely. We had already decided to excavate on a site between the back of the Tombstone magazine and the ruined cottages. We started to dig a series of trenches, but had considerable difficulty in keeping them straight because of the rocky ground. In fact they grew more and more irregular as we went along. We found a number of pieces of pottery, as well as nails, bolts and wire which the troops had left behind. The pottery told us that we were in the vicinity of the priory, but work was slow and it was obvious that a great many more visits would have to be made before we reach any conclusions.

During the afternoon I went down to the beach to see how the cave explorers were faring. At low tide a rocky shelf surrounds Steep Holm, broken by pebble beaches on the south and east sides, but the caves are on the north side and here exploration is difficult. The explorers were making their way along the ledges of rock, left wet and slippery by the receding tide. One of them did slip into the sea and was hauled out soaked and shivering. The rest disappeared round a corner and came to a small beach with a sea cave at the back of it. A single-chambered cave, it is flooded at high tide and is of no archæological interest.

Farther along the northern side, a narrow sea gulley led to a smooth rounded recess in the cliffs. At the top of the recess, about forty feet up, was the entrance to another cave. It was impossible to descend by rope from the top, because of overhanging rocks, and the only way was to tackle the slippery climb up the face of the recess. The cave consisted of a chamber of two levels. The upper one was reached by a short climb over stalagmite. The chamber was not very large, and unlike the cave nearer the landing beach, it was not formed by sea action. That morning the explorers had found another cave of similar origin on the north side of the island. It was close to the top of the cliff and was reached by rope down the grass slope between the cliff and the perimeter path. It was a single-chambered cave and was entered through the roof, which was partly open to the sky. Like the last cave, it contained a small amount of cave earth, and the Bristol Folk House Archæological Club intends to investigate both these caves in the future.

There is reputed to be a large cave called "The Church" on the island, and although the description of the approach is not unlike that of the cave found that morning, the size is very different, so that there seems to be at least one cave not yet explored on Steep Holm.

All too soon it was time to carry our bedding and equipment down to the beach again. As we sat on the beach, waiting for the boat and looking out across the channel towards the main range of Mendip, I thought of the little garrison, the cruiser pounding away at Rudder Rock, the smugglers' inn, back to Prior William and his tiny community of monks and back to the monk Gildas. Then I saw a small speck bobbing up and down off Knightstone Harbour. It made over towards Brean Down, and as it turned out to sea I could see it dipping down into the troughs of the waves. In forty minutes we heard the chug of its engine off the beach and we left the island to the peregrine falcons, the cormorants, and the gulls.

If it had not been for this book, perhaps I would never have gone to Steep Holm. I went for the first time with my friend and co-author, Bill Coysh. It was on this occasion that I met Mrs Dorothy Rowlands who was writing a radio feature on the island. From this broadcast I first heard some of the stories of people who had once lived there.

Since then I have returned there again and again with parties of archæologists, birdwatchers, and cave explorers. Interest in the island grew rapidly. Now several local natural history and archæological societies have formed a Steep Holm Trust. The Trust has taken a lease to preserve Steep Holm as a sanctuary for bird and plant life and to explore the foundations of the old priory and the much more ancient cave deposits. Much has been done since the Trust was formed. A laboratory exists on the island to deal with the birds, the barracks are no longer without windows and the coffin-lid has been removed from the old sidearms store to the shelter of the barracks. The work of the Trust has added much to our knowledge of the island but the peregrines, sadly, have left.

CHAPTER VII

THE ROYAL FOREST OF MENDIP

FOR most of us the Saxon period in English history is a confused story of barbarism, bloodshed, and treachery diversified by occasional bouts of boisterous wassailing and energetic hunting expeditions. Only a few well-remembered stories serve to recall the chief characters of this shadowy era, and one of the most interesting of them is to be found in a manuscript still preserved in Axbridge. It tells of King Edmund's miraculous deliverance from death on Cheddar Cliffs and of Saint Dunstan's consequent recall from banishment.

"Sometimes for the sake of hunting [so runs the old document] the King spent the summer about the forest of Mendip, wherein there were at that time numerous stags and several other kinds of wild beasts, and he came to the said forest to hunt; Axbridge being then a Royal Borough. The King three days previously had dismissed Saint Dunstan from his court with great indignation and lack of honour, which done, he proceeded to the wood to hunt. This wood covers a mountain of great height which, being separated at its summit, exhibits to the spectator an immense precipice and horrid gulf called by the inhabitants Cheddre Clyff. When, therefore, the King was chasing the flying stag here and there, on its coming to the craggy gulf the stag rushed into it and being dashed to atoms, perished. Similar ruin involved the pursuing dogs; and the horse on which the King rode, having broken its reins, became unmanageable and in an obstinate course carries the King after the hounds, and the gulf lying open before him threatens the King with certain death; he trembles and is at his last shift. In the interval his injustice recently offered to Saint Dunstan occurs to his mind; he wails it and instantly vows to God that he would as speedily as possible recompense such injustice by a manifold amendment if God would only for the moment avert the death which deservedly threatened him. God immediately hearing the preparation of his heart took pity on him; inasmuch as the horse instantly stopped short, and to the glory of God caused the King, thus snatched from the perils of death, most unfeignedly to give thanks unto God. Having returned thence to his house, that is to the borough of Axbridge, and being joined by his nobles, the King recounted to them the course of the adventure which had happened; and commanded Dunstan to be recalled with honour and reverence; after which he esteemed him in all transactions as his most sincere friend."

Most people are surprised to know that the "Forest of Mendip" was thus once a favourite hunting resort of kings and that a district now so sparsely wooded should once have been a forest, but there is a common confusion about the real meaning of the ancient term "forest", which only in a popular and comparatively modern sense signifies a great tract of trees. Originally it was an unenclosed district over which the king strictly reserved all rights of hunting, and to preserve these rights there were special forest laws administered by forest courts over which the ordinary courts had no control. The ancient "forest" often included extensive woodland, but its essential feature was that it was "privileged for wild beasts and fowls . . . to rest and abide in, in the safe protection of the king, for his princely delight and pleasure". At one time the Mendips probably had quite large tracts of woodland, but the Romans must have taken a fair toll of the timber for strategic purposes and to clear a way for their roads, and also for fuel to smelt the ore of the Mendip mines. Building needs encroached still further on the timber, and in Saxon times when development of the mines required increasing amounts of charcoal, woods so conveniently to hand must have been even more heavily depleted.

There were no less than five royal forests in Somerset; of these Exmoor is the only district which in modern times is popularly associated with the ancient "chase", but for the royal hunter of Saxon and Norman times Mendip Forest was a favourite hunting territory—a territory which (according to one report) stretched "from the place called *Cotellis Ach*, now Cottle's Oak, near the town of Frome, as far as the rock called Blackstone in the western sea". From other documents it appears originally to have comprised little more than the manors of Axbridge and Cheddar. The Saxon kings were keen hunters, even the more serious-minded rulers like Alfred and Edward the Confessor, and there are several contemporary records of their sporting expeditions in this district. The ancient borough of Axbridge thrived on Mendip hunting; it may even in part have owed its importance to its proximity to the forest. Under an old charter certain of its municipal officers were charged with the duty of providing royal hunting parties with food and wine when they were visiting the district—no light responsibility in those days of almost boundless appetites and thirsts.

The Norman kings were mighty hunters, too, and followed their predecessors' example in regarding Mendip Forest as a favourite hunting district. Before the county was finally subdued by William the Conqueror there must have been many rebel Saxons hiding in the forest waiting for Harold's sons to make a more successful bid to regain the crown than the mere marauding raids they had attempted on the Severn coast from their stronghold in Ireland. In any case we know that Gytha, Harold's mother, fled to Mendip after her grandsons' defeat at Exeter; but as William marched from Devon through Dorset and into Somerset, leaving a trail of ruthless destruction and devastation behind him, she realised that not even this hiding-place was safe and she escaped through the forest to the coast and eventually landed safely in Flanders.

William the Conqueror himself, who "loved the red deer as if he were their father", must often have hunted here, especially in the early years of his reign before his New Forest was ready for his "princely delight and pleasure"; but of all the Norman and Plantagenet kings perhaps the most familiar figure in the Mendip district was King John. A picturesque old house overlooking the Square at Axbridge is traditionally known as King John's Hunting Box, and the little head carved in wood on its wall is popularly supposed to represent the king. The building is in fact much later than John's reign—no older than the sixteenth century—but its name serves to show how strongly the memory of this king's visits to Mendip Forest has persisted through the centuries. Axbridge, Cheddar, and Wells must often have been the scene of gay hunting parties led by this sporting monarch, who, according to the chronicler Holinshed, was often "of right merry humour" and "thought it scoffery to pursue any fallow deer with hounds, but tired them out with his own travel on foot"—a surprising holiday picture of the shifty ruler who in school textbooks is shown chewing the Runnymede turf in undignified rage before signing Magna Carta.

The picturesque side of the mediæval hunt has been well described by Chaucer, who was himself the deputy forester of a Somerset forest. The reader will remember that the yeoman of the *Canterbury Tales* was a forester:

Of woodecraft wel koude he al the usage.
Upon his arm he baar a gay bracer,
And by his syde a swerd and a bokeler,
And on that oother syde a gay daggere,
Harneised wel and sharpe as point of spere;
A Cristophere on his brest of silver sheene;
An horn he bar, the bawdryk was of grene.
A forster was he, soothly as I gesse.

Chaucer showed an intimate knowledge not only of the chase but also of forest woodcraft. It is no mere amateur who wrote the list of trees in *The Parlement of Foules* and noted their characteristics; and there is a fine description of a hunt in *The Dethe of Blaunche the Duchesse* which recaptures all the freshness and vigour of this colourful age. But Chaucer was a poet, and ordinary folk must have regarded royal forests less romantically than a poet with courtly connections and holding office as a deputy forester. The severest penalties for infringement of the forest laws had been introduced by the Norman kings, who were particularly jealous of their hunting rights. The original punishment for killing a deer was death, and barbarous mutilation was prescribed for unlawfully hunting lesser beasts of the forest like the wild boar or the wolf. Savage fines were imposed even for killing the humble rabbit or squirrel, and the honey of the wild bees was just as stringently protected. Permission could be obtained to feed swine, cattle, and horses in the forest at certain fixed periods, but heavy payments were demanded for this privilege which were rigorously enforced by the forest official called the *agister*. It is interesting to note that goats were not allowed in the forest at all, because they were supposed not only to spoil the pasture but also to repel the deer. It was with the greatest difficulty that permission could be obtained even to drive these ostracised animals through the forest. Timber and fuel was guarded by the *woodward*, and to spoil the vert by felling trees without licence was an offence punishable by severe penalties.

The judges who toured the countryside administering the forest laws sometimes held their court as Wells, and in the short, dry reports of the trials may be found the outlines of many exciting stories of the ceaseless war waged by the king's foresters and verderers against wily and sometimes desperate poachers. Thus in 1216 a Mendip forester, James de Thurlebere, was riding over the hills above Cheddar when he heard the yelping of dogs and the crashing of branches. A young buck burst into view pursued by three mastiffs urged on by their owner, who was caught red-handed by the forester. Thurlebere discovered that the poacher's name was Richard le Marshal and that he came from Congresbury. His mastiffs were confiscated and he was taken back to Cheddar, where several people offered to go bail for his appearance at the next forest court. The forester then released Richard—rather too credulously as it turned out, for at the next meeting of the forest court the offender was nowhere to be found; and to add still further to the forester's chagrin one of the men who had so readily offered bail for the accused had also disappeared, another was discovered to be a pauper, and a third had died in the meantime.

Members of the clergy were not above an occasional poaching expedition. This same forester James de Thurlebere had also caught the rector of Shipham (very properly assisted by his clerk) taking shots at a hart in Mendip Forest. The Bishop of Bath and Wells had been ordered by the King's forest justices to produce this sporting parson for trial, but the Bishop could not find him, or pretended he could not find him, so the rector was pronounced an exile. On another occasion in 1260 a poaching party from Witham Priory led by an enterprising lay brother was found in the forest above Cheddar lugging one deer they had already killed and chasing another with mastiffs. Brother William, it appeared, had his own special and very effective method of hunting deer. He prepared wooden staves with sharp points which he hardened in the fire. He then drove these staves, business end uppermost, into the ground, blocking the gaps through which the deer generally passed. Then the mastiffs were set loose and the deer were driven against this home-made trap. The Prior of Witham was ordered to bring Brother William and the other lawless members of the priory household before the forest court to receive due punishment for their misdeeds. Sometimes a whole village would be called upon to bear the brunt of a culprit's punishment when he could not be found. Thus during the reign of Henry III the forest court squeezed a large fine out of the four villages of Banwell, Christon, Hutton, and Loxton because two men of Bleadon had killed a buck on Mendip and failed to appear before the judges.

The account of another interesting quarrel over forest rights has been quoted at length by F. A. Knight from the Register of Bishop Ralph of Shrewsbury for the year 1332. Three royal foresters with the sturdy names of John le Champion, John le Knyght, and Clement le Forester swooped down on a party of Bishop Ralph's men who were cutting wood in Mendip Forest. The foresters confiscated the timber, claiming with all legal right on their side that the Bishop's men were committing a trespass against royal property and a grave breach of the forest laws. The Bishop retaliated by sending letters to the clergy of Axbridge, Cheddar, Winscombe, Rowberrow, and Compton Bishop, ordering them to pronounce sentence of excommunication "with due solemnity, with the tolling of bells, with candles lighted and extinguished, and with cross held up by hand", against the three "malefactors who had robbed the Bishop's manors of Axebrugge and Cheddre".

The three foresters were furthermore ordered to do penance in

Wells Cathedral and the parish churches of Axbridge and Cheddar. The Bishop's letter, still preserved, ordered that each of them

> "while the ceremonies of the mass are being performed, shall stand by the font in a penitential attitude, with feet bare, having laid aside his cloak, and clad only in a shirt, in a public and conspicuous place where the congregation there assembled shall be able to discern and see him, and there he shall remain, holding in his hand a lighted candle or taper; and this, when the rites of the mass are finished, he shall offer on the high altar."

Clement le Forester "duly and in all respects calmly and humbly" performed his penance to the Church's satisfaction, but the Vicar of Cheddar reported to the Bishop that John le Knyght during his penance "was not careful to hold the lighted candle in his hand all the time as he had been enjoined, or to stand where the congregation might be the better able to see him".

When King Edward III heard of this treatment of his officers he sent an angry letter to the Bishop supporting the foresters who had tried to protect the royal forest. It was illegal for the Bishop's men to fell

> "divers oaks and other trees in the wood of Cheddre, within our forest of Menydep, pertaining to the manor of Cheddre which is of the ancient demesne of the crown of England, and which you hold at fee farm . . . without the view of the foresters and officers and against the assize of the forest. . . . You caused our said foresters and officers to be cited before you, and because they did not appear before you, you fulminated the sentence of excommunication on them in contempt of us and the right of our crown. We prohibit that you attempt anything which may turn to the prejudice of us or of our crown, and if anything has been unduly attempted by you or yours we will cause it to be revoked without delay."

It is tantalising that the records do not contain the Bishop's reply to the King (if he ever sent one), nor any further reference to the three foresters who had so sturdily maintained their king's forest rights, but the whole quarrel is typical of the complications which arose owing to the difficulties of administering an intricate forest law and land law side by side. Nor was the harshness of the forest laws the only grievance of Mendip landowners. The continual encroachment of forest bounds on private land also caused bitter complaints. Originally the forest comprised little more than the manors of Axbridge and Cheddar, but the boundaries spread farther and farther as successive kings suddenly declared parts of private property to be royal forest, until finally it stretched from the bounds of Cottle's Oak near Frome to Black Rock at the mouth of the River Axe near Uphill. There was a continual struggle to get the limits of the royal forests defined, and one of the clauses of Magna Carta declared that "all forests which have been afforested in our time shall be immediately disafforested". Two years later a Forest Charter was issued by Henry III ordering that all lands which had been afforested during the preceding half-century should be viewed by "good and legal men" with the object of returning them to their rightful private owners.

Yet it was not until 1298, some eighty years later, that officials made a formal "Perambulation" of Mendip Forest and declared on oath what its true boundaries were. And these enclosed a territory which, as the Victoria County History of Somerset points out, did not embrace much more than the parishes of Axbridge and Cheddar, and the officials of the perambulation recommended the return of twenty manors (Banwell, Blagdon, Burrington, Chewton, Christon, Churchill, Compton, East Harptree, West Harptree, Hutton, Langford, Loxton, Priddy, Rowberrow, Shipham, Ubley, Uphill, Whatley, Winscombe, Worle) to private landowners, so that the extent of the forest was reduced once more to its original bounds. In this restricted area the forest laws were enforced more and more sporadically after the Middle Ages as the forest courts decayed, so that in 1535 when Leland visited the district on his "Itinerary" he noted that "Mendepe Forest" was formerly "well furnished with dere; but, anon, aftar, for riots and trespassys done in huntyngs it was deforestyd and so yet remaineth".

In the seventeenth century Charles I made an attempt to revive the forest courts in all their mediæval vigour. Fines were levied for "encroachment" on royal hunting land dating back to the distant past, and an attempt was made to cancel titles to the land which had been restored to private owners after the Perambulation of 1298. This revival of an obsolete royal prerogative aroused intense opposition, and organised poaching raids became a kind of local sport during the Civil War. At last after the Revolution of 1688 the forest laws were dropped once and for all, and the process of disafforestation of Mendip was hastened by enclosures on the hills for grazing sheep. In 1790 the Somerset historian Collinson recalled that "this forest was in ancient times well stocked with deer, nor was it infrequently supplied with wood, but since its disafforestation it has degenerated into a wild and woodless plain, retaining no longer the dignity of its pristine title, nor generally known but by the name of Mendip Hills". Mendip Forest was thus even then nothing more than a memory; today it is generally forgotten even as a name, although the Mendip Hunt and Weston Harriers ride from their kennels to chase the fox and hare over hills where kings once hunted the deer, the wolf, and the wild boar. And Mendip farmers set off in the evenings, gun in hand, over land where centuries ago to be seen taking a rabbit would have incurred all the dire penalties of the royal forest courts.

CHAPTER VIII

TOWERS AND BATTLEMENTS

COLERIDGE had a theory that spires are seen to their greatest advantage in flat country, for an instinctive taste teaches men to build their churches in these parts with spire steeples which, "as they cannot be referred to any other object, point as with silent finger to the sky and stars". Perhaps he may have remembered that as a kind of converse of his theory some of the finest towers without spires are set in the hills of Somerset, where he had spent the early years of his married life. It is true that there are some score of spires in the county (six of them in the Mendip country *), but Somerset is, as Dr F. J. Allen expresses it, "the chief centre for towers without spires . . . it was here during the Perpendicular period that spireless towers attained their greatest perfection, and the county contains nearly as many notable towers as the rest of England together".

But many churches had been built in Mendip towns and villages long before the English builders developed the Perpendicular style about the second half of the fourteenth century, and there are some striking examples of earlier ecclesiastical building in the district. No Saxon church architecture has been preserved, but the large number of Mendip churches with Norman fonts bears witness to earlier buildings, and more extensive Norman work has been preserved in the churches of Compton Martin and Christon. Compton Martin's church is, in fact, the finest example of Norman work in the county, but it was only by an odd freak of chance that it escaped destruction at the hands of the industrious and sometimes ruthless builders of the Perpendicular period. These seem to have planned a complete rebuilding of the old Norman church, and they began work on the chancel arch. As they worked the foundations must have started to sink, flattening out their pointed arch and tilting one of the pillars awry. This distorted arch can still be seen today, for the builders obviously decided not to meddle any further with the old church. But they did "twist" one of the squat Norman pillars in the nave—that is, they carved spiral cable fluting round and round the column, producing a remarkable

* At Croscombe, Doulting, Frome, West Harptree, Whatley and Ubley.

illusion of a twisted pillar. The church would be worth a visit if only to see this odd feature. The Norman church at Christon with its finely carved south doorway is much smaller and simpler, but it is so beautifully situated in its tiny village among the hills, facing the bold outline of Crook's Peak, that it is difficult to understand why Norman building should ever have been characterised as heavy and clumsy.

When towards the end of the twelfth century English builders, like their Continental fellow-craftsmen, discovered how to use a pointed arch instead of the rounded Norman arch, the pillars and some other features of their new arch still had for a time much of the appearance of the old Norman style. There is an excellent example of this "Transitional" building in the north porch of Wells Cathedral, where there are two lines of Norman zigzag moulding round an arch which is pointed and decorated with leaves in the later Gothic manner. The whole of Wells Cathedral is in fact a practical illustration of the history of English architecture in itself, with examples of various styles of building from the Transitional style up to the Perpendicular period. The pure Early English style which developed out of the Transitional style can be seen in the famous West Front and in the Central Tower up to the level of the roof; the flowing lines of the Decorated style which followed the Early English towards the end of the fourteenth century is illustrated in the upper two stages of the Tower, the Chapter House, and the Lady Chapel; and the upper portions of the two Western Towers are Perpendicular.

The skill of the English builders had brought the art of the Decorated style to the peak of its achievement, and then suddenly disaster struck the country, for by 1348 the dreaded Black Death had reached our shores. During this terrible scourge of the bubonic plague, carried by rat-infested ships from China to Europe, between one-half and one-third of the population of England was swept away. When we read how whole families perished, how the dead lay unburied in the streets of the towns, and how in the country the harvest rotted and the ground was untilled, and "sheep and cattle strayed through the fields and corn, and there were none left who could drive them", we realise how completely all industry was paralysed. There are churches in England which still show with what dramatic suddenness the builders were struck down by the disease. Certain details have been left unfinished or were completed at a later date and in a different style. For when the pestilence had finally died away, and life in England began gradually to return to normal, so that building could be resumed, the English builders for the first time developed a national variation of Gothic architecture—the Perpendicular style.

This national variation of Gothic architecture which English builders then developed is very characteristically represented in Mendip churches with their fine towers and their windows of vertical lines—the stone upright mullions crossed at right angles by the horizontal transoms, making a number of narrow rectangles so different in effect from the flowing tracery of the Decorated period. These Perpendicular churches show other rectangular characteristics: in the battlements and panelling of the tower, in the square frames of doorways surmounted by vertical moulding, and even, as at Axbridge, in the panelled ornamentation of the stem and bowl of a font. This continual repetition of the same type of tracery and ornamentation has been criticised by some as rigid and monotonous, and indeed the Perpendicular style as a whole has been the subject of keen controversy. Some have described it as a degeneration after the variety and grace of the Decorated style, while others claim that it is the dignified climax of English Gothic architecture of which we have every right to be proud when we compare it with the fussy Flamboyant style which was developed on the Continent. After seeing a dozen Mendip churches you will doubtless have formed your own opinion, but most people would agree that at least the Perpendicular tower as represented in this district is a magnificent achievement.

The traditional explanation of the large number and rich splendour of these towers in Somerset is repeated by Rutter when he suggests they "can only be accounted for by the probable supposition that they were amongst those erected by Henry VII when he came to the crown in 1485, as a reward for the attachment which the county of Somerset had evinced towards the Lancastrian party during the civil wars"—that is, the Wars of the Roses. Yet Henry VII's notorious avarice and the fact that some of the towers are of earlier date than his accession make this an unlikely theory, and a much more reasonable explanation is to be found in the wealth of Somerset wool merchants in the fifteenth century. It was their money and their enthusiasm which gave the impetus to this magnificent building all over the county. The Mendip district was also fortunate in having plenty of easily worked stone at hand which provided excellent building material for the local masons. Thus the creamy limestone of Doulting quarries which provided the stone for Wells Cathedral is still being worked today.

There have been several attempts to classify Somerset Perpendicular towers, and while most of us are content merely to enjoy them without troubling about their classification it is certainly interesting to realise the remarkable resemblances between certain groups of towers as they have been classified by Professor Freeman, R. P. Brereton, or Dr F. J. Allen. One of the earliest of Somerset Perpendicular towers is at Shepton Mallet, and here the base of a projected spire is clearly visible even from the ground. It is not known why the builders so suddenly abandoned this spire, but it has been suggested that they were afterwards so satisfied with the pleasing proportions of the tower without its spire that it was made the prototype of the spireless tower so characteristic not only of the Mendip district but of the whole county. The typical Mendip tower is square and stands as a rule at the west end, with a west window and outside stair turret; it is crowned with battlements and pinnacles which generally form a beautifully proportioned whole, except in those rare cases when the pinnacles are over-elaborate and are themselves provided with flying buttresses, so that the final stage of the tower has the appearance of a top-heavy lid.

Dr Allen has pointed out that the slightly later towers of Banwell and Cheddar also have signs of foundations prepared for spires which were never built, perhaps another proof that the builders realised they had discovered the art of constructing a beautifully proportioned tower without a spire. It is easy to see signs of the same building tradition—perhaps even of the same guild of masons—in most Mendip church towers, but there is no lack of variety in the superb examples of their skill to be found in almost any village of the district. The genius which could produce towers as diversified as those of Winscombe, Cheddar, Chewton Mendip, Leigh-on-Mendip, and St Cuthbert's, Wells, not to mention scores of other outstanding examples, can hardly be characterised as monotonous.

Panelled oak roofs like those of the churches at Shepton Mallet and Axbridge and the carved bench ends at Cheddar and Winscombe remind us that the Perpendicular period was also notable for the skill and invention of the mediæval craftsman working in wood. A later period is represented in Croscombe church, where there is a display of Jacobean woodwork of almost bewildering richness. An enormous screen reaches almost to the top of the chancel arch, the bench ends and roof are equally elaborate, and the pulpit is an astonishing *tour de force* of the wood-carver's art. Equally interesting from an entirely different point of view are the modern bench-ends at Mells and Rodney Stoke, which are the work of local carvers—an outstanding proof that the fine Mendip tradition of amateur craftsmanship was still alive at the beginning of the twentieth century.

Arthur Mee's book on Somerset reminds us that the county "has more mediæval stone pulpits than any other county in the land—twenty out of about sixty in all England". Some of the finest of them are to be found in Mendip churches: Shepton Mallet (perhaps the finest of them all), Banwell, Bleadon, Cheddar, Compton Bishop, Hutton, and Loxton. Dinder church has something still rarer—a stone pulpit of the seventeenth century. It is a fine work of art, carved with royal roses and fleurs-de-lis.

There is still preserved in some Mendip churchyards, either in original form or partly restored, the old cross which in mediæval times was the meeting-place when itinerant preachers came to the village or travelling merchants set up their stalls. There are particularly fine specimens at Bleadon and Chewton Mendip, the latter an unusual "canopied" variety with the figures at the top of the cross set under cover. According to Charles Pooley, the original shaft of the Bleadon cross was taken away, an iron hook was driven into it, and it was set up in the village as a "hitch-stone" to tie up horses. In 1929 the rector of Bleadon when he first came to the parish "searched for this piece of shaft as it was no longer where Pooley saw it—against the wall of a farmhouse close by the church. Ultimately a part of it was found on the same farm supporting a fowl roost in an outhouse," from which place he rescued it and placed it in the church.

The well-known market-cross at Cheddar has a roof, arches, and steps, although these are obviously later additions to the 15th-century central shaft of the cross. It has often been remarked how skilfully the six-sided roof and steps have been grafted on to the eight-sided shaft. A market-cross of still more elaborate design stands in the market-place at Shepton Mallet, but this is a nineteenth-century replica of the original, which had to be pulled down in 1841, having decayed beyond repair. Another fine market-cross which stood in the market square of Axbridge was taken down during the second half of the eighteenth century and never rebuilt, and about the same time Wells lost a magnificent example of a covered cross because it had become dangerous through long neglect. Perhaps any regret we may feel at the loss of these picturesque links with the past is dispelled by the thought of the added difficulties they would cause in streets already much too narrow for modern traffic.

It might be expected that the Mendips would have several mediæval fortresses still crowning the hilltops, but there are in fact only two ruined castles remaining in the district, at Nunney and at East Harptree. Perhaps it would be more accurate to say that only one remains, as there are only a few fragments of Richmont Castle at East Harptree. The castle at Nunney is still impressive and stands brooding in an kind of magnificent dilapidation, giving the authentic mediæval air to the little village which clusters round it. The history of the castle has been written by C. E. Giles, and he points out that unlike so many other castles it was never the residence of a great feudal lord but of a local knight or gentleman. Its origin has been traced back to a building begun by Sir Elias de la Mare in the latter years of Edward I's reign, but its real history begins in 1372 after a certain Sir John de la Mare returned home from the French wars laden with booty and was granted permission "to fortify and crenellate his manse at Nunney in the county of Somerset with a wall of stone and lime".

In the reign of Henry VIII Leland described the castle as:

> "a pretty castle at the west end of the parish church, having at each end by the north and south two pretty towers gathered by compass to join into one.* The walls be very strong and thick, the stairs narrow, the lodging within somewhat dark. It standeth on the left bank of the river which divideth it from the churchyard. The castle is moated about, and this moat is served by the water conveyed into it out of the river. There is a strong wall without the moat round about, saving at the east part of the castle where it is defended by the brook."

The only exciting period of the castle's history was its last—during the Civil War, when its owner, Colonel Prater, garrisoned it for King Charles I, and stored what the Parliamentarians imagined to be a large stock of ammunition within its walls. In 1645 Fairfax and Cromwell, on the way from Sherborne in Dorset to Bristol, arrived at Castle Cary and despatched two regiments to Nunney with orders to subdue the castle and if possible to capture the store of ammunition intact. Fairfax himself rode over to examine the defences of the castle and declared it "very strong, but not very large".

C. E. Giles quotes one amusing story about the siege. In order to deceive the besiegers the garrison of Nunney Castle punctually every day at ten o'clock used to carry up into one of the towers a young pig which they happened to have kept inside the castle. Then they pulled the tail and ears of the long-suffering animal until its squeals could be distinctly heard by the soldiers outside, who thus imagined that the besieged Royalists had sufficient provisions to be able to have fresh pork every day. Unfortunately a deserter from the castle went over to the Parliamentary army one night and revealed the trick, and turned the

* That is, the building was such a narrow rectangle that the towers at each end were practically touching one another.

King John's Hunting Box, Axbridge

joke against the garrison. It was probably this same deserter who showed the besiegers the thin part of the wall where the staircase led to the upper apartments. They directed their cannon at this point and battered a way through, making a large breach in the wall.

Colonel Prater was unwilling to see his property completely destroyed and after a short parley he agreed not only to surrender but also to change his allegiance. The garrison was found to consist of some eighty men, mostly Irish mercenaries, under a Captain Turberville, and with them "some others, refugees, and a good store of papists". But the victors must have been sadly disappointed in the amount of ammunition they captured—only small arms for 200 men and two small kegs of gunpowder.

> "Seven of the besiegers were killed, and mostly by one marksman who, watching his opportunity from the turrets, seldom failed to strike his man. The besieged lost none but the above-mentioned deserter. One of the besiegers in contempt of the small garrison had the audacity to climb a fruit tree in a garden which was so near the castle that he was brought down by the first shot from the watchful marksman on the walls."

One description shows that the besieged garrison had flown above the castle a red standard "and in the midst thereof a fair crucifix cross". This roused the anger of the Parliamentarians and as the garrison "had fought under such a popish symbol the prisoners were set down almost all as papists, and the flag was sent to London as a trophy and exhibited to the Parliament at Westminster". As for Colonel Prater's hurried change-over from the Royalist side to the Parliamentarians, this seems to have been of little use to him. Parliament voted that the castle should be rendered useless for any further warlike purpose; its interior was destroyed, its roof was stripped, and in addition the remainder of the colonel's property was declared forfeit to the Commonwealth as a punishment for his "treason".

When C. E. Giles wrote his account of the castle the breach made by the Parliamentary cannon in the north-west wall was still clearly visible, but on December 25th, 1910, the greater part of this damaged wall collapsed, and no attempt was made to repair the remainder of the fast crumbling castle until in 1926 it was scheduled by the Ministry of Works as an Ancient Monument. Some necessary repairs were carried out, the moat was cleared, and this interesting example of a fortified house was preserved for the nation.

The curious shape of the castle—a very narrow rectangle with a cylindrical tower at each corner—explains the unusual arrangements

Chewton Mendip church

of the rooms. Some of them were excessively cramped and, as Leland remarks, "the lodging within somewhat dark", but after his time the narrow slits in the walls were replaced by the large windows we see today. It is still possible to work out the general plan of the original interior; the kitchen with its huge fireplace and oven was evidently on the ground floor, and probably all the other domestic offices were grouped around it, together with accommodation for men and horses. The hall must have occupied the central portion of the first floor and was apparently of considerable size, extending the whole width of the castle and lighted by four large windows. In the south-west tower on the second floor there is a perfect example of a domestic chapel of the period. Its door is on the west side, opening in a very interesting and curious manner through the jamb of a deeply recessed window. The other window opens to the east, and its sill, jutting out, forms the altar which is still intact with its consecration crosses. There is also the piscina remaining on the right of the window. In the walls of the north-east and south-east towers it is still possible to trace the shaft of a *garde-robe*, that remarkable mediæval concession to the necessity for some kind of primitive plumbing.

In 1950 the castle, together with its moat, lawns, and water, and described in the auctioneer's catalogue as "a valuable relic of domestic architecture of the late fourteenth century or Plantagenet era", was put up for auction. The bidding opened with an offer of only £150, and finally the castle, together with the title of "Lord of the Manor", was knocked down to a purchaser for £600.

Richmont Castle at East Harptree was a much older building than Nunney; it was, in fact, one of the many Norman castles which sprang up all over the country after the Conquest. The castle is always associated with the family of de Harptree, which later assumed the name de Gourney, but its original owner was Azeline de Perceval, generally known by the unenviable nickname of "Lupus", the "Wolf". He certainly showed a wolf-like cunning when he chose this magnificent site for his stronghold. The castle stood on the brow of a hillside with a clear view of the surrounding countryside, and protected by a deep, thickly-wooded valley and a stream.

Richmont sustained the one great siege of its history during the troubled years which followed Henry I's death, when the crown should have passed to his daughter Matilda. Many of the more powerful nobles scorned the idea of a woman as ruler and preferred to support the claims of Matilda's cousin Stephen, but the masterful and capable Matilda soon rallied followers prepared to fight for her.

In the West Country particularly she had powerful supporters, among them Sir William de Harptree who garrisoned Richmont Castle for "Queen" Matilda and fortified it in anticipation of a siege by the other side. The garrison did not have long to wait; during the following year, after laying siege to Bristol, Stephen himself led an army to East Harptree and settled down before Richmont Castle with the apparent intention of undertaking a long siege. To draw de Harptree's men away from their almost impregnable position Stephen then made a feint retreat, and the impatient defenders, tired of skulking behind their walls, were deceived by this old trick. They rushed out and swarmed down the wooded slope of the valley to attack the rear of Stephen's supposedly retreating army. For once this king seized his opportunity shrewdly and promptly: he hurried his cavalry to the rear of the castle before the besieged garrison could fall back to defend it. The gates were fired, scaling ladders were set against the walls, and Stephen's soldiers poured into the inner wards of the castle and took possession of it while the surprised defenders were still trying to fight their way back up the steep sides of the valley.

The castle remained in a good state of preservation for many years after this, and it was not until Henry VIII's reign that its owner, Sir John Newton, finally pulled it down and used its stone to build the house of Eastwood a short distance outside the village. The effigy of Sir John in the south porch of East Harptree Church shows him with a family of eight sons and twelve daughters—which doubtless explains his anxiety to build a more commodious and convenient dwelling than Richmont Castle.

The remains of the castle are somewhat difficult to find without specific detailed directions; most guide-books speak vaguely of "castle remains about half a mile north-west of the church", as if its ruined walls could be seen from a distance. In actual fact only a few crumbling foundations of Richmont Castle can now be seen jutting out through the turf and tangled undergrowth, but somehow this is quite enough to stir the imagination in surroundings so romantic and so unspoilt.

The simplest way to find the castle remains is to continue up the road past the church until you come to a letter-box in the wall bearing the curious name of "Proud Cross". Then take the lane to the right, over a stile through a farmyard, to another stile and on to a well-marked path leading up to the hillside. You follow the path over uneven ground, bearing to your right so that you keep towards the edge overlooking the wooded valley, which begins to deepen as you go along. The path leads you between two hollows in the hillside which seem to show some signs of the foundations of castle out-buildings or perhaps a wall. You continue straight on until you come to a beech tree with a bole blackened by fires which have been lighted up against it; and there ahead of you are the ivy-covered foundations of the great round keep of Richmont Castle which once towered above the sheer sides of this deep valley. If you clamber over the top to the path just below on what must have been an outer rampart the stone-work is still more clearly visible, and exploration a short distance away will reveal further remains.

The whole place is impressive at any time of the year, but perhaps it is specially attractive in spring and in autumn. In spring the wood is full of birds' songs and a haze of light green hangs over the slopes of the valley. In autumn it glows with a rich warm brown colour; only the rustle of your own footsteps over the fallen leaves and beech-mast breaks a stillness so mysterious and so expectant that as you make your way back over the uneven turf which covers so many stones of that ancient stronghold shadows seem to glide among the trees to remind you that this is haunted ground, peopled by the ghosts of

. . . old, unhappy, far-off things,
And battles long ago.

Chapter IX

"SOMETHING MUST BE DONE FOR CHEDDAR"

One fine August morning in 1789 a small carriage drove slowly through the village of Cheddar towards the cliffs which even in the eighteenth century were one of the recognised show-places of Great Britain. As it went past the straggling line of wretched poverty-stricken cottages small groups of dirty, half-naked children ran along beside it jeering and throwing stones. Dull-eyed, slatternly women in tattered clothes stared sullenly from the doors of their hovels, but they little guessed what the result of this visit to their village would be. For the man inside the carriage was William Wilberforce, the famous philanthropist and slave liberator, who as a direct result of this journey to Cheddar inspired the devoted work of Hannah More for the Mendip miners and agricultural workers. It is a remarkable story of courage, patience, and determination which is still remembered in the Mendip country.

Yet it is surprising how few people outside the West Country know even the name of Hannah More, who was once famous as the friend of Dr Johnson, Boswell, Garrick, Reynolds, and Horace Walpole; as a best-selling writer; and as the woman who altered the lives of countless Mendip villagers. The latest edition of a well-known encyclopædia gives the extraordinary information that she is best remembered for the schools she set up in *Cheshire*—a misprint for Cheddar which most West Country people would consider inexcusable. Most remarkable of all, it was an *American* who wrote the first really new biography of Hannah More for nearly a hundred years.

Hannah More was one of the five daughters of the headmaster of the Free School at Fishponds near Bristol. She started her career with her sisters when as five penniless and inexperienced young women they set up a school in Bristol. It became a very well-known institution, and the five sisters were able to retire with reasonable incomes when Hannah was only forty-five. Meantime her astonishing success in London was largely due to her friendship with Garrick. He encouraged her to write a tragedy, *Percy*, which was produced with great success at the Covent

Garden Theatre in 1777. One critic has charitably said that although this play "is often ridiculous yet it is never undignified". Perhaps it is nearer the truth to say that it is a sobering reflection on eighteenth-century taste that such a fustian piece of nonsense should have been received with rapture, making "strong men shed tears", selling 4,000 copies in a fortnight, and earning for its author a substantial sum in royalties—altogether the kind of success which in our century is mostly reserved for musical comedies.

On the sudden death of Garrick two years later Hannah More resolved never to enter a theatre again, to give up writing for the stage, and to retire to Cowslip Green, a small country house in the beautiful Wrington Vale facing the Mendip Hills. Here she planned to devote herself to serious literary work in the peaceful surroundings of country life, but her friend Wilberforce came to the house and paid his visit to Cheddar. It was a very shocked Wilberforce who returned to Cowslip Green and said: "Miss Hannah More, something must be done for Cheddar. If you will be at the trouble, I will be at the expense."

That Wilberforce had not exaggerated the poverty and squalor he had seen is amply proved by another description of a visit to Cheddar, this time some fifty years later. The visitor was the Rev. Henry Thompson, who stressed that Hannah More's work had greatly altered conditions in Cheddar, and yet

> "some traces of former barbarism are still in existence. It is not more than four years since the writer visited the last surviving inhabitant of *a cave* in the Cheddar cliffs. The abode, far better adapted for a sepulchre than a dwelling, extended a considerable distance into the rock. A narrow fissure served to carry off the smoke while the inner part of the cavern, ceiled with stalactites, was on every side dripping with damp. A rough wooden door rudely following the outline of the cavern's mouth was the only protection against external violence. In this habitation a human being had existed for upwards of thirty years. This woman, wild and squalid as her dwelling, was only one individual of a class who although inhabiting more humanising abodes were neither less ignorant nor less barbarous. Females, whom nothing less but their female garb could associate in the traveller's mind with an idea of the sex, hung on his path at every step, vending the mineral productions of the country and the seeds of the Cheddar pink, and not infrequently engaging in furious and even sanguinary contention when any of the unsightly sisterhood appeared to have been more successful in such attempts than the rest."

These conditions were no worse than those of many other rural parishes in the eighteenth century when the influence of the church was at its lowest ebb and organised religion had been brought into disrepute by the lax morals of many of the clergy and by the abuses of pluralities which turned

> "the wealthier and more learned of them into absentees * while the bulk of them were indolent, poor and without consideration. At the other end of the social scale lay the masses; they were ignorant and brutal to a degree which it is hard to conceive, for the vast increase of population had been met by no effort for their religious and educational improvement. Not a new parish had been created; hardly a single new church had been built. Schools there were none, save the Grammar Schools of Edward or Elizabeth. The rural peasantry were left without moral or religious training of any sort."

This description gives some idea of the problems which faced Hannah More and her sister when at Wilberforce's earnest request they undertook to improve conditions in Cheddar. A number of possible schemes were discussed and finally they decided to establish "a Sunday School for the instruction of the poor in the village". After Wilberforce had left Cowslip Green they drove over to Cheddar and put up for a few days at the George Hotel, a humble little public-house near the Market Cross, so that they could find out how to begin, for, as Hannah More herself confessed, they were utterly at a loss.

> "We found more than two thousand people in the parish almost all very poor; no gentry, a dozen wealthy farmers, hard, brutal and ignorant. We went to every house in the place and found every house a scene of the greatest ignorance and vice. We saw but one Bible in all the parish and that was used to prop a flower pot. No clergyman had resided here for forty years. One rode over from Wells to preach once a Sunday, but no weekly duty was done or sick persons visited, and children were often buried without any funeral service. Eight people in the morning and twenty in the afternoon was a good congregation."

One of the first things to be done, of course, was to enlist the co-operation of the wealthy farmers in the locality. Hannah More realised that she would encounter a great deal of opposition from them on the grounds that education was "the most unsettling thing in the world for the poor", but the two sisters boldly visited them all, finding out at each house the name and character of the next farmer, "for all the world

* One Welsh bishop confessed he had visited his diocese only once since his appointment, as he preferred to live in the Lake District.

like fortune-tellers". Shortly afterwards a letter was sent to Wilberforce to report progress.

George Hotel, Cheddar, 1789

Dear Sir,

Though this is but a *romantic place* yet you would laugh to see the bustle I am in. I was told we should meet with great opposition if I did not try to propitiate the chief despot of the village, who is very rich and very brutal; so I ventured to the den of this monster in a country as savage as himself near Bridgwater. He begged I would not think of bringing any religion into the country; it was the worst thing in the world for the poor for it made them lazy and useless. In vain I represented to him that they would be more industrious as they were better principled; and that for my part I had no selfish views in what I was doing. He gave me to understand that he knew the world too well to believe either the one or the other.

Somewhat dismayed to find that my success bore no proportion to my submissions I was almost discouraged from more visits, but I found that friends must be secured at all events, for if these rich savages set their faces against us and influenced the poor people I saw that nothing but hostilities would ensue, so I made eleven of these agreeable visits and as I improved in the art of canvassing, had better success. Miss Wilberforce would have been shocked had she seen the petty tyrants whose insolence I stroked and tamed, the ugly children I praised, the pointers and spaniels I caressed, the cider I commended and the wine I swallowed. After these irresistible flatteries I inquired of each if he could recommend me to a house, and said that I had a little plan which I hoped would secure their orchards from being robbed, their rabbits from being shot, their game from being stolen, and which might lower the poor-rates. If effect be the best proof of eloquence then mine was a good speech, for I gained at length the hearty concurrence of the whole people.

Patty, who is with me, says she has good hope that the hearts of some of these rich poor wretches may be touched. They are as ignorant as the beasts that perish, intoxicated every day before dinner and plunged in such vices as make me begin to think London a virtuous place. One of the farmers seemed especially pleased and civil. He is rich but covetous, a hard drinker, and his wife a woman of loose morals but good natural sense. She became our friend sooner than some of the more decent and formal. By their assistance I procured immediately a good house which when a partition is taken down and a window added will receive a great number of children. The house and an excellent garden of almost an acre of ground I have taken at once for six guineas and a half per year. I have ventured to take it for *seven years*—there is courage for you!

> I asked the farmers if they had no resident curate. They told me they had a right to insist on one; which right, they confessed they had never ventured to exercise for fear *their tithes should be raised.* I blushed for my species. The Vicarage of Cheddar is in the gift of the Dean of Wells; the value nearly fifty pounds per annum. The incumbent has something to do (but I cannot find out what) in the University of Oxford where he resides. The curate lives at Wells; they have only service once a week, and there is scarcely an instance of a poor person being visited or prayed with.
>
> The living of Axbridge belongs to the Prebendary of Wiveliscombe in the Cathedral of Wells; the annual value about fifty pounds; the incumbent, the Rev. Gould, is about sixty years of age and is intoxicated about six times a week, and very frequently prevented from preaching by two black eyes honestly earned by fighting.

On the following day the two sisters began a systematic visitation of the families in the village itself and drew up an exact list of the characters of the parents, their employment, wages, and the number of their children. Here again a good deal of opposition was encountered. Some refused even to think of sending their children to the school unless they received a payment for doing so; others suspected that the whole scheme was a plot to kidnap children and sell them as slaves. It was all most discouraging, but in spite of continual ill health Hannah More overcame all these difficulties by sheer strength of will; a schoolmistress was appointed and at last the Cheddar school was opened. No less than 170 children were present, and "it was an affecting sight", she wrote to Wilberforce. "Several of the grown-up youths present had been tried at the last assizes; three were the children of a person lately condemned to be hanged; many were thieves, all ignorant, profane and vicious beyond belief."

Yet there were other Mendip villages which were even more savage and uncontrollable than Cheddar. It was common knowledge that no constable would dare to arrest a Shipham man for fear he should himself be waylaid, murdered, and concealed in one of the many mining pits around the village. This method of disposing of over-zealous legal officers had in fact been employed several times in Shipham, according to Hannah More. The neighbouring mining village of Rowberrow was quite as lawless, and the sisters were warned that they might receive actual physical violence from the inhabitants. It was characteristic of their courage that this made them all the more determined in their efforts, and shortly afterwards schools were established in both these villages as well as at Axbridge, Winscombe, Banwell, Blagdon, and other neighbouring places.

It was a heavy and unrewarding task at first, for Hannah More had to combat not only the depravity and ignorance of the villagers but also the malice and jealousy of many of the gentry and church dignitaries. She was accused of teaching false doctrine, of encouraging subversive political activities, and even of "seditiously praying for our enemies, the French, and introducing their revolutionary ideas". The schools were scattered over a wide area, and visiting them all with conscientious regularity and thoroughness was a severe strain on Hannah More's precarious health. In spite of all these handicaps the schools gradually became the most respected and flourishing institutions of their villages, especially when Hannah More decided that

> "surely no harm can arise from giving leave to such parents as desire to hear their children instructed to come in the evening and be instructed themselves. We will at first limit the number; as to the time an hour will be quite sufficient; more would break in upon the children's time and take parents too long from their families. They are so ignorant that they need to be taught the very elements of Christianity."

Hannah More soon realised that religious instruction by itself was not enough; practical measures would have to be taken to do something towards relieving the poverty of these Mendip villages. Rich influential friends like Wilberforce and the famous banker Henry Thornton were badgered for subscriptions, and a scheme for teaching the village women to spin worsted was started in Cheddar. Hannah More had arranged for an Uxbridge manufacturer to buy the yarn at current market prices and also as many stockings as the women cared to knit. In addition girls were given an opportunity of being trained for domestic service, and servants from the "Cheddar School" soon had a reputation for reliability and efficiency.

It was quite as important to instil some notion of thrift into these wild, feckless, undisciplined Mendip villagers, and various "Female Friendly Societies" were organised which in return for the modest sum of three halfpence a week paid out benefits to members—"a sick woman receives three shillings a week, seven shillings and sixpence for lying-in, etc." Reluctantly Hannah More allowed the grant of one guinea for a funeral, the one benefit which seemed really to interest the village women and to obtain which they were even prepared to "relinquish the comforts and blessings of assistance at their lyings-in, for what did a woman work for but in hopes she should be put out of the world in a tidy way?" In 1816 two societies alone had a membership of three hundred women, and in twenty years over £1,000 had been paid out in benefits—a remarkable record, although Hannah More records that at one of the Society meetings "two or three ungrateful members came determined to complain that their good health had always prevented their taking out any benefit!"

These practical adjuncts to Hannah More's introduction of religious teaching into Mendip villages were strictly supervised. Old folk in the almshouses who regularly attended the morning and evening prayers instituted by Hannah More for them were rewarded at Christmas-time, and Martha More's diary tells the story of one old woman of Shipham "who came with the rest for her promised reward of a shilling, a piece of beef and some peas. It was found on inquiry that she had never attended the prayers once. . . .So as she refused the benefit of prayer she was also denied the pleasure of beef."

In her diary Martha More gives a full description of the first "Mendip Feast", a remarkable outing which took place on Callow Hill above Cheddar Wood:

> "We had long promised the schools a dinner as a bribe for good behaviour, and the prospect of the *feast* as they called it was a charm so captivating that it procured many a task to be learned with pleasure for the sake of obtaining one good dinner. On the 4th of August [1791] on Callow Hill, a high part of Mendip, all our children were assembled (except the new schools—without them we had five hundred and seventeen). We left Cowslip Green in the morning with some friends, mounted in a waggon dressed out with greens, flowers, etc. Another followed with the servants, thirteen large pieces of beef, forty-five great plumb-puddings, six hundred cakes, several loaves, and a great cask of cider. The children by order were concealed in a valley whilst all the preparations were making, such as railing in a large piece of ground and placing the dinner upon the ground to the best advantage. In the meantime we were arranging the children below. At the sound of the horn the procession began. A boy of the best character carried a little flag; we walked next, then Mrs Baber followed by the Cheddar children and so on according to seniority, all the schools, one after another, singing psalms. Upwards of 4,000 people were assembled to see this interesting sight. After marching round our little railing all were seated in pairs as they walked. The dinner was then carved and each child had at his feet a large slice of beef, another of plumb-pudding and a cake. The instant they were served all arose and six clergymen who were present said grace. All were again seated and were permitted to eat as much as their stomachs would hold, and talk as much as their tongues would go. At the conclusion Hannah permitted a general chorus of "God

Save the King", telling them that loyalty should make a part of their religion. We all parted with the most perfect peace, having fed about nine hundred people for less than a *fine* dinner for twenty costs. The day was the finest imaginable and we got home safe in our waggons."

Hannah More's anxiety to encourage some feelings of patriotism among the Mendip children (if only by making them sing the national anthem at the conclusion of this almost too well disciplined picnic) is readily understandable when we recollect that by 1791 revolutionary doctrines were already beginning to spread from France to England, and agents of the Convention were intriguing with discontented elements in this country. To combat these seditious forces Hannah More wrote a series of simple popular tracts which had the enormous sale of no less than two million copies in one year and contributed, according to one contemporary, "very essentially to counteract the poison of impious and immoral pamphlets which were dispersed over the kingdom in such numbers by societies of republicans".

But in the Mendip district it was the schools and Hannah More's own practical philanthropy which had the greatest effect. The Rev. James Jones, who when curate of Shipham had found the poor in such an uncivilised state, could now as rector write:

> "I attend our school every Sunday and it gives me pleasure to observe that the most regular attendants at church are they who attend the school. A weekly school of industry and a benefit society for the poor women were established here by Hannah More, all of which institutions in a place of such extreme poverty are eminently advantageous, and their good effects are evident in the gradual diminution of vice, and the growth of industry and morality."

Meanwhile the war with France which had broken out in 1793 was bringing considerable hardship to the Mendip district, especially to the two mining villages of Shipham and Rowberrow, where there was no longer any demand for the calamine ore and some 1,200 miners were out of work and almost destitute. The distress was so great that Hannah More and a friend began to purchase a certain amount of the ore every week, storing it in a warehouse until better times returned, and in addition she "laboured hard to prevail on the *real* merchants to renew the trade by the time these purchases were exhausted". The poor of Shipham had by now become so accustomed to look to Hannah More for help in time of trouble that scarcely a day passed without someone knocking at her door and applying for relief.

There is no doubt that this ready practical philanthropy had its effect on the characters of these rough mining villagers, for although during the troubled years after Waterloo "seditious discontent began to assume a menacing appearance; when nightly assemblages were held, threatening letters were sent; and houses, barns and rick-yards were set on fire, displaying melancholy proofs of the degradation of national character produced by long distress", yet it is recorded that in Shipham, where after the distress of the war years discontent might well have been dangerous,

> "every single effective male inhabitant came forward begging permission to enrol himself in an association if it were necessary, or at any rate requesting that their little community might send up an address expressive of their horror of revolutionary principles and their desire to prove their loyalty on any suitable occasion. The address was prepared and sent up to Lord Sidmouth accompanied with an intimation that these were the same patriotic fellows who, when the French landed at Fishguard some years since, were suddenly seen marching in military order to Bristol."

Hannah More died in Clifton on September 7th, 1833. She had every reason to look back with quiet satisfaction on the result of her life's work in the Mendips, but she could hardly have imagined that such a remarkable tribute of respect and affection would be paid to her on her last journey to Wrington, where she was to be buried in the family vault with her four sisters. She had always expressed a wish that her funeral should be private, but a great number of people in deep mourning joined the funeral procession as it passed through Bristol. Shops were closed and the bells of all the churches tolled. On its arrival at Barley Wood it was joined by a large body of the neighbouring clergy, gentry, and yeomanry, accompanied by children from her schools, who on arriving at the churchyard lined the pathway to the door.

It is only natural that Hannah More had critics as well as admirers. Cobbett scoffed at what he called "the old Bishop in petticoats"; de Quincey published (anonymously) a vitriolic attack on "Holy Hannah" three months after her death; and Augustine Birrell sneered at her writing and at her philanthropy.

> "She was one of the most detestable writers that ever held a pen [he wrote], and she flounders like a huge conger eel in an ocean of dingy morality. She was the first of a large class which may be described as 'the well-to-do Christian'. It inhabited snug places in the country and kept an excellent if not dainty table. Outside its garden wall lived the poor who, if virtuous, were for ever curtseying

to the ground or wearing neat uniforms, except when expiring upon truckle-beds beseeching God to bless the young ladies of The Grange or the Manor House as the case might be."

In spite of these gibes the fact remains that it was the practical humanitarianism and energetic personal example of Hannah More in that age of lazy complacency which drew attention to the physical and moral needs of a neglected agricultural and mining community. As a writer she may be deservedly forgotten, but her influence in the Mendip villages was profound and lasting. There her memory is still respected, although derelict chimneys and deserted sunken hollows are now the only remains of that vanished race of miners.

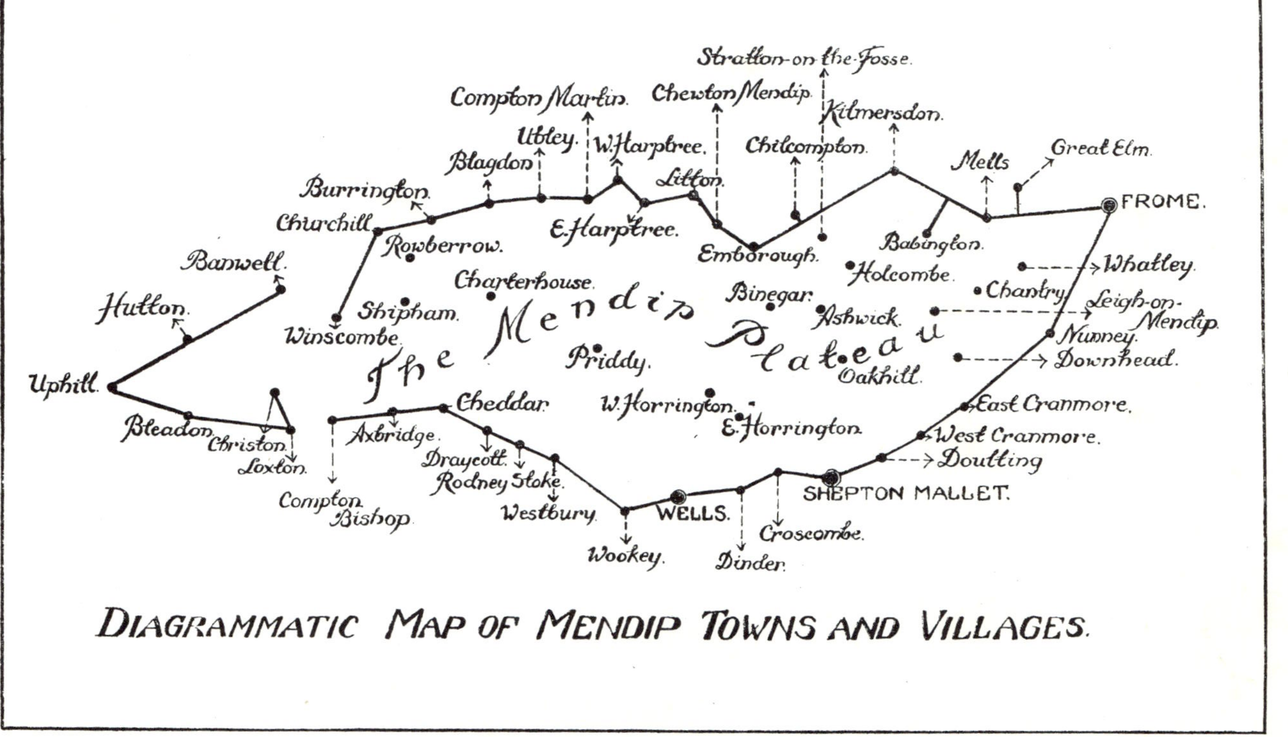

Diagrammatic map of Mendip towns and villages

Old Uphill church

Chapter X

THE WESTERN RIDGES

The western ridges of the Mendips, separated from the main range of the hills by the Lox Yeo valley, slope away to the west at Bleadon, narrowing to a rise at Uphill, and then thrusting into the sea they come to an end in the strange monster-like shape of Brean Down, only to reappear once again two miles away as the rocky island of Steep Holm. The villages of this part of Mendip lie all around the foot of the slopes and the best roads link these villages by encircling the base of the hills. To cut right across the ridges, say from Bleadon to Banwell, or from Hutton to Christon, you must be prepared to walk at least some of the way or to subject your car or bicycle to rather rough treatment. All the same, these exhilarating hill roads should not be entirely neglected if magnificent and ever-changing views of countryside, hill, and sea appeal to you. Even without walking, a car or bicycle will take you comfortably to some of the finest vantage points.

I always regard Banwell as the capital, so to speak, of this part of Mendip, first because of its antiquity, and then because it has so much of interest for even the casual and hurried visitor. Its quiet preoccupation with the orderly bustle of everyday village life only serves to conceal history so rich and varied that it is difficult to know what to mention and what to omit. First in chronological order, of course, is the prehistoric hill camp which lies to the left of the road leading into Banwell from Churchill off the main Bristol–Bridgwater road and the caves, but the first in general interest is the church. The fine slender proportions of its tower are best appreciated from the high parts of the village which clambers picturesquely up the steep sides of the Mendip ridge. On the south side of the tower there are two figures which in my boyhood days *both* had a carved lily and vase on the sills beside them. Apparently the left-hand figure's floral decoration was added in the nineteenth century because the two figures were popularly supposed to represent Henry VI and his wife, and it was felt that the king should be symmetrically honoured with his queen. A wiser generation realised that the figure with the original lily is the Madonna and the other represents the angel Gabriel. I see that the latter's

The Norman church at Christon

gratuitous lily has recently been removed. Of the general appearance of the church the historian Freeman remarked:

> "I am inclined on the whole to set down the nave and aisles of Banwell as, externally, the most thoroughly beautiful I know among churches of its own kind; the proportions of the aisle and clerestory are absolutely perfect. I have hinted that the Perpendicular clere-stories are, if anything, a little too low and the windows a little too small. Banwell has hit the exact mean; its range of three-light windows with pointed arches is most stately."

Inside, the magnificently carved rood-screen set up about 1521 and the fine timber roof are perhaps the features which will attract most attention, but the church also has a stone pulpit (hardly improved by the extra "wing" added in Victorian times) and in the vestry some delightful little panels of Flemish glass collected by a former vicar which represent various incidents from the Book of Tobit, featuring in particular Tobias, Sara, and of course the dog. The heavy-looking font is Norman, but the stem carving around the bowl was obviously added at a much later date. In the churchyard close by the path passing along the south side of the chancel is a curiously foreign-looking carved stone bust of the local archæologist William Beard.

Next door to the church is the so-called Banwell "Abbey", a private residence which was built in the nineteenth century but incorporated some of the stonework of the ancient episcopal palace or manor-house originally belonging to Thomas Beckington, the great fifteenth-century Bishop of Bath and Wells. Banwell is closely associated with several Bishops of Bath and Wells. One of them, Thomas Godwin, built a summer residence here called Towerhead about 1584. In Rutter's time it was still "a large substantial structure in the Elizabethan style, retaining much of its original character". Later, however, it was pulled down, and the present Towerhead Farm which stands by the road under the slopes of Banwell Camp retains only a few traces of the old building—some original stone doorways and a carved stone shield bearing the arms of Bishop Godwin and his punning motto: WYN GOD WYN ALL. This bishop's summer months at Towerhead were clouded by trouble with Queen Elizabeth when (to quote Harrington's *Life of Godwin*)

> "aged upwards of seventy years and very infirm he married his third wife, a widow much younger than himself. Sir Walter Raleigh, coveting the manor of Banwell and being very well aware of the Queen's dislike to marriages of her clergy represented it to her

Majesty as a heinous offence that the bishop had married a girl of *twenty*, when he was so gouty that he was unable to stand at the time of his marriage. The courtier finally begged that the bishop might be deprived of his possessions at Banwell and that they might be granted to himself by lease for one hundred years. The queen's favourite, the Earl of Leicester, defended the character of the bishop, and the Earl of Bedford assured her that 'though he knew not how much the woman was above twenty yet he did know that she had a son near forty". This rather irritated than soothed the queen who replied, 'He hath the greater sin. There are three kinds of marriages: first, of God's making, when two young folks are coupled; second of man's making, when one is young and the other is old; and third, of the devil's making, when two old folks are married, not for comfort, but for covetousness, and such is this of the bishop's.' The good bishop was much perplexed by this sudden tempest and withstood several severe messages from the queen, probably similar to the one she sent to the Bishop of Ely, viz.

Proud Prelate,
I understand you are backward in complying with our agreement, but I would have you know that I, who made you what you are, can unmake you; and if you do not forthwith fulfil your engagement, by God I will immediately unfrock you.

Yours, as you demean yourself,
ELIZABETH

Fearing that he should lose his favourite manor of Banwell the Bishop relinquished that of Wiveliscombe for ninety-nine years and by this means purchased his peace."

The unhappy Lady Sybil did not long survive this unseemly treatment of her husband and the parish records say she was buried in Banwell church under the Bishop's great pew, which was later removed.

It is unnecessary to remark that Banwell Castle for all its specious air of antiquity is a modern building—unnecessary because the present owner in order to ward off the more persistent type of sightseer has set up the whimsical notice:

"Built in the 19th century and has no historic or other interest. Kindly remember that this Englishman's castle is his home and do not intrude."

But a strange turf mound in the shape of a cross close by the castle is genuinely ancient. It is situated on top of the hill, which can be approached by the gateway opposite the castle entrance. An almost square surrounding rampart and ditch enclose this mysterious cross, which is still clearly visible although covered over with a tangle of weeds. It is scheduled as an Ancient Monument, but no satisfactory explanation of its purpose has ever been given by archæologists. At various times it has been described as a special kind of fortification, a Roman boundary mark, an ancient cattle-shelter, and even a meeting-place of primitive Christians.

The chief landmark of Banwell, visible for miles around, is the tower which crowns Banwell Hill. It was built about 1840 by another Bishop of Bath and Wells, G. H. Law, who also planted avenues of trees about the hill and laid out walks in the manner of a park. It is an easy climb up to this interesting tower if you go up the lane leading off the turning near Banwell Castle. You pass through a gate and continue between lines of larches along a fine ridge walk with superb views on both sides. The avenue of trees swings to the left and you go between two ruined pillars which might once have supported an arch or perhaps an ornamental gate. The track continues to climb gently up to a small archway which is blocked up, but there is an easy entrance on the left which leads into the last narrow overgrown path.

I have climbed up to Banwell many times—on summer days when the crowded trees have been motionless and heavy with the heat; on winter days when the branches were bare and a cold wind rustled the dry bushes, and I always feel the same atmosphere of mystery, of hushed expectancy, directly I enter this last stretch of track. And I never fail to recall those haunting lines of Wordsworth's:

I heard among the solitary hills
Low breathing coming after me, and sounds
Of indistinguishable motion, steps
Almost as silent as the turf they trod.

There are rough stone pillars at intervals all along this track which leads straight to the small mound on which the tower stands. You can still mount the winding stone steps almost to the top, and through a window guess what a panorama was once visible over the parapet which has recently crumbled away and crashed to the ground. It is sad to see that the whole tower is rapidly falling into a state of dilapidation and soon this interesting Mendip landmark will be beyond repair.

As you go out of Banwell to continue your journey round the western ridges to Hutton you will notice a remarkably handsome bowling green in the centre of the village. In my boyhood days this area was covered by an ancient pool fed by the well which gave the village its name, but in recent years this familiar feature was drained and covered over, and the well water was diverted elsewhere—not, I understand, without a certain amount of heart-burning and belated opposition in Banwell. Rutter gives a full description of Banwell pond as it was in the eighteenth century:

> "The large sheet of water in the middle of the village is ornamented by a graceful weeping willow on a small island in the centre and a pair of handsome swans. It forms a pleasing object from the street. This beautiful spring of water which is said never to be frozen works an extensive writing paper manufactory."

and according to F. A. Knight this paper was later used for making Bank of England notes, until the factory became a brewery, which has in its turn disappeared.

For a short distance we follow the main Weston-super-Mare road, and on our left Bishop Law's tower makes a conspicuous landmark on the top of Banwell Hill. Then we branch off to the left for Hutton along a road which hugs the side of the hills and from which there is a wide view over the level land to the sea. The narrow road which leads off to the left before we come to the village of Hutton winds up through a small wooded valley and then peters out into a rough track climbing right to the top of the hill which in my schoolboy days we always called "Caterpillar Hill". This odd name was probably suggested by the bristling line of trees along its crest, which when seen from a distance gave it the appearance of a rough hairy ridge. Unfortunately the trees have now been so thinned out by wind, weather, age, and disease that the old name has lost its original appropriateness.

Hutton itself nestles under its wooded hill sheltering its church and ancient manor-house which lie tucked under the trees away from the main road. It is difficult to realise that this tiny place has a history which even in written records dates back to the Domesday Book. Later in Henry III's reign it is mentioned as one of the four Mendip villages which had to share the fine levied on two Bleadon poachers who failed to appear before the forest courts. In its church there are two outstanding treasures: a stone pulpit and a pair of ancient brasses. The pulpit is superbly carved and set at such an astonishing height above the floor (there are nine steps leading up to it) that listening to a sermon must be a neck-cricking penance in the front pews.

Both the brasses commemorate members of the Payne family and they are each adorned with a bevy of eleven children. The older brass of the two is to be found underneath the strip of carpet within the altar rails. It is to the memory of John Payne who died in 1496, and it shows him in knightly armour with sword and dagger. Facing him is his wife, and beneath them, boys below the father, girls under the mother, are the effigies of their four sons and seven daughters. It seems almost impossible that this monument is over four and a half centuries old, so well has it been preserved, and so clearly marked are the lines in the metal. The other brass, in the recess of the north wall of the chancel, is to John Payne's son, Thomas, who died in 1528. Behind him kneel eight sons, and behind his wife there are three daughters; thus did father and son both just fall short of a dozen in their family figure.

Church registers are generally inaccessible to the ordinary visitor, and in any case most of them make difficult and not always interesting reading. But there is one unforgettable entry from the Hutton church register for 1793 which was quoted by F. A. Knight. The rector who married William Pimm and Diana Brooks in that year added the following note about the service: "When I came to that part of the ceremony on the woman's part 'Obey him', etc., Pimm bawled out, 'Stop, sir; please to read that over again. The women don't rightly understand it.' " In 1805 the register notes that prayers were said in the church "on account of a compleat victory over the French fleet off Trafalgar by Adm'l Nelson who lost his life in the battle", and in 1815 "for the splendid victory gained by the Duke of Wellington over Buonaparte at Waterloo, which decided the war".

The attractive manor-house, Hutton Court, is close by the church, Its oldest portions are the dining-hall, which has a fine old timber roof, and the square tower at its side. These may very well have been built by the John Payne who lies buried before the altar in the church.

The road from Hutton continues to cling to the side of the hills, and then, dipping sharply, it crosses the main Bridgwater to Weston-super-Mare road and leads into Uphill. Uphill was once a somewhat isolated little village, and even now, in spite of being very much of a crowded "far end of Weston", it has managed to preserve something of a character of its own. The Roman associations of the place have already been described and today its most obvious landmark is the little ruined church which stands with a kind of sturdy bleakness on the hill looking out to sea. This old building was most suitably dedicated to Saint Nicholas, the patron and guardian of seamen, since for centuries it has been a landmark for ships sailing the Severn sea. In Rutter's time it was, in fact, frequently whitewashed, which must have made it even more conspicuous, but whitewashing seems to have been the general method of treating most Mendip buildings at that period. Rutter himself criticised the practice saying:

> "It is common in this part of the country for public and private edifices, and to a stranger arriving at the edge of the lofty Mendip Hills above Blagdon and Burrington the whiteness of the distant buildings below him affords a pleasant mixture with the more natural objects of the vale; but on approaching the several edifices the fine effect of strong masonry is quite destroyed by the unmeaning uniformity of the whitewash."

Perhaps its romantic situation on the cliff gives this forlorn little ruin its undeniable attractiveness, but it might be added that those who are sufficiently energetic to clamber up the hill to examine the building at close quarters will be rewarded by the view and the interest of the church itself. It was about 1840 that the parish of Uphill began to think of deserting their old church. It was showing signs of serious dilapidation and its position on the hill was a great handicap to older parishioners. A new church of Saint Nicholas was built in a more accessible part of the village and consecrated in 1844, but for two years services were still held in the old church on alternate Sundays, until finally it was closed up. About twenty years later the roof became dangerous and was taken down; at the same time the chancel was converted into a mortuary chapel for burials, which still take place in the churchyard. You can walk through the north door into the roofless grassy nave, and a door set in the chancel leads into the tiny chapel, where ever since 1894 a yearly service has been held every second Sunday in July. Traces of the original Norman building can still be seen in the north porch and in the small arched doorway of the south wall. On the south side of the squat tower is an odd three-headed gargoyle which may possibly have been the somewhat ingenuous anthropomorphic representation of the Trinity carved by a local stonemason.

Near the church is a round tower, the remains of an old windmill, which have fortunately been preserved as a vantage point from which there is a magnificent panoramic view of the surrounding countryside.

Rutter mentions Uphill's "coal wharf on the river Axe where vessels from sixty to eighty tons may conveniently unload". At the foot of the quarry under the hill the remains of this old quayside can still be traced, and farther along the river mouth, opposite the small Black Rock which once marked the western limit of the Forest of Mendip, a ferry plies across to Brean Down. At low tide, when the mouth of the Axe here is reduced to a muddy trickle, "crossing over by the ferry" consists merely of walking across the almost grounded boat from one end to the other and disembarking on a flight of slippery steps covered with glutinous grey mud; but the saving of time for anyone intending to explore Brean Down is considerable, as it obviates a long circuitous detour by road.

From Uphill to Bleadon there is a steep climb over the southern slopes of this western ridge of the Mendips. The southern aspect, extensive views, and close proximity to Weston have encouraged a fair amount of building along this road in recent years, but Bleadon itself is still a small village—a rather sternly grey village which stretches down to the moorland at the foot of the hills. There is an ancient tradition connected with Bleadon at the time of the Danish raids on England which is quoted by C. W. Dymond in his account of Worlebury. A party of Danish marauders had settled themselves on Steep Holm so that they could more easily make raids on the mainland. On one occasion they crossed over to Uphill and

> "fastened their ships to the shore, left them and marched up into the country for booty. All the inhabitants fled away before them, one poor lame woman excepted, who hid in a rock near the ships. When she was near spent with hunger she was necessitated to adventure down to the ships for relief, but coming thither and searching from ship to ship and finding no living creature, at length espying a hatchet, took it and with it chopped off all the cables which anchored the ships to the shore, and sent them to sea where they quickly perished. The Danes, having gotten intelligence of the loss of some of their ships, speedily returned to save themselves and the rest, but the people of the country, having intelligence that all their ships were cast away, took courage, pursued them to Bleadon and there fought and destroyed them with such a bloody slaughter that from thence the place took and ever since hath kept the name Bleadon, alias Bleed-down or Blood-down, to this day."

This ingenious but quite inaccurate explanation of the name of the village is followed by an account of Bleadon ploughmen, who when they "plough their grounds find multitudes of men's teeth there which, being naturally the hardest bones in the body, are almost as permanent as little stones". Finally, to complete the story of this traditional battle, "a gentleman, having bought a piece of moorland ground lying at the foot of the said Bleadon, had his labourers renew the dyke filled up about it, and they found great heaps of men's skulls and human bones as entire as ever they had been".

Bleadon figures in the pages of verifiable history as belonging to

Githa, Harold's mother, who escaped to Mendip Forest after her grandsons had been defeated by William the Conqueror at Exeter.

There is a very fine specimen of a village cross just outside the churchyard wall, and the remarkable story of how its lost shaft was found has already been told in Chapter VIII. The head of the cross is modern, but the figures now set in the right wall of the church porch may very possibly have been the original head, for this curious piece of canopied sculpture is certainly very reminiscent of the covered figures crowning the cross at Chewton Mendip. Inside the church the most interesting things to be seen are the richly carved octagonal stone pulpit, the tub-shaped Norman font, and the two weather-beaten stone effigies dating probably from the fourteenth century which were moved from the churchyard and now lie on the floor of the nave.

After Bleadon the road winds along the base of the hills, which now show cultivated fields and woods stretching halfway up the gentler southern slopes. To the right the Somerset flats recede into the distance with a network of rhines and pollarded willow trees. Then the bold outline of Crook's Peak stands out against the skyline and a sharp turn left over a little stone bridge leads up to the picturesque village of Loxton which clambers up the steep hillside beside the road. The church, which is well below the road, has an attractive setting of really unspoilt rusticity. A farmyard flanks the churchyard wall, and cows stare in mild surprise at the visitor passing through the gate under the great yew-tree which spreads right up to the tower. This tower has some traces of Norman work and the lower part of it forms the porch, in which there is a curious squint-hole cut right through the wall at such an angle that the altar can be seen.

Another of the magnificent Mendip stone pulpits belongs to the church, carved out of one single block of stone, and resting on the stone figure of a man. The little sixteenth-century oak screen across the chancel has a pleasing simplicity, but perhaps the most interesting treasure of the church is some fragmentary fourteenth-century stained glass in the delightful chapel which has been made out of a former vestry. A typical example of the robust eighteenth-century brand of practical piety is shown on a board fixed to the north wall of the nave. It gives details of the fifty pounds left in 1765 by Mrs Ann Gadd, who directed in her will that the interest obtained from it when "lent out on the best security" was to be spent in teaching "the poor children of Loxton parish to read and to knit". In 1829 Rutter wrote, "A poor woman is appointed by the present rector to teach six or eight poor children to read and knit, for which she is paid 25*s.* half yearly from the interest of this money." When the present rector first came to the parish he discovered that the Gadd Bequest was being used to provide a gift of money to each of the Loxton children who were in the village school at Christmas-time. This hardly seemed to have been Mrs Ann Gadd's intentions, and in order to carry out the terms of the will more closely it was decided in 1951 that the benefit of the charity should be used for "the purchase of Bibles, Prayer Books and other material for the use of the Sunday School (or Children's Service) of Loxton Parish Church to enable the children of the parish to read the Holy Scriptures and other religious literature for their spiritual edification".

Just outside the porch, shadowed by the yew-tree, is a well-proportioned fifteenth-century churchyard cross. The original head has been lost, but it has been replaced with a very beautiful and most effective modern replica of an ancient canopied head with figures.

Not even the pylons which stride along this green Lox Yeo valley can detract from its peaceful, unassuming charm, and Christon, the next village, is as attractive a place as the most hardened and fastidious traveller could wish to come across on a summer evening. It has none of the neat, well-ordered quaintness of the typical "postcard" village, but its simplicity is quite unspoilt. Its tiny Norman church has an especially fine doorway from which there is an impressive view of Crook's Peak on the other side of the valley.

> "No one who has seen this porch [says Arthur Mee], framing in its arch this perfect Norman doorway, can forget it. There are few who will not accept the invitation of the ancient stone seats to stay awhile by this rough horseshoe arch, those lovely mouldings, and look out at the other picture in this frame, where Crook's Peak shoots up like a miniature volcano from the Mendip ridge."

The nave and chancel arches and the small font are equally good examples of Norman work, and it is interesting to notice how the chancel is deflected (to represent the drooping of Christ's head at the Crucifixion) and how skilfully the steps are shaped to fit the awkward turn of the chancel arch. The vaulted roof under the tower is spanned by ribs which end in an odd dragon-like head, and it is worth while examining the outside of this squat tower to see the amusing little animals and human faces which the Norman craftsmen carved around it.

Recently a new reredos of light oak has been built in front of the former stone one, and the altar has been moved forward. This has solved in an ingenious way the problem of providing the church with a much needed vestry, which is now tucked away behind the new reredos.

The farmhouse to the west of the church is the rebuilt manor-house, most of which was pulled down in 1822 and the remaining portions greatly altered. In front of the old mansion there was, according to Rutter, a richly decorated porch, and over it the arms of the Vaughan family sculptured in stone, but in his day this lay "neglected in the enclosed garden", which still retained its "ancient gravelled terrace, 64 yards in length".

On leaving Christon the road continues to wind along the side of the valley right under the brow of Banwell Hill, and then after a stiff climb it leads past Banwell Castle to the starting point of this round tour of the western ridges of the Mendips.

Recently the "peaceful unassuming charm" of the Lox Yeo valley has been rudely shattered by the road building works which are thrusting a continuation of the M5 motorway towards Highbridge. The giant shovels, bulldozers and lorries have poured into this green and fertile place with all their usual concomitant ugly noise and the scattering of clouds of choking red dust. Local inhabitants have stared aghast at the ruin modern progress has made as it destroys or irredeemably changes the familiar features of this Mendip valley in the interests of speed. All they can hope is that when the motorway is completed and the cars are hurtling along its carriageways it may possibly blend with the landscape more happily than they dare to hope at present.

CHAPTFR XI

THE MENDIP PLATEAU

THE capital and centre of the Mendip plateau is Priddy, a village as cheerless and grey as Mendip stone walls, sheltering in a hollow around its green where a famous sheep fair is held every August. Its church stands on rising ground above the village, and its sturdy tower is fretted by the bleak winds which whistle over the cottages in the wild winter weather. There is something particularly appealing about the rough workmanship of this lonely church. It has an enormous Norman font and a crudely made stone pulpit now superseded by a smaller substitute north of the chancel steps. An interesting embroidered altar cloth of the fifteenth century which was formerly kept framed in the church is at present in the vicarage so that its faded colours may be preserved from damp.

Perhaps it is hardly surprising that such an isolated village in the heart of a mining district should once have had a reputation for a love of violence tempered with a respect for rough justice. As far back as 1225 a document records that a Priddy man with the extraordinary name of John Swete-bi-the-bone "killed Richard the Shepherd and fled. Therefore let him be exacted and outlawed. He had no chattels." And in the days of the *little ol' men* there were many tales told *down under Mendip* of the wild doings *up to Priddy*. Yet with all this lawlessness Priddy always jealously guarded old customs, and even today Priddy folk maintain a skill in folk dancing and still cherish the charming (although not very ancient) tradition that Christ came to their village as a boy when Joseph of Arimathea journeyed here to trade for metal.

Shipham was also closely connected with Mendip mining, and the land around the village is still honeycombed with mounds and hollows. Francis Knight's book *A Corner of Arcady*, which describes the building of a house near Shipham for his retirement, has several good stories about the treacherous nature of this "gruffy ground" with its hidden pits and galleries just below the surface. When his household belongings were brought up to the new home the drivers of the vans refused to risk themselves until they had "liquored up for four hours at a wayside tavern—another proof of the dryness of the district". The *minedry* or old mine refuse spread over much of the land makes it sour and difficult to cultivate. Until he enriched the soil Knight had in his kitchen only stunted sickly yellow cabbages, shrivelled turnips, and no peas, beans or onions at all. "Us told 'ee zo," the locals had said; "'tis that there minedry; you won't never be able to grow nothing there."

Two wars, the motor-car and the wireless have done much to eradicate the soft-sounding dialect of Mendip countryfolk, but at the beginning of the century when Knight's book appeared it was still possible to hear the infinitive ending in *y* and the rough breathing *hr* before the letter *r*—"It do hrainy vor zure; but Jesse did tell I as how Mr Clark did tell 'ee, whether 'twere Zaturday or Zunday a could'n zahy, as how it did hrain vor dree hours, down the maash." Thirty years before *Agrikler* had published a "Grammar" of Mendip speech and gave the conjugation of the verb "to be" as follows:

Present Tense	*Past Tense*
I be	I were
Thee beest	Thee wert
He, she, it be	He, she, it were
We'm	We was
You'm	You was
They'm	They was

Present Negative Interrogative	
Bain't I?	Bain't us?
Bisn't thee?	Bain't 'ee?
Banner?	Bain't 'em?

Although in recent years Shipham has become a place of residence for more and more Bristol and Weston townspeople with a taste for village life, it still retains something of its old mining-village characteristics and it has an irregular network of narrow lanes winding through a number of sternly grey cottages. Its church is a Victorian building with an octagonal tower and an interior almost forbiddingly austere. It has a window to the memory of Hannah More, and an interesting font cover which was made in Shipham out of a massive oak door from the original church after it was pulled down about 1840. Old drawings of the original St Leonard's show it as a small building with a plain square tower crowned by a low spire. It has been suggested that the gargoyles on the present tower were saved from the previous building.

Another former mining village, Rowberrow, lies under the Dolebury Warren less than a mile from Shipham. Its picturesque little church has a sturdy fifteenth-century tower of a beautiful warm red stone, but the remainder of the church was rebuilt in the nineteenth century. Its most interesting possession was dug up at the time of the rebuilding and is now preserved in the north wall of the nave. It is a carved stone with an intertwining pattern and a snake-like motif suggesting that it was once part of an early Saxon cross.

It is the district around Shipham, Rowberrow and Charterhouse which forms the background of *Two Men O' Mendip*, perhaps the most successful book of the Somerset novelist Walter Raymond, and an excellent picture of life in this part of Mendip at the end of the eighteenth century. Charterhouse lies halfway between Shipham and Priddy, a lonely, wind-swept place surrounded by deserted mine workings, dark moorland and rough stone walls, all of which seem to enhance the friendly, simple beauty of its whitewashed gabled church. Inside there is some excellent modern carving, and an open fireplace in the north wall gives a unique touch of homeliness to this delightful little building. The name Charterhouse is connected with the monastic cell which is traditionally supposed to have been founded in this isolated parish as an offshoot of the original Carthusian monastery at Witham, about three miles south of Nunney. Witham was the first Carthusian religious community set up in England, the direct result of Henry II's penance for the murder of Thomas à Becket after the Pope had commuted the original penalty of a three years' crusade into the building of three monasteries, of which one was to be a Carthusian community. In the royal deed granting land to the small band of monks who came from La Chartreuse to Witham about 1180 there is included the gift of a large tract of land on Mendip, where later these austere followers of St Bruno's rule worked the lead mines and kept large flocks of the now extinct breed of Mendip sheep. The prior at Witham signed a surrender of all the monastery's buildings and lands at the "Dissolution," and the cell at Charterhouse has long since disappeared, even its position being now only conjectural.

The central area of the Mendip plateau is a district of farms, many of them with strange picturesque names like Crapnell Farm, Roemead Farm, Thrupemarsh Farm, Burnthouse Farm, and Washingpool Farm. Here are very few villages and they are of little interest. Binegar is an exposed little place locally well known for an annual horse-fair held at Whitsuntide. Except for its attractive, rather prim-looking tower, the whole of the church was rebuilt in Victorian times, and although it has a pleasant enough exterior it is hardly worth a visit inside. The name of Gurney Slade promises more interest, suggesting romantic connections with the famous Gurney family, but in spite of the Downside School song which extols the attractions of the Abbey Water Works Pumping Station here it is nothing more than a characterless main road hamlet. Oakhill, with the important exception of a large brewery, has even less to offer the interested traveller, and its near neighbour Ashwick has only a graceful Perpendicular tower left to suggest what its church was like before it was rebuilt in Victorian Early English with pitchpine furnishings.

East and West Horrington are two breezy villages situated high above Wells on either side of a main road, with little apart from fine views to interest the casual passer-by. The one village in this district which draws many thousands of visitors every year is Stratton-on-the Fosse, where the great attraction is the magnificent Benedictine Downside Abbey set about with green trees and lawns, and with its lofty tower standing high above the surrounding countryside. This great building was begun in the nineteenth century as the permanent home of this branch of the English Benedictine community of St Gregory after their long period of exile. For after they had been driven abroad from this country by the Reformation they settled at Douai until 1793, and then the French Revolution forced them to move again and once more they came to England to find refuge. For nearly a quarter of a century they had a home at Acton Burnell in Shropshire and then finally settled here at Downside with their now famous school. It would be impossible to describe here the rich details of the Abbey church: its lofty nave and spacious choir; its numerous chapels and elaborate carvings; and its magnificent organ with a system of reversible luminous stop buttons which have a double-touch cancelling action. Downside Abbey can be appreciated only after several visits and with attention to all its details as well as to the general effect, which is one of exhilarating spaciousness and gracefulness combined with dignity and restraint.

On the other side of the village street, once a section of the Fosseway, is Stratton's parish church dedicated to St Vigor—a dedication shared by only one other church in England. It would be interesting to know how many of the visitors to the great Abbey ever search out this unassuming little building, and yet as a village church it has nothing to be ashamed of. With its attractive porch, Norman font and dainty stone pulpit it is the perfect foil to its majestic neighbour.

A glance at the map will show that the eastern side of the Mendip plateau is criss-crossed by a bewildering network of roads linking up a few scattered villages in an apparently haphazard fashion. The long straight roads of the old Roman mining district come to an end here, with the important exception of the highway above Shepton Mallet, which climbs over Beacon Hill and gives a vast and impressive view. It is from this road that a track leads up to Cranmore Tower, another Mendip "Folly" which stands high on the hills. This was once the property of the Paget family, who used to allow the public to climb its spiral stairway to the top balcony and view the magnificent expanse of countryside spread out below that great height. Now the Forestry Commission has the land and Shepton Forest has been planted about the tall grey tower which has become a neglected ruin with split walls and crumbling steps.

Whatley, the plateau town nearest Frome, is a quiet place where R. W. Church was rector for nineteen years before becoming a well-known Dean of St Paul's. He came from Oxford as a newly ordained priest to this little agricultural community and found here a dilapidated church, a tumbledown rectory, and indifferent or suspicious parishioners, but no one could have played the part of a country parson with more tact, energy, and enthusiasm. Soon a new relationship of respect and affection grew up between him and the villagers; he was their friend and counsellor, but at the same time he was not afraid of showing the sternest disapproval of parishioners' failings. It used to be said that during his time at Whatley "a man durs'n any more beat his old woman else parson 'ud be down on 'un", and in any drunken brawl he would always be sent for to stop the dispute and if need be to step in and part the combatants. One occasion of this sort was long remembered in the village. After being sent for late one night to stop a fight between two men, both very drunk and very violent, the rector fearlessly seized the more powerful of the two and forced him to walk up and down the road, until at last the man, sobered and quietened, turned and shook his hand, saying, "Thank 'ee, zur, I think I've walked far enough now, and zo I'll go a-bed."

In 1871 Gladstone offered the rector of this obscure little Mendip village the Deanery of St Paul's. After much hesitation on his part and much pressure from his friends R. W. Church finally accepted, but not without some misgivings that he had made a great mistake in exchanging his peaceful life at Whatley, where he could work calmly and at his leisure, for the tangle and whirlpool of ecclesiastical problems and quarrels in which his new appointment would involve him.

> "You will not mind my telling you before the treadmill begins [he wrote to a friend] how happy my life has been at Whatley these nineteen years, what blessings I have enjoyed in the sense of liberty, in being able to worship and serve away from the strife of tongues, in the perpetual delight of the beauty of nature all round, of sun and

Downside Abbey

air, and green fields and flowers, in the kindness of friends of high estate and still more of low. I have not valued them or used them as I ought, but it is very bitter to take leave of them and to know that they will never come again as they have been."

At the close of his life Dean Church had always expressed a wish to be buried in the Mendip village where he had spent some of the happiest years of his life as rector, and his simple grave may be seen close to the south wall of the chancel of the church, a small building in the Decorated style with a simple but graceful octagonal spire over the tower which gives it a special interest in this landscape. The interior was extensively restored when Dean Church was rector, largely at his own expense, but there is a good Norman doorway in the porch and a magnificent fourteenth-century stone effigy of Sir Oliver de Cervyngton in the chantry chapel.

About a mile beyond Whatley church on a spur of the hills is the village of Chantry, with an interesting Victorian Gothic church designed by Sir Gilbert Scott. Chantry is a scattered parish consisting of four groups of houses: Chantry, Little Elm, Bull's Green, and Deadwoman's Bottom—a grim name which recalls the equally sinister Murder Combe and Mary's Grave nearby. Downhead, a little way off the main road, has a small church which has fortunately managed to preserve eight fantastic gargoyles on the tower and a Norman font in spite of some ruthless nineteenth-century restoration work.

The glory of Leigh-on-Mendip is its magnificent church tower, but it is in itself a pleasant, straggling little place with all the colour and characteristics of a bleak upland village. On old maps it is written as *Lye-under-Mendyp* and this pronunciation is still retained in spite of the modern spelling. In this part of Mendip the name is a kind of shibboleth and a stranger is immediately recognised when he asks the way to "Lea". Leigh is justly proud of its lovely church—one of the loveliest in the whole of Somerset. Seen from the village the grandeur of the tower seems out of all proportion to the more modest size of the rest of the building, but this disparity is forgotten once you are inside. Here the magnificent roofs supported by thirty stone angels give an effect of dignity and space which is all the more striking if you have just come from the rather stuffy stained-glass obscurity of Chantry church. The old oak benches are particularly fine. One of them, the last on the north side, has a series of notches cut into it which are generally supposed to be the tally-marks made by some bored fifteenth-century parishioner to register the turns of the pulpit sand-glass. Another interesting feature of the church can be seen above the doors in the chancel, where there

Modern bench end, Rodney Stoke church; old bench end, Cheddar church

are two small corbels which must originally have been used for supporting the veil spread before the rood during Lent in pre-Reformation times.

There is little of interest in Coleford, which still looks like a small and not unattractive mining village; Stoke Lane (*alias* Stoke St Michael), although situated pleasantly enough in a miniature valley, is hardly worth a special visit. Except for the tower its church was completely rebuilt in the nineteenth century, but all the old monuments were meticulously preserved. Some of them have been fixed to the new walls, including one clumsy seventeenth-century gravestone which stands out incongruously against its Victorian surroundings.

Holcombe is a village which should on no account be missed, not that it is particularly interesting in itself, but about a mile away you will find its former parish church surrounded by green fields, and now used only occasionally for a service, because a modern church has been built more conveniently in the village. But the villagers have not allowed their old church to become a neglected ruin, and this beautiful little building is one of the most satisfying sights in the whole of the Mendip district. A farm at the end of a lane supplies the key, and a path across the fields leads to the simple grey church, which has a perfect Norman arch at the south porch with a finely carved angel as its key-stone and on one of its capitals a strange inscription apparently scratched upside down. The inside, of almost Quaker-like simplicity, is furnished with quaint box-pews painted white and still provided with old-fashioned candlesticks.

For all its artless simplicity this little church has great associations and recalls one of the most moving episodes in the history of British exploration. For in its graveyard members of the Scott family lie buried, and the famous explorer of the Antarctic himself once stood beside the grave which now bears the added inscription:

> *And in memory of Robert Falcon Scott, C.V.O., Captain, R.N., who in returning from the south pole with his companions was translated by a glorious death, March, 1912.*

CHAPTER XII

THE NORTHERN FRINGE

THE northern fringe of the Mendips is bounded by roads which from Winscombe to West Harptree run under the shadow of steep hills; and then from West Harptree to Frome they pass over the gently undulating country which slopes away from the irregular plateau of eastern Mendip.

Winscombe has had the good fortune to attract two sympathetic local chroniclers in Theodore Compton and Francis Knight. Compton's *A Mendip Valley* has long been out of print, but anyone fortunate enough to come across a second-hand copy will find it a delightful study of Mendip village life at the end of the nineteenth century. In its modest way the book does for Winscombe what Gilbert White's classic did for Selborne and it has something of the flavour of its famous predecessor. Francis Knight spent the greater part of his life as boy and master at Sidcot School, and besides being the author of the authoritative *History of Sidcot School* he has also written with knowledge, affection and humour of Winscombe and its people in *The Heart of Mendip* and *A Corner of Arcady*.

Even in Compton's day the chief centre of the village was not by the church, as one might imagine, but in what was then the small hamlet of Woodborough.

> "Though it boasts of a 'street' [he wrote], and even a *square*, there is not a row of houses in the actual village of Winscombe. The street is without shop, footpath or lamp-post and the square is simply a meeting of lanes. There is not even a public-house; an attempt was made some years ago to supply this uncommon want, and a vermilion sign swung for a while from a small farmhouse heralding *The Rising Sun*, but the vermilion faded, the sign broke down, and so did the publican. The *Rising Sun* set, to rise no more. It is the central hamlet of Woodborough which has an inn, a Congregational Chapel, a Board School, a lecture and temperance hall, the Post Office and the shops."

The shop which combined the business of post-office and general stores with a kind of benevolent chaos and which I knew so well in my schoolboy days had been transformed into a private residence; Winscombe now has a smart new building used solely for the transaction of postal business under the direction of efficient officials, but Compton's description of the old régime arouses affectionate memories:

> "In the Post Office . . . may be purchased at all prices from a halfpenny upwards those variously tinted portraits of the Sovereign which transport anything they stick to from Woodborough to the ends of the earth. Next is the counter for stationery and drapery, and on a shelf opposite the door is a display of crockery. The shelf below is more attractive to the young. Sweetmeats allure the tender mind and, if nursery morals be sound, spoil the teeth; but here are other bottles to counteract the ill effect of lollies and bull-eyes; the bane and antidote are both before us, as in the days of Cato and Shakespeare. The other end of the shop is devoted to grocery and the provision trade; while over your head hang boots and shoes with formidable hob nails and iron heels, intermingled with spades and shovels, brushes and brooms, baskets and buckets, candles and curry-combs."

Originally the parish name of Winscombe was relatively unfamiliar, as Compton points out:

> "Woodborough is in the centre of Winscombe valley and parish, and the Post Office and Inn being there the name is more familiar to drivers from Weston-super-Mare than that of the parish itself. The station itself is in Woodborough and was at first called by that name, but there being another Woodborough station in Wiltshire, and mistakes having been made, our station received the more distinguishing, comprehensive and correct name of the parish and valley. It is the only Winscombe in the whole island, perhaps in the whole world."

As a boy I was told the story of the renaming of the railway station—a story which Francis Knight has recalled in *The Heart of Mendip*. Having decided to change the name the railway authorities in Bristol sent down a board inscribed with the name "Winscombe" and gave instructions that it should be set up in place of the old "Woodborough". A local carpenter employed for the job spent a laborious afternoon and evening fixing the new board. For years this old man had successfully concealed the fact that he was unable to read, but the secret was out next morning when passengers for the first train stared in amazement at the board bearing the curious name ƎBWOƆSNIM.

The Cheddar Valley Line, completed in 1876, has now been closed under the Beeching plan after nearly a century of useful life. A contemporary Bristol newspaper described the official opening of the first section of the railway:

> "Notwithstanding that a soaking rain fell all the morning the proceedings were attended with considerable éclat and excited much interest throughout the district generally. Leaving the main line at Yatton the branch proceeds through nearly ten miles of some of the most beautiful and picturesque scenery of mid-Somerset. The making of the track for a considerable part of the route has been comparatively easy; the natural level of the valley has been followed as much as possible, and the line passes over and under some half a dozen bridges in its course. It is only when Axbridge is approached that there is anything like a heavy cutting, and before getting to that station there is a short tunnel through the limestone rock.
>
> "At eleven o'clock a special train left Yatton containing in an elegant saloon carriage nearly all the directors of the railway and passed slowly through the several stations. At Axbridge a number of flags were exhibited, the Union drum and fife band played and the bells of the church rang merrily. At Cheddar the directors were invited into the station where an elegant refection of cake and champagne was prepared for their refreshment. The vicar said he was deputed to welcome them to Cheddar. In his opinion the main cause of the prosperity of the railway was that the directors were a God-fearing body (*hear, hear*). They had not run on the Lord's Day those monster excursion trains by which the people were demoralised. He wished them all success for their line (*loud applause*). Several bottles of champagne were then opened and the usual toasts were drunk without stint."

The part of the village around the parish church is still quite unspoilt and as tranquil as ever it was in Compton's time. There are one or two new houses, but the road which climbs up the hillside is still narrow and comparatively unfrequented.

The church has a fine tower which R. P. Brereton considered the most graceful example of the Cheddar Valley type. Inside the north porch a stair turret leads to what was once a room over the porch, and the position of the original floor is still clearly visible. The most noteworthy possession of the church is the rich fifteenth-century and sixteenth-century glass, which although it suffered some mutilation during the nineteenth-century restoration of the church is still a wonder of colour. The most interesting and complete windows are in the north wall of the chancel and at the east end of the north aisle; and as an attractive example of the soft glowing colours which former craftsmen could produce in glass the ancient fragments in the small window over the priest's doorway in the south wall of the chancel are well worth examining. Of original woodwork there remain ten bench-ends carved with a pleasing simple design, and the fine roof of the north aisle is genuine Perpendicular craftsmanship, with which it is interesting to compare the very competent copy in the south aisle.

One quite illegible memorial on the south wall under the tower commemorates Mrs Whalley, the mother of Thomas Sedgwick Whalley of Mendip Lodge. Another memorial on the opposite wall is to Samuel Knollys, First-Lieutenant in the 21st Regiment of Foot who

> "when just recovered from the Yellow Fever which in six weeks had carried off thirteen of his brother officers at Antigua, volunteered his services against Guadéloupe, and the captain under sickness confiding the command thereat to him, he as its leader, after giving many signal proofs of his courage in the attack against the town of Pointe-à-Pitre (defended by the French), received a mortal wound on the 2nd of July, 1794, whereof he died the day following in the 21st year of his age."

Sidcot, on the east side of the main Bristol to Bridgwater road, is mostly a collection of houses gathered around the well-known Quaker school. There had been a school here as early as 1699 under the patronage of the Society of Friends but not under their direct control. The present school traces its history back to 1808, when a new constitution superseded private enterprise and a committee of Quakers appointed John Benwell superintendent. After an early experiment in mixed-class teaching the school adopted co-education at the beginning of this century, a daring venture in those days.

Francis Knight's history of the school is a fascinating study of progress in education, and for the Sidcot scholar of today it must seem almost as much an historical curiosity as the Stone Age to read of a syllabus restricted to "Reading, Writing, English Grammar, Arithmetic, and Geography"; of a headmaster who roughly reproved a boy's whistling with the words, "Does thou not know that whistling is the next door to swearing?"; of "three boxes of proper dimensions for the solitary confinement of refractory boys"; of the rule that "a boy must stand with his face to the wall while the girl walks quickly past him" in the case of an accidental meeting in a passage; of a hungry young Quaker Oliver Twist who when he ventured to ask for more was told by the scandalised mistress, "holding her hands together as if she had just caught a cricket ball, 'Dost thou not know that little boys' stomachs are only *so* big?' "

Perhaps it is only fair to add that it is not only the school authorities who have become more enlightened. Francis Knight has described a remarkable game of the old days called Mad-Ball which

> "was played once a year only at the General Meeting. Every fellow who could provided himself with a supply of small hard balls—surreptitiously, for the authorities strongly objected to the sport, and no wonder—and on the two days of the General Meeting it was considered the proper thing to pelt the visitors, male and female, old and young alike, without the least respect of persons. It is forty years since, but I can still see our white-haired master, standing bareheaded at the door, calling vainly to us to desist, when a stray ball struck him in the face and smashed his spectacles to atoms."

Another Sidcot story concerns an eighteenth-century poltergeist. In a cottage opposite the old Meeting House there lived a man called George Beacham who had something of a local reputation not only as a horse-doctor but also as a wizard. Before his death he directed his wife to have him buried not in consecrated ground but under a tree in his garden. "If 'ee don't," said the old man, "I'll trouble 'ee." His last request was not complied with, however, and the parish register records his burial in the churchyard on July 27th, 1788. A year later, on the anniversary of his death, the Sidcot Friends were sitting quietly in meeting when a terrified old woman rushed in crying out, "Oh, neighbours, do 'ee come out; there be all Joan Beacham's things a-vallin' about the vloor!"

And so indeed they were. When two members of the congregation crossed the lane and entered the cottage a heavy chair lurched forward to meet them; tables were dancing about the room; pots and pans were flung violently about; old Joan's great pastry pan rocked to and fro as if moved by invisible hands; and the dead man's boots clattered noisily downstairs into the kitchen. The astonished neighbours crowded round to watch these disturbances, which after a while ceased as suddenly as they had begun. Various people tried to find the cause of the strange phenomenon; even Hannah More drove over from Cowslip Green to make enquiries about it, but in spite of the most rigorous search no explanation was discovered and no trickery exposed.

The most interesting part of Churchill lies some little way from the main Bristol to Bridgwater road. This little village is doubly connected with the family of the Duke of Marlborough, and thus with Sir Winston Churchill—first, because the ancestor of Sarah Jennings who married the first Duke of Marlborough, once owned Churchill Court, the attractive house, largely rebuilt, which is close to the church; and secondly, because this house was sold in 1652 to Sir John Churchill who was himself a cousin of the Duke's.

There are several good things to be seen in the pleasant little church, especially the two stone effigies, presumably of the former lord of Churchill Manor, Sir Roger Fitzpayne, and of his wife, which now lie in the porch; the Jennings brass; and the Latch monument. The picturesque brass is at the east end of the south aisle and is a memorial to "Raphe Jenyns" and his wife, "Jhone", who were sixteenth-century great-great-grandparents of the famous Duchess of Marlborough, one-time confidante of Queen Anne. Ralph Jenning's will had directed that after his death his executors were to "provide one great marble stone to lie upon my grave and a picture of my wife and my eight children with the daye, month and yeare of my buriall to be made and graven in latten, and fixed on the same stone". In Collinson's time the brass effigies of the five sons and three daughters were still there, but some vandal must have removed them later to squeeze in the white marble gravestone which is now below it.

The Latch monument is a handsome but rather macabre piece of work in the north wall of the chancel. It shows Sir John Latch (a seventeenth-century owner of Langford Court) lying full-length, leaning on one elbow and looking with a tragic expression of sorrow at the waxen face of his dead wife Sarah which can just be seen through a slit of her burial shroud as she lies beside him. Below them are the small kneeling figures of their eleven children, seven boys and four girls; four of the children are carrying skulls to show that they were dead when the effigies were made. Beside the first son there is the figure of a babe swathed in black.

The traditional story which has been handed down for generations to explain this gruesome tableau recounts that Sir John Latch returned home from the Battle of Newbury in 1644 to find his wife had died in childbirth the day before. So great was his grief as he gazed on the corpse of his beloved one that he himself "was immediately struck down by the hand of death".

Two windows on the north wall contain some beautiful pieces of old glass presented to the church by the present owner of Churchill Court. They have an interesting history, which is best told in the words of the donor:

> "This fourteenth, fifteenth, and sixteenth century glass was originally in Wakefield Parish Church but was turned out by Gilbert Scott when he 'restored' the church in 1861. It lay for many years in the plumber's shop, but was bought in 1905 by J. W. Walker who

offered to replace it in that church, but the offer was declined because 'it did not match the new glass by Kempe'. Thus it found its way to Churchill."

From Churchill it is another "A" road which runs north of the Mendips as far as West Harptree, but it is a main road of great beauty, banked on one side by wooded hills and with wide views on the other First there is the strange outline of Dolebury Warren on our right and then Mendip Lodge woods sweep right from the very crest of the hill down to the side of the road. The Lodge itself has been demolished but for years it glimmered ghostly white against the enveloping trees, and indeed it was a ghost—or rather the derelict skeleton—of a very remarkable house built by a very remarkable man, the Rev. Dr Thomas Whalley.

As a boy I had always stared with interest at this strange, Italian-looking house with its long arcaded verandahs, which seemed perched at an impossible angle on the steep side of the hill. Not until years after did I hear of Dr Whalley and read the caustic account of him and of his house written by De Quincey in his most acrimonious vein.

Thomas Sedgwick Whalley, the son of a Regius Professor of Divinity at Cambridge University, was born in 1746. He was ordained as a matter of course in the somewhat irreverent fashion of the times and after making something of a name for himself as a poet he spent his time as a young man travelling widely on the Continent. He had always had connections with the Mendip district, as his mother was the daughter of a Chancellor of Wells Cathedral who owned Winscombe Court. This connection was still further strengthened when Whalley married the heiress of Langford Court. His bride was a widow and some years older than himself, but she was very wealthy and the young clergyman lived very happily with her in spite of the fact that he proceeded very rapidly to reduce her very considerable fortune by his extravagance. For without having any positive vices Dr Whalley was a notorious spendthrift. In addition to running the luxurious household of Langford Court he bought a house in the fashionable Royal Crescent at Bath, where he entertained on the most lavish scale, and he became a conspicuous figure in the set that fluttered around the spa squandering money in liberal hospitality. To servants he distributed largesse like a prince, and in Bath the post-boys used to fight for the honour of driving him. About this time Fanny Burney met him and described him as "immensely tall, thin, and handsome, but affected, delicate, and sentimentally pathetic."

Ten years later his finances were in such confusion that he had to let Langford Court, and it was then that he began to build Mendip Lodge.

One of Dr Whalley's lifelong friends has left a detailed description of the house as it was at the end of the eighteenth century:

> "It is the loveliest architectural luxury I ever saw, being seated on a slope of the Mendips at the east end of Dolebury Warren. It hangs over the traveller at a considerable distance and at first sight appears inaccessible, but the ascent is so gradual and easy that we are soon surprised to find ourselves on an Italian verandah, 84 feet long, looking down on innumerable towers, steeples and villages. In every direction are steep and verdant walks, and the grounds contain fifty-two grottos, one for every week in the year.
>
> "Recently I passed six weeks in this Alpine habitation. It is peculiarly calculated for the almost dizzy elevation on which it stands and for the extreme of light which it catches and which is given by large windows the whole height of the appartments, from every one of which on the second floor we step out into the gay verandah. Here twenty-four large china jars had been filled with autumnal flowers and one of them placed under every arch. There is a noble dining-room at the back of the house adorned with fine pictures, the chief glory of which is a full-length portrait of Mrs Siddons by Hamilton. It is a speaking, a beautiful, an exquisite likeness, by which her charming face and figure, drawn in the prime of her life and beauty, should go down to posterity. The state bedroom, like the dining-room, is at the back, and was fitted up with much magnificence in expectation of its being occupied by the late Duchess of York on an intended visit to this spot."

There was also a description of what was perhaps the most remarkable feature of the inside of the house—"the painted rooms", in which landscapes in trellised frames had been painted on the walls, apparently by some of the French prisoners who were drafted into Bristol during the Napoleonic wars.

In 1801 Dr Whalley's first wife died, and two years later he married Miss Heathcote, a rich Wiltshire lady, who brought him another small fortune to squander. During the winter months they used to close up Mendip Lodge and live at Bath. Reports of his social activities here brought a letter of sharp reproof from a friend, who complained that "one lady had amused a circle of company with accounts that Dr Whalley had permitted a public display of his bride's night-clothes decorated with lace of the most profuse expense".

And yet this eccentric clergyman had as frequent visitors to Mendip Lodge many other more orthodox and more worthy celebrities such as Mrs Piozzi, Mrs Siddons, and Hannah More, with whom he maintained a lifelong friendship. William Wilberforce, who met him during his visit to Cowslip Green, shrewdly summed him up as "a sensible, well-informed and educated, polished, well-beneficed, nobleman's and gentleman's house-frequenting, literary and chess-playing divine—of the best sort". Another visitor to Wrington who met him about the same time was the young De Quincey, who regarded both Mendip Lodge and its owner in a very different light.

> "Mendip Lodge [he wrote] was a show place in which a vast deal of money had been sunk upon two follies equally unproductive of pleasure to the beholder and of anything approaching a pecuniary compensation to the owner. The villa, with its embellishments, was supposed to have cost at least sixty thousand pounds, of which one half had been absorbed, partly by a contest with the natural obstacles of the situation, and partly by the frailest of all ornaments—vast china jars, vases and other knick-knackery baubles which held their very existence by so frail a tenure as the carefulness of a housemaid, and which at all events, if they should survive the accidents of life, never are known to reproduce to the possessor one-tenth part of what they cost.
>
> "Out of doors there are terraces of a mile long, one rising above another and carried by mere artifice of mechanic skill along the perpendicular face of a lofty rock. Had they when finished any particular beauty? Not at all. Considered as a pleasure ground they formed a far less delightful landscape and a far less alluring haunt, than most of the uncostly shrubberies which were seen below in unpretending situations and upon the ordinary level of the vale.
>
> "What a record of imbecility! For all Dr Whalley's pains and expense in forming this costly 'folly' his reward was daily anxiety, and one solitary *bon mot* which he used to record of some man who on being asked what he thought of the house replied that 'he thought the Devil had tempted the Rev. Doctor up to an exceedingly high place'. No part of the grounds, nor the house itself, was at all the better because originally it has been beyond measure difficult to build it—so difficult that, according to Dr Johnson's witty remark on another occasion, there was good reason for wishing that it had been impossible."

Whalley's second wife died two years after their wedding and the widower spent the next eight years squandering the remainder of her fortune. Then, heavily encumbered with debt, he cast around for a third wife and married an eccentric widow named Mrs Horneck, of Bath, in circumstances described at caustic length by De Quincey:

> "Finding himself in difficulties by the expenses of this villa going on concurrently with another large establishment, he looked out for

> a good third marriage as the sole means within his reach of clearing off his embarrassments without proportionable curtailment of his expenses. It happened, unhappily for both parties, that he fell in with a widow lady who was cruising about the world with precisely the same views and in precisely the same difficulties. Each (or the friends of each) held out a false flag, magnifying their incomes respectively, and sinking the embarrassments. Mutally deceived they married, and one change immediately introduced at the splendid villa was the occupation of an entire wing by a lunatic brother of the lady's. the care of whom with a large allowance had been made to her by the Court of Chancery. This, of itself, shed a gloom over the place, which defeated the primary purpose of the Doctor (as explained by himself) in erecting it. Windows barred, maniacal howls, gloomy attendants from a lunatic hospital ranging about—these were the sad disturbances to the Doctor's rose-leaf system of life."

The ill-assorted couple agreed to separate and Whalley had to arrange a settlement for this third wife and also gave her a large house in Bath, where she became famous for her grand parties. The doctor for his part was suddenly struck with remorse for the way he had wasted money in extravagance and vanity, and he determined to sell Mendip Lodge so that his financial affairs should be set in order before his death.

As he was asking £30,000 for the house, it is hardly surprising that it was never sold. The disconsolate old man wandered from acquaintances to relations and from relations back to acquaintances; or he travelled abroad to divert himself. At the age of eighty he decided to set up a home again and bought a house in Windsor Terrace, Clifton, but he left it in the following year, as he considered that the fogs from the River Avon made it unhealthy. He later offered it to his old friend Hannah More, who spent her last years in it after selling up Barley Wood.

At the age of eighty-two he left England for the last time on a visit to a favourite niece at La Flèche. Although he took the journey in easy stages he was so frail that it proved too much for him. He died a few weeks after his arrival in France, "in a common lodging-house", according to De Quincey, "and in all things the very antithesis of that splendid abode which he had planned for the consolation of his melancholy and the gay beguilement of his old age".

Some twenty years later a member of the Somers family bought Mendip Lodge, which had been in Chancery since Whalley's death. I have seen a series of photographs showing how carefully the interior, the gardens and the walks had been restored to their original beauty. The house was sold again about 1904, and after various vicissitudes of occupation and vacancy it fell into disrepair and finally decay and its owner abandoned the idea of renovating it in these difficult days of expensive building materials and had it pulled down.

It was shortly after discovering the whole of this strange story of Dr Whalley and Mendip Lodge that I went to explore the house itself. Although the little twin lodges on either side of the gates facing the main road were in ruins and the fine drive winding through the trees was rutted and overgrown, yet the house itself looked in what gardeners call "reasonably good heart". It was therefore all the more curious to find on drawing nearer that its front assumed first the blank appearance of an empty house and then finally the desolation of a derelict ruin. Surely never did a house hide its dilapidation more successfully.

The stables were still occupied but the house had fallen into a sorry state of decay. Paths were strangled by weeds and overhanging bushes; windows were smashed; the roof was stripped; and damp had rotted the woodwork. A rusty gate screeched on its hinges opening on to the lower verandah tangled with the wilderness of brambles now covering the slopes which were once smooth green lawns. Inside the house reigned destruction, decay and an uneasy stillness. I opened a shutter to let a shaft of sunlight into one end of Dr Whalley's "long suite of rooms"; there were still mirrors on the inside of the shutters, but the paper hung down in festoons from the ceiling and floorboards had been ripped up. The walls of the "painted rooms" had been stripped, and the wistaria outside the Duchess of York's bedroom had run amok, pushed its way between the window sashes and was clambering across the floor and up the walls. Only the view from the upper verandah remained unspoilt—a superb view of landscape spread out below, shining in that clear light which a northerly vista always seems to give.

As I passed out of this chill, mouldering, empty shell of Dr Whalley's "architectural luxury" and left its shuttered ruined rooms once more to the throng of silent ghosts who must have been waiting to emerge from their shadowy hiding-places, I could not help thinking with what sardonic relish De Quincey would have viewed this pathetic ruin as a fulfilment of his prophecy that "Mendip Lodge was a monument to the vanity of human wishes and a melancholy comment upon the blindness of human foresight".

For most people Burrington means Burrington Combe (generally visited as a prelude to the vaster and grander Cheddar Gorge) and the "Rock of Ages". Hardly any of the thousands of sightseers who flock up the Combe during the summer months on a "round trip" to

Cheddar make the short detour to the village of Burrington; consequently it has preserved a peaceful charm which is quite remarkable for a place so near a popular tourist centre. As the narrow road leads nowhere there is practically no traffic, the grey walls are brave with a mass of bright valerian, and the cottages are gay with flowers. The church is small and neat, with a most elaborate stair-turret which formerly led to a rood-loft. The turret itself is surmounted by a tall, graceful spire which makes it seem taller and more striking than the squat tower at the west end of the church. A well-restored cross stands just inside the churchyard, which also contains some interesting gravestones, set up on end, to various members of the families of Jones and Somers. One odd inscription to Edward Jones states that he was "born Novr. ye 15th 1708 and Dyed March ye 14th 1708". This apparent error is in fact a correct statement, because before the introduction of the New Style of calendar in 1752 a new year did not begin until March 25th. There are some amusing, nightmarish gargoyles on the north wall of the church, one of them a hideous animal whose mouth is stretched open by a monkey.

Inside it is a pleasure to see how well the church is cared for, but there is not much of striking interest apart from the ancient sculptured slab (probably part of a tomb) which was discovered under the plaster of the south wall of the sanctuary.

The two tattered flags hanging on either side of the tower arch with their device "Who is afraid?" are the last remnants of the colours of the East Battalion of the Mendip Legion of Cavalry Volunteers, which was formed in 1803 at the time of the French wars and when the invasion scare was at its height. The colonel of this nineteenth-century equivalent of the Home Guard was John Hiley Addington, who bought Langford Court when Dr Whalley was in financial difficulties. This John Addington was the brother of the Prime Minister who is chiefly remembered by the contemporary epigram:

Pitt is to Addington
What London is to Paddington.

The "No Thoroughfare" road up the hill past the church leads to an attractive walk over the "Ham" commonland, with fine views of the Wrington Vale, the Channel and the background of Welsh mountains. On the other side of the hidden Burrington Combe rises the dark outline of Blackdown, the highest point of the Mendips with its 1,067 feet.

From the Ham it is possible to continue on foot down to the top of the Combe, which is bleakly impressive, with an attraction of its own quite different from that of Cheddar Gorge. The famous Rock of Ages is a cleft in the side of the cliff near the bottom of the Combe. The story is well known how the Rev. Augustus Toplady, then curate-in-charge at Blagdon, took shelter in this somewhat inadequate crevice and was inspired to write the hymn which is sung by English-speaking people all over the world:

Rock of Ages, cleft for me,
Let me hide myself in Thee.

The tradition is now well established and an inscription on the face of the rock says:

ROCK OF AGES
This rock derives its name
from the well-known hymn written about 1762
by The Rev. A. M. Toplady
Who was inspired whilst sheltering in this cleft during a storm

The road from Burrington to Blagdon is particularly beautiful, twisting among thickly wooded hills past an enchanting little waterfall and pool, in the middle of which there is a miniature island covered with rhododendron bushes, and then there is a steady climb up through a tree-clad valley past Coombe Lodge.

On the whole the best things about Blagdon are its church and its setting. It stands high up on the side of the Mendips overlooking the Yeo Reservoir, which with the green fields sloping right down to its blue water has all the beauty of a natural lake. Even the bizarre red-brick waterworks building with its appearance of a grotesque cathedral adds a further interest to the view.

It is not often that a church is twice rebuilt in less than a century: St Andrew's, Blagdon, has this distinction, for apart from its fine Perpendicular tower, which has been preserved, it was first entirely rebuilt in 1822 and then largely altered again in 1909. Rutter described the first rebuilt church as having "a not very elegant exterior, but the interior is spacious, light and strikingly handsome". The present church was the gift of Lord Winterstoke, formerly Mr W. H. Wills of the famous tobacco family. Certainly this building is handsome and spacious enough; indeed, like Downside Abbey, it restores faith in the skill and imagination of modern ecclesiastical building. "The church is great in its simplicity," says one admirer, "with no intricate beauty, no richness of decoration, no hundred-and-one things to draw the eye. It is fine for its stone, the splendour of its oak, and the beauty of its glass." Formerly the chancel was too dark, but in 1965 windows were inserted in the north and south walls in memory of Jean, Lady Wills, and it is now possible to see in daylight the unusual reredos painting of the Last Supper.

For two miles the road continues with extensive views over Blagdon "lake" along the side of the hills to Ubley, which stands a short distance away from the main road like Burrington, and like Burrington it has preserved an atmosphere of peaceful rusticity in spite of its proximity to a busy highway. In the centre of a small cluster of houses is a diminutive village green, almost entirely covered by a fine cross which was rebuilt in 1901. The squat tower of the church has a short spire with an odd, lop-sided appearance caused by the stair turret bulging out beside it. It is well worth going round to the south wall to see the six gargoyles there; they set a high standard of whimsical grotesqueness even for gargoyles.

The road runs very closely under the hills from Ubley to Compton Martin, where the thickly wooded sides of the Mendips climb steeply up right behind the village which Collinson describes as "a large parish lying under the east and north-east sides of Mendip in a delightful woody vale. From the south side of the village, which is more than half a mile in length, consisting chiefly of one street, the hills rise finely vested with woods, and very high and steep, the ridge being the top of Mendip." Compton Martin must certainly once have had great charm, but somehow it seems now to have lost something of its individuality and it is very much a main-road village, although the church perched on the side of the hill and the village pond opposite with its bevy of ducks still make an attractive picture.

The church contains some of the finest Norman work in the whole county of Somerset, and some of its most interesting features have already been described in Chapter VIII. In the north aisle there is a stone effigy of Thomas de Moreton which was discovered quite by accident during extensive renovations to the church in 1858. The family of Moretons flourished in this district for several generations and their name is still preserved in the hamlet two miles to the north of the village. The carved oak screen which encloses the east end of the south aisle also has a history, for it was taken from Bickfield Nunnery, the remains of which may still be seen in the moated Bickfield Farm situated in a lane off the Chew Stoke road. The well-designed pews in oak recently placed in the church add considerably to its dignity.

West Harptree is the meeting-place of several busy roads, but it seems to have the secret of preserving an unruffled tranquillity in spite of the traffic that sometimes bustles through its pleasant wide streets.

Compton Martin church

Wendy

The church has been spoilt by nineteenth-century renovations, but the tower is Norman, however hard the addition of an ugly little slated spire may try to hide its antiquity. Much more attractive than the church are the two ancient manor-houses of the village. Gournay Court stands opposite the church. According to Rutter this beautiful house, built in a warm reddish-brown stone quarried from land close by, stands on the site of a mansion which was the property of the Gournay family, who also owned Richmont Castle. One story suggests that it was because one member of the family, Sir Thomas Gournay, was implicated in the murder of Edward II at Berkeley Castle that the property was confiscated by the Crown. It passed into private hands in 1928.

The present building was begun towards the end of the sixteenth century by a Francis Buckland who had been granted a lease of the property by the Duchy of Cornwall. Sir Geoffrey Hippisley-Cox's *Notes on Gournay Court* tells us that:

> "After the close of the 17th century the property seems to have become a farm, and it continued as such until it was restored to its former estate 1908–9, it is understood, at the instance of Queen Mary, then Princess of Wales. Little structural alteration was made. A new passage was contrived on the ground and first floors at the rear of the east side of the house, and small rooms placed in the angles in the inner courtyard to provide necessary offices. The stables were converted into a servants' wing."

The house on the opposite side of the road near the church is Tilly Manor, now a very attractive farmhouse. Only the central portion remains of the original double-winged building, but the coats of arms over the front windows have been well preserved and give some indication of its former dignity.

East Harptree is reached by turning off the main road to the right; it is a straggling village which climbs up the lower slopes of the Mendips. The remains of the De Gournays' Richmont Castle have already been described in Chapter VIII, but there is also a church here well worth visiting if only to see its south porch with its curiously shaped Norman doorway and its effigy of Sir John Newton who built Eastwood House with material from the ruins of Richmont Castle. The figures of his family, twelve girls and eight boys, make an imposing array at the base of the monument. Perhaps the greatest treasure of the church is in the showcase which contains the pewter jar and some of the 1,496 Roman coins discovered in it when a local farmer was

Cheap Street, Frome

digging in a nearby field. Some of the other coins of this ancient hoard are preserved in the British Museum as "The Harptree Collection".

A sign directing the way to "The King's Arms, a fifteenth-century Inn" probably attracts a number of people to Litton who would otherwise never turn off the main road to see this village in its delightful little winding valley. The cottages of its steep streets are so neat and trim that it was something of an anticlimax to find such a disappointing church. The tower has some impressive gargoyles, and the interior in spite of its awkwardly added north aisle, its ugly organ and the distortion of its Jacobean pulpit by a modern book-rest, might be transformed into a simple, dignified village church. Even its most interesting possession, a great stone bowl which might be the font of a Saxon church on this site, I found sadly neglected on the north side of the churchyard. Recently the appearance of the building has greatly improved.

From Litton the road winds in and out among the slopes of the Mendip foothills until the stately tower of Chewton Mendip church can be seen high on the rising ground behind the grey cottages of the village. "Chewton Mendip, or the town upon the Chew," says Collinson, "is additionally styled Mendip by reason of its situation under that mountain. It lies in the great turnpike road from Bristol to Wells, and consists of one street nearly a mile in length." The village still has a picturesque dignity as if it was proud of its long and interesting history and felt with A. L. Rowse that "history isn't something that is dead and done with; it is something that is alive and all around us, in our blood and bones, in our memories, in our head—if we have any head—in the things we see before our eyes".

Before the Norman Conquest Chewton Mendip was in the possession of Queen Edith, wife of Edward the Confessor, and it was among the first manors to be seized by William I after the Conquest, although he granted the church and its tithes as a reward to the great Benedictine Abbey of Jumièges in Normandy, in whose hands it remained until 1414, when Henry V confiscated all priories dependent on foreign monasteries. By the middle of the fourteenth century the manor was held by the family of Henry Fitz-Roger, whose effigy lies beside that of his wife in the church. The part played by Chewton in settling the laws of the Mendip miners has already been described in Chapter IV.

Then in 1553 Queen Mary granted Chewton to Sir Edward Waldegrave, a member of her royal household, and thus began the connection of the village with this family which has continued right up to the present day. In 1643 Charles I rewarded one member of the family for loyal services by making him a baronet, and about half a century later his grandson was created Baron Waldegrave by James II and appointed Comptroller of the King's Household. When the Revolution broke out and James fled to France this first Lord Waldegrave followed him into exile and died in Paris in 1689, but his eldest son, "being a person of great honour and abilities", served George I and George II as ambassador in Vienna and Paris, and was rewarded in 1729 with the titles of Viscount Chewton and Earl Waldegrave.

In spite of this long association of the Waldegrave family with the village it was not until Victorian times that a family seat, Chewton Priory, was built here. It has always been popularly supposed that this house was built on the site of an ancient Benedictine priory, but this appears to be nothing more than a fanciful tradition, and the decision of the present earl to pull down "an ugly Victorian monstrosity" has revealed that the original core of Chewton "Priory" was much more likely to have been the "neat seat of Richard Jenkins Esq., built in a very elegant Gothic style" of architecture which is mentioned by Collinson.

A narrow cul-de-sac off the main Bristol to Wells road leads to the church, which has many points of great interest besides its famous tower of which the village and indeed the whole county of Somerset are justly proud. The churchyard has a fine canopied cross and several ancient yew trees, one of which has been carefully supported by stonework set in its decaying trunk. There is also in the churchyard a remarkable rusty *iron* tombstone to Jane and Henry Box—surely a unique specimen of nineteenth-century uncomeliness.

The church is an interesting mixture of various styles: the tower is a magnificent example of Perpendicular work at its best, the arches of the nave are Early English, and there would be some fine Norman building still left if the Perpendicular craftsmen had not been as destructive in their alterations as any Victorian restorers. For obviously the chancel of the church must originally have had three Norman arches, but during the fifteenth century the present ugly arch was inserted, bulging clumsily into the south chancel wall. One of the Norman chancel arches still remains, however, and there is a finely moulded Norman arch leading into the north door of the church. It has even been suggested that this was the central arch which the fifteenth-century builders removed from the chancel. Another example of inartistic fifteenth-century meddling is the sedilia on the south side of the sanctuary; although attractive in themselves they utterly spoil the graceful proportions of the Early English arch into which they are fitted.

In the north wall of the sanctuary is the famous "frid" or "frith" seat which is one of the great features of interest in the church. A frid stool was "a seat or chair of stone placed near the altar and the last and most sacred refuge for those who claimed sanctuary, and for the violation of which the most severe punishment was decreed". It is said that there are only two other frid stools still in existence today—one at Hexham in Northumberland and the other at Beverley in Yorkshire.

There is a good example of fifteenth-century woodwork in the original bench-ends which have been left, and the fine altar made in the village from English oak shows that this local tradition of craftsmanship is still alive in the village. The original altar is now placed in the Lady Chapel and it is a very fair specimen of good Jacobean work. Another seventeenth-century treasure of the church is the fascinating wooden lectern and the first edition of the Authorised Version of the Bible which until recently was used for the Lessons. Now very wisely it is kept in a glass case near the tower, and it is displayed open at Ruth iii. 15 to show the misprint: "and *he* went into the city" instead of "and *she* went into the city".

The chapel south of the sanctuary contains an impressive stone effigy of Sir Henry Fitz-Roger and his wife, and also several tablets to members of the Waldegrave family, including one set up by her fourth husband, Lord Carlingford, to Frances, Countess Waldegrave, a famous society beauty of the Victorian age. "Her brilliant gifts, her noble and beautiful character, made her the centre of a wide and worthy influence and attracted to her an extraordinary amount of friendship and affection."

A change in the general character of the Mendips is noticeable as far back as East Harptree even from the road. The steep slopes gradually sink down to undulating pasture land, and the bold bleak outline of the western ridges gives way to the softer green tableland of the eastern side. Sometimes the upland nature of the hills is almost lost in the gentle rise and fall of the scenery, so that it is often difficult to decide exactly what is true Mendip country. At Chewton Mendip there is a choice of roads to Frome, and any choice must necessarily be arbitrary, but the road through Farrington Gurney, Midsomer Norton, and Radstock does seem to be something of a detour and too far north to be "on Mendip", and therefore we shall decide on the shorter road which rises up the Mendip flank to Emborough, a lonely little village standing high above the surrounding fields which slope away to the north.

There is something about Emborough, in spite of its well-cared-for farmland, which always reminds me of Goldsmith's *Deserted Village*.

Perhaps it is the disconsolate appearance of its bleak little church with its overgrown paths and crumbling gravestones and its farmhouse huddled up against it as if for protection and warmth. It is worth while obtaining the church key from the farm to see the quaint inside with its whitewashed ceiling and diminutive chancel from which rough uneven steps lead up to the tower. On a small stone south of the sanctuary are the crudely drawn heads of two children and below them these lines can still be traced:

These pretty babes for long did play
Before the Lord called them away.

At the west end of the church there is a sturdy little Norman font and an odd clumsy-looking musicians' gallery supported on oak pillars. The church register shows that the church was "re-opened on 17 October, 1926, after restoration". The interior badly needs restoration again, but it was heartening to see (in 1952) some repair work had been done on the exterior and more recently on the interior.

Emborough Pool, south of the Wells road, was described at some length as early as 1791 by Collinson:

> "At the bottom of a steep declivity is a fine lake called by the different names of Emberrow and Leachmore pond, containing nearly ten acres. It lies in a vale extending almost east and west with a beautiful plantation of firs, beeches and sycamores on the slopes of the hills on each side. On the eastern boundary is a small cottage and a boat-house; at the west end is a marsh, and below that another lake much smaller."

The appearance of the pool varies capriciously with the weather: on a sunny day it is pleasant enough with its shady, tree-lined walks around the edge, but when the skies are clouded it might be the "standing pool" of which poor Tom in *King Lear* "drank the green mantle", or perhaps the scene of Keats' *La Belle Dame sans Merci*:

O what can ail thee, knight-at-arms,
Alone and palely loitering?
The sedge is wither'd from the lake,
And no birds sing.

Of course this atmosphere is pure fancy, otherwise the boys of Downside School would not roar out a hearty song about the place:

Keep your trotters off the ice
Until it's hard as eggs boiled twice.
Not so many years all told,
A gang from Downside waxed too bold.

The ice chucked,
And the skates bucked,
The water sucked,
And the gang were ducked.

All the same, it was an Emborough man who said to me in all seriousness, "They do zay as how Emboro' Pool is hreally the crater of a volcanny. That's why no one has never bin able to measure the depth of the middle of 'un!"

The road to Kilmersdon continues past the seventeenth-century Old Down Inn and farther on away in the distance you can see the waste tips of the Radstock coal mines in their incongruous setting of green fields. Chilcompton lies in a rather stuffy little hollow off the main road; the stream which cascades down the side of its street gives the village a certain fictitious charm, but Dinder does the same sort of thing so much more delightfully that there seems little to lose by making direct for Kilmersdon.

Kilmersdon is a village which it would be difficult to overpraise. It has character, grace, dignity, and what might be described as "proportion", for the church is an integral part of the place and its noble tower does not overpower the individuality of its setting. It is a village which has escaped the doubtful favour of popular classification as a show place and thus it is attractive without a trace of self-consciousness. It reveals fresh beauties at every visit and at every season. Even its approach is beautiful: the tall column in Ammerdown Park is silhouetted against the skyline as you draw near and then the tree-lined road dips down to a fold in the hills past a Lilliputian toll-house, a telephone box discreetly painted brown, and a dapper little post-office and you come to the open space in front of the church.

The tower has some fine gargoyles and there is an especially rich collection of carved figures all round the walls. As you pass through the west door, its nails showing the date 1766, you will see two royal figures on either side with their crowns still just recognisable. One striking feature of the interior is the collection of ten angels which are the original corbels of the roof, which was raised a considerable distance above them in the fifteenth century. The tower arch and chancel arch are both richly panelled in Perpendicular style and the elegantly carved font and six remaining original bench-ends belong to the same period. One Norman slit window has been left in the south wall—a remarkable concession on the part of such ruthless rebuilders as the craftsmen of the Perpendicular period. A massive door with the original lock and key leads into the vestry which was formerly the south porch. There is an ancient stone monument here dated 1528, but perhaps the most valuable of all the treasures of this church is the gracefully proportioned stone screen of the chantry chapel in the north aisle.

Two other buildings in the village are of special interest. The first, opposite the inn, is a small square stone building colloquially known as "The Blind House", which was once the lock-up for local offenders against the law. The other, a short distance from the church, is a picturesque gabled building, now a private house, which was built in 1707 by the Rev. Henry Shute as a Free School "for the teaching of 40 poor children to read, write, cast Accounts and the Church Catechism"—a remarkable contribution towards popular education in an age when learning was the privilege of the few. A collection of manuscripts preserved by the school shows that eighteenth-century schoolmasters often had the same problems to face as their modern counterparts. There is, for example, a letter written by the master, John Hughes, to his "reverend patron", Mr Shute, complaining that "Roder, an ale-house keeper, with a loud drunken noise, abundance of ill language and whole volleys of execrable oaths, and a rabble rout at his heels," had abused the master for threatening to chastise his son. The school continued its useful work in its original building right up to 1900, when the old premises were sold and the proceeds given towards building the new school on the hill opposite.

A fascinating *History of Kilmersdon* was written in 1910 by the late Lord Hylton which is a model of what a parish history should be. It includes a series of extracts taken from the churchwardens' accounts over a number of years, and from them the following curious items are taken:

1778	5th November. For a bassoon for the use of the Singers	£4		
1785	For Quarrying of Stones to build the Guard-House	1	16	5
	Hauling sd. stones	4	10	0
	Lime and carriage	3	8	6
	Abraham Hobbs and his sons for building ye sd. house	6	9	11
	Joseph Cox's bill for work done at sd. house	4	8	4
1786	11 June. For beer for putting Charles and John Abraham in the Guard-house	0	0	5
	6 August. John Hall for a pole-cat	0	0	4
	Wm. More for hedgehogs	0	0	10
	September. Expenses putting a Soldier in the Guard-House	0	0	4
	For 6 dozen sparrows	0	1	6
1796	For a lock for the Stocks	0	1	2
	Amending the lock of the Blind-House	0	2	0
1800	For beer for the men in holding a person in a rope to weed the Tower	0	3	6

Details of memoranda written by a William Wallen who lived at Kilmersdon and from the year 1600 onwards acted as local deputy of the lord's steward give an authentic picture of contemporary social and economic conditions in a flourishing Mendip village:

> "At this period and at a much later date the manufacture of cloth was a great and thriving industry throughout this part of the country; many small towns and villages in Somerset still contain fine old houses built by the wealthy clothiers of those days, and there must have been a brisk demand and a lucrative price for wool to supply the manufacturers. Wallen's accounts contain lists of the produce of his fleeces or, as he wrote them, 'flizes' or 'wolles'. In 1619 his wool fetched 27*s.* 6*d.* per thirty pounds. In 1622 he bought eleven wether sheep at 5*s.* 2*d.* apiece and other from 5*s.* 8*d.* to 6*s.* 2*d.*"

Echoes of the Civil War now reached Kilmersdon and £2 8*s.* 8*d.* was paid for a rate made "for the maintenance of soldiers in Bath and Bristol for the safety of the county". Charles I on the march through the West halted at Sir John Horner's house at Mells and his escort was quartered at Kilmersdon, but unfortunately Wallen's book contains no reference to this stirring episode in the village annals, and he contents himself with quietly copying out more rates for the maintenance of soldiers.

Lord Hylton refers to the precautions taken round about Kilmersdon against possible invasion during the Napoleonic wars:

> "The beacons on Mendip which had been prepared to warn the Somerset of Elizabeth should the Spaniards effect a landing and to rouse the colliers from their 'sunless caves' to defend their homes, were now replaced by an elaborate system of martello towers along the coast and of semaphores or 'telegraphs' to convey instant intelligence of any French invasion. Local volunteer forces of every description, such as the Mendip Legion, the Selwood Cavalry and others were enrolled under the direct command of the Lord-Lieutenant and a methodical system for utilising in case of need all horse, livestock and waggons was set on foot in every district."

During the last war descendants of those Kilmersdon men who had enrolled in the Mendip Legion or Selwood Cavalry were serving in the Home Guard; and so history repeated itself throughout those six long years until at last the bell in their village church bearing the words *Peace and Prosperity to this Parish* could once again peal out.

The road from Kilmersdon to Mells rises out of the small valley and passes a now disused lodge gate of Ammerdown House, the seat of

Lord Hylton. Ammerdown House was designed by the well-known eighteenth-century architect James Wyatt, whose wholesale demolition of beautiful mediæval buildings in the interests of "restoration" earned him the nickname "the Destroyer". His most notorious architectural experiment was the neo-Gothic Fonthill Abbey in Wiltshire which was built for the eccentric William Beckford, one-time M.P. for Wells, but Ammerdown House is designed in the orthodox classical style. The tall column which stands out against the sky in the highest part of the park was built about 1854. An inscription in Latin, French, and English explains that it is a monument set up in memory of a member of the Jolliffe family.

It is well worth turning off the main road through a drive which leads to Babington church, a fascinating little Georgian building which stands like a private chapel right in the grounds of Babington House with its gravestones invading the very lawns before its front door. It seems clear that Wren cannot be claimed (as he sometimes is) as the architect of this church without a village, but even so such an interesting little church with its apse, domed chancel roof, finely moulded east end wall, and tiny pulpit deserves some attention to prevent it from falling into more serious ruin.

The village of Mells has long been considered one of the show places of Somerset and writers as distant and different from each other as Leland and George Birmingham have described it at some length. In Leland's account we read:

> "Melles hath bene a praty Townelet of Clothing. It longgid unto Glessenbyri. The church is faire and buildid in tyme of mynde ex lapide quadrato by the hole Paroche. Ther is a praty Maner Place of Stone harde at the West Ende of the Chirche. This be likelihod was partely buildid by Abbate Selwoode of Glasteinbyri syns it servid the Farmer of the Lordeship. Now Mr Horner hath boute the Lordeship of the King."

The novelist George Birmingham has written in a more intimate vein of the village in *Pleasant Places*, for as Canon J. O. Hannay he was rector of Mells from 1924 to 1934. An Irishman who had worked for twenty years in a country parish in the west of Ireland, he had accepted the living with some misgivings. Before he gained their confidence and affection he confessed the "tongue-tied restraint" of the villagers had puzzled him, and compared with his Irish mountains the scenery of this part of eastern Mendip was, as he said, "undulating fields, no more", but from the very beginning it was the village itself which had attracted him and he has left a striking description of his first sight of Mells church:

> "In front of me rose the tower, purple in the strong sunlight, and its broad shadow fell black over the grass and the grey tombstones to the north of it. I looked at the great west door of the church, its clusters of columns rising from the ground in stages, till they bent towards each other in an untroubled curve and met in the points of the arch. Above them rose the stonework of the window, slender shafts with spaces between them of dull leaded glass, faintly pitted and dented by the rains and storms of centuries. High up the shafts broke in solemn playfulness into the simple patterns of perpendicular design. Then above the door and window rose the square flat front of the tower itself—strength, calm, changeless endurance, supreme and confident superiority to all foolishness, all fussiness, all passion."

When such unstinted praise has been lavished on Mells by so many people it may seem ungracious to suggest that there is nevertheless something disappointing about the village as a whole. It is only fair to say that the least satisfactory view is from the west, and it must be seen from the other side, coming from Frome, in order to appreciate the attractive grouping of the cottages in the foreground and the fine proportions of the tower against the sky. Even so I have only once known Mells to have the irresistible beauty it is always described as having, and that was one autumn evening when in the setting sun church and cottages faded away like a dream village into a golden haze of twilight.

Leland's remark that "Mr Horner hath boute the lordeship of the King" is a reminder that the manor of Mells has been owned by a Horner from the days of Henry VIII until the death of the late Sir John Horner. His son Edward Horner, the last direct male heir to the estate, was killed at the Battle of Cambrai in 1917 and Mells manor passed to the Asquith family by reason of the marriage of Sir John Horner's daughter with Raymond Asquith, who also fell in action during the first world war.

Mells and the Horner family have popularly but erroneously been connected with the old nursery rhyme of "Little Jack Horner", for according to the traditional story the Abbot of Glastonbury at the time of the dissolution of the monasteries hoped to placate Thomas Cromwell with a bribe. Accordingly he sent Jack Horner, the Abbey's steward, to present Cromwell with a pie containing the title-deeds of twelve manors belonging to Glastonbury. On the way the steward lifted the crust, "put in his thum and pulled out the plum" of the manor of Mells for himself. It is a delightful story, but in justice to the Horner family it must be added that in fact Mells was, as Leland remarks, bought from Henry VIII by Thomas Horner, and the legal deeds of conveyance are still preserved.

Mells Park House, the seat of the Horner family, stood in the beautiful grounds on the western outskirts of the village, but the mansion was virtually destroyed by fire in 1917 and a modern house has been built in its place. The five-gabled Manor House adjoining the church was originally built in the shape of the letter H, but part of it has since been pulled down. It is an early Elizabethan building and it was for some time used as a farmhouse. During the middle of the nineteenth century it was converted into a school for theological students, and then finally Sir John Horner made it into a private residence once more. It was in this house that Charles I slept one July night in 1644 during the Civil War. The squire, another Sir John Horner, was not there to play the host to his King, for he was in disgrace as a staunch Parliamentarian. The King was on his way from Bath to Exeter and a contemporary diarist records that "the King lay at Sir John Horner's house at Mells, a fine large house of stone, very strong, in the form of an H with two courts. The church is very large and faire, adjoining. Horner is in rebellion, his estates sequestered." Many of the Royalist soldiers were sent to find quarters for themselves at the Joliffe Inn at Kilmersdon.

The richly decorated tower of the church is best seen at a distance, for at close quarters its breadth seems over-accentuated by its buttresses and pinnacles. The elaborate porch is beautifully groined and inside the church there is some fine fan vaulting under the tower. On the south wall of the tower there is a memorial designed by Sir Edwin Lutyens to Raymond Asquith, son of the Liberal Prime Minister, who was killed at the Battle of the Somme in 1916. On the opposite wall is a remarkable plaque to the memory of Mrs Alfred Lyttleton, another member of the Horner family. It was designed by Burne-Jones and represents a peacock perched on a tomb. The translation of part of the Latin epitaph written by Dean Church runs: "Thou liest in the far north, O most beloved, but here also we who loved thee have set up a stone in token of our inconsolable grief." A few of the original Jacobean pews have been preserved in this part of the church; the other seats were all carved in Mells by village people, and every design on the bench-ends is different. The font is a fine example of Norman work with a rope device carved round the base.

South of the chancel behind the organ there is a bust of George Birmingham hidden away in the gloom above a door which leads into an oddly shaped vestry. Leland gives the information that "one Garlande, a draper of London, gave frely to the building of the vestiarie, a fine and curiose pece of Worke." The rich glass in this room, and also that of the clerestory windows, was made by local craftsmen in Mells in 1860. Above the vestry is another room of similar shape which has some beautiful pieces of ancient stained glass.

The Horner chapel on the north side of the church is almost filled by the striking equestrian statue of Edward Horner designed by Sir Alfred Munnings. The garish stained-glass window in the chapel representing Saint Francis preaching to the birds and fishes is the work of Sir William Nicholson, the well-known portrait-painter.

The church has eight bells and four chimes playing the tunes *Mells*, *Holsworthy*, *London New*, and *Hanover*. An old tradition sets the following words to the ancient Mells tune:

The man who made these bells is dead,
He'll make these bells no more.
He used to wear a snuff-brown coat
That buttoned down before.

and the guide to Mells church says that "this is supposed to refer to John Wesley who visited and preached in the neighbourhood". In his Journal Wesley wrote under the date Wednesday, September 7th, 1785:

> "I preached . . . in an open place near the road at Mells. Just as I began a wasp though unprovoked stung me upon the lip. I was afraid it would swell so as to hinder my speaking, but it did not. I spoke distinctly nearly two hours in all and was no worse for it."

Two roads lead to Frome from Mells, offering the invidious choice of going through either "Murder Combe" or "Bedlam". If you choose the latter you pass the tiny village of Great Elm and you will be able to see for yourself that the tree on its village green after which it was named has now been replaced by a sturdy young oak. You can also take the narrow lane to the right opposite the church (which has a quaint saddle-back tower and some supposedly Saxon herring-bone stonework in the south wall), climb down to the head of the attractive Vallis Vale and then join up with the other more direct road just before it enters the outskirts of the last town of the Mendips.

If Mells has always had a generous share of praise the town of Frome has sometimes been unduly disparaged by writers. John Wesley, who visited the town no less than nineteen times, called it a "dry, barren, uncomfortable place"; and John Foster the essayist, who was a Baptist minister here for a time, gave it the derogatory description of "a large and surpassingly ugly town in Somerset". There is no doubt that Frome is a place that grows on you; merely to pass through it gives little impression of the unexpected charm hidden in its narrow, steeply climbing streets. The focal point of the town is the wide market-place, from which the attractive Cheap Street, with its open rivulet of clear water, leads up to the church, and Frome needs exploration on foot to discover the astonishing variety of picturesque streets which clamber precipitously uphill and down.

As you go through the side-streets you come upon quaint names like Blind House Lane, Stony Street, Willow Vale, Apple Alley and Pudding-bag Lane, and you turn suddenly into unexpected beauty like the old cobbled Gentle Street, or Paul Street which gives the impression of a Cornish fishing village, or the view from the north porch of the church somehow reminiscent of the background of a Brueghel picture. It is only in this leisurely fashion that old-world Frome reveals its charm.

Frome stood on the northern limits of Selwood Forest, one of the five ancient royal forests of Somerset, and for that reason it was often known as Frome-Selwood, although it was never reckoned to belong to that forest, nor did the forest laws apply to its inhabitants. "Cottle's Oak" which marked the eastern limit of the Forest of Mendip was outside the town's boundaries, but the name is still preserved today in the district south of Vallis Road. Selwood was disafforested by Charles I "with all the deer therein in such manner as was most convenient to his Majesty's profit", but right up to the eighteenth century Frome still suffered marauding raids from a band of desperadoes who had concealed themselves in what remained of the forest round about Woodlands.

It has been said that the happiest women are those who have no history; if the same test applies to a town then Frome may be considered fortunate indeed. Even during the Civil War when the town's Roundhead sympathies might have attracted the attention of the Royalists it was the nearby Nunney Castle which bore the brunt of a siege. During the Monmouth Rebellion the townsfolk were enthusiastically for the Duke, but it was fortunate for them that the loyal Earl of Pembroke had entered the town and disarmed all the inhabitants before Monmouth and his rabble army arrived, tired and dispirited after their skirmish with the King's forces at Norton St Philip. The town could thus give no help to the Duke apart from finding him lodging in a house in Cork Street (then known as Hill Lane), so that when the day of reckoning came at the Bloody Assizes only twelve men were hanged in Frome, and two of these, aged sixty and seventy respectively, were not inhabitants of the town at all and protested that they had not been in the least implicated in the rebellion but that having been taken on suspicion they had imprudently pleaded "Guilty" in the hope of being pardoned more quickly.

From Tudor times the cloth trade was an important industry in Frome side by side with agriculture, and by the beginning of the eighteenth century it had become the staple industry of the town. Then came the beginning of the industrial crisis; machine looms and the shifting of the industry to the North brought distress and hardship to the town. A contemporary newspaper reported changed conditions:

> "From Frome, that once wealthy clothing town, we have such melancholy accounts of the misery of the inhabitants as are almost incredible. The people are wholly out of employ and in want of the common necessaries of life; their Poor Rates amount to twelve shillings in the pound and though they made no less than 96 books the last year the necessitous in their workhouses were almost starved."

Just about a century after Defoe's visit the honest, cantankerous William Cobbett rode into the town and found everywhere "proofs of the irretrievable decay of the place". Two or three hundred unemployed weavers who had pawned all their possessions were cracking stones for a living. In his typical fashion Cobbett railed against their former employers. "I remembered how ready the bluff manufacturers had been to call in the troops. Let them, said I to myself, call the troops in now to make the trade revive."

Most of the smaller firms went bankrupt, but Sheppards kept going by adapting their work to the new conditions and by gradually introducing steam-power machinery in spite of much bitter opposition. Up to that time the yarn had been sent out to houses in the town and almost everywhere the visitor to Frome could hear the noise of the shuttle. A man would hire a loom and set it up in his downstairs room; the yarn would be sent to him from the mill on a spindle and would then be worked up. Often the single loom grew into three or four and a shed would be built on to the house to accommodate them, and these sheds became a common feature of the town. It is said that in the days before the Crimean War the breeches worn by the Czar's Imperial Bodyguard were always made of Frome cloth because its home-spun yarn made it the finest obtainable of its kind.

It was fortunate that Frome did not have all its industrial eggs in one basket. The firm of Cockey which had cast bells for churches in Somerset during the eighteenth century became one of the biggest manufacturers of gas-holders in the country. John Webb Singer founded a firm which began manufacturing ornamental metalwork at the beginning of the nineteenth century and which became well known enough to be chosen to cast the famous Boadicea statue near the Houses of Parliament. Most remarkable of all was the rise of the printing firm of Butler and Tanner. from the humble beginning of a small press set up in an enterprising chemist's outhouse about 1790 it now provides the main industry of the town. And in spite of Cobbett's gloomy prognostication the woollen industry is not entirely dead in Frome, for the firm of Alfred Tucker continues to make West of England cloth at their Wallbridge mills.

The parish church of St John the Baptist is often criticised adversely, but there is no denying that it is an impressive building. The odd position of its tower which carries a fine spire—quite a feature for a Somerset church—gives its exterior an untidy appearance, but this is more than offset by the fine site of the building. Every approach to the church is attractive. If you go up Bath Street (that steep hill down which exuberant Protestant inhabitants of Frome used in the old days to hurtle blazing tar-barrels on Guy Fawkes' Day) you enter by the west door after passing through an elaborate stone gateway into a spacious parvis. If you approach by the narrow little Cheap Street you can climb up the picturesque steps to the west door or turn aside up to the north porch past the *Via Crucis*, a quite remarkable series of sculptured panels, whatever may be thought of their artistic merit.

The church traces its foundation back to St Aldhelm, who died at Doulting in 709 and who built a church and monastery here. The church was destroyed, probably during the Danish raids, although the curious Saxon carvings on the stones fitted into the interior of the present tower are traditionally said to be from St Aldhelm's original building. The church today is an astonishing mixture of various styles inside. There is a Norman doorway leading into the Lady Chapel; an Early English chancel arch and tower base; an arcade of the Decorated period in the eastern portion; and a great deal of Perpendicular work everywhere. Finally, the whole building was much restored in the nineteenth century by the Rev. W. J. E. Bennett, a notable figure in the High Church movement, who was vicar here for fourteen years. Father Bennett had been vicar of St Paul's, Knightsbridge, until a number of riots provoked by his advanced ritualistic practices compelled his resignation. Then the Marquess of Bath offered him the living of Frome, which he accepted. He had naturally to face a good deal of opposition from the town's strongly Protestant element, but even his opponents admitted his energy, zeal, and devotion as a parish priest, and at the end of his life he had gained everyone's respect even if he had not won everyone's approval.

Of his restoration of the church it might be said that his zeal outran his discretion, for the building has, as one critic so rightly says, "too much of everything, and somebody has not been able to leave it alone". The bewildering number of its stone figures, its carvings, its corbel heads, its kinds of coloured marble, its medallions above the arches of the nave, its figured titles, and a hundred and one other things need a handbook to appreciate. For those who boggle at the thought of such detail I suggest three outstanding things of interest (besides the two Saxon stones built into the tower), all of them monuments.

First there is the somewhat ghoulish *memento mori* in the Lady Chapel—the emaciated figure of a man under a stone slab who is traditionally supposed to be Edmund Leversedge of Vallis House, about whom the following story is told. After coming into possession of the family estates he began to meddle with the black art of magic and lived a wild life of dissipation until one day he was struck down and died during one of his orgies. He was carried to the Leversedge vault in Frome church by torchlight at night to avoid inciting the anger of the townspeople, who objected to the burial of such a dissolute scoundrel in consecrated ground. As they made their way towards the church the bearers fancied they felt movements inside the coffin; they stopped and uncovered the bier, and there was the wasted form of Edmund Leversedge breathing and alive. At length he sat up and told how he had been held in a trance and had been taken through the other world, had seen heaven and hell, and was restored to live an altered life. When he did at last die this shrunken effigy was by his desire carved on his tomb "as a witness to all how God had dealt with him".

The second memorial is to be found on the north wall of the aisle over a stone staircase. It is an odd painting on metal, badly needing restoration, showing a Mr Avery of Frome with his wife and eleven children. This local lawyer is said to have been responsible for the removal and destruction of all the coloured glass in the church during the Cromwellian period.

The third monument is the most famous of them all, for it is over the grave of Thomas Ken, the saintly bishop of Bath and Wells. The tomb itself is modern, a stone canopy over a curious iron framework with an iron mitre and pastoral staff. Bishop Ken's career was remarkable in

Croscombe church

many ways—he wrote two of the best-known hymns in the English language; he refused Nell Gwyn accommodation in his Winchester house when Charles II was visiting the city, and in return the King rewarded "the little black fellow who refused his lodging to poor Nell" with the bishopric of Bath and Wells; he was imprisoned by James II for refusing to read the Declaration of Indulgence; he was deprived of his bishopric by William and Mary because he declared their accession unconstitutional; and he was awarded a pension by Queen Anne to relieve the poverty of his old age. He spent his last days at Longleat and at his death he was buried according to his own wish "at the rising of the sun in the nearest parish of my old diocese", and the epitaph ordered by himself has been set up over his grave:

> *May the here interred Thomas Ken, Bishop of Bath and Wells, uncanonically deprived for not transferring his allegiance, have a perfect consummation of blisse, both of body and soul—of which God keep me always mindful.*

There is one other cleric connected with Frome who should not be forgotten. It may seem a far cry from this Somerset town to Oxford, but when Matthew Arnold wrote *The Scholar Gipsy* he took

> *The story of that Oxford scholar poor,*
> *Of pregnant parts and quick inventive brain,*

from a book written by a seventeenth-century vicar of this parish, Joseph Glanvill, whose preoccupation with sorcery and witchcraft must have been a source of uneasy interest among his parishioners.

The bells of the church recall the century of bell-making by the local firm of Cockey, for three of them were made by William Cockey, and one bears the inscription:

> *God made Cockey and Cockey made me*
> *In the year of our Lord 1743.*

But one was made by the rival Somerset firm of Bilbie at Chew Stoke, and this in its turn reminds us of the challenge written on a bell in Kilmersdon church:

> *You, Ruddle and Cockey, come hither and see*
> *Which is the best workman of all us three.*
> *Thomas Bilbee cast me.*

Two other churches are worth seeing in Frome. They are both modern, but Holy Trinity has a good collection of windows designed

Dinder

by Burne-Jones, and Christ Church has one of the most dignified and convincing modern Gothic exteriors I have ever seen—but if you wish to preserve the illusion you should not go inside.

John Wesley noted in his Journal the extraordinary number of sects existing in Frome in his time—"Anabaptists, Quakers, Presbyterians, Arians, Antinomians, Moravians and whatnot", so it is not surprising that you have here Nonconformist chapels which are almost as interesting as the parish church. The Wesleyans have not only an imposing chapel at Butt's Hill but also houses for two resident ministers, a school and a master's house—an impressive group of buildings which testify to the prosperity of nineteenth-century Wesleyans in Frome. The organ in the chapel is something of a curiosity on account of its cathedral-like proportions; it has great, swell, choir, solo, and echo, organs, and a 32-foot pedal-stop. In 1889 it had the distinction of being officially opened by Sir John Bridge, the organist of Westminster Abbey.

The Rook Lane Congregational Chapel in Bath Street, one of the most attractive buildings in the town, was built at the beginning of the eighteenth century, although its origin dates back to 1662, the year of the Act of Uniformity to which something like two thousand English clergymen refused to subscribe. Among them was the vicar of Frome, and a memorial tablet in the chapel tells us that:

> "The Rev. John Humfry was ejected from the parish church of Frome and founded this congregation. On the passing of the 'Five Mile Act' he removed to London and ministered to the congregation there. He died in London 1719 after surviving nearly all the ejected ministers of the Kingdom."

Every summer since 1932 local cricket lovers have had a chance of seeing their county play on the town ground. It was here that a then unknown young man of twenty-one from a farm at Watchet—Harold Gimblett—scored 123 against Essex in 63 minutes—the fastest century of the season.

Before leaving Frome one little legend often innocently repeated by its inhabitants must be contradicted. Gentle street is not "the old-fashioned street of the old-fashioned town" in the famous song: the composer, W. H. Squire, has told me categorically that his words refer to Witney in Oxfordshire. But the people of Frome need not be disappointed at this disclosure: their Gentle Street is none the less charming.

Chapter XIII

THE SOUTHERN FRINGE

The main road from Frome through Shepton Mallet and Wells to Weston-super-Mare follows the north-westerly direction of the hills so closely that there is no difficulty in deciding the limits of the southern fringe of the Mendips, although the road as far as Nunney rarely shows more than a slight rise to the north.

The entry into Nunney never fails to have the sudden delight of surprise, with its unexpected view of the castle rising up like some dream of the Middle Ages, the glimpse of the church tower, and then the picturesque bridge over the village stream and the old-fashioned inn sign straddled right across the street. As the castle has already been fully described in Chapter VIII there remains only the church to examine, which was recently in the throes of restoration. The village gallantly faced the task of dealing with the chaos caused by worm, beetle, and dry rot in the roof; the nave was temporarily covered with corrugated iron and the church was re-roofed section by section as funds permitted, and the visitor had to pick his way through the debris of the nave to see the fine stone effigies of members of the De la Mare family. Now, however, the restoration and renovation of this interesting old building have at last been completed.

The road out of Nunney rises slightly, but the hills still have the appearance of rolling tableland as far as the little village of Leighton. Cranmore Tower stands out against the skyline on the right, but the village of East Cranmore is off the main road on our left. Cranmore Hall, once a stately country house, is now a school. West Cranmore, farther along this side road, is an attractive little place with a church which has a dainty replica of Shepton Mallet's tower without the spire base. The interior is spoilt by a garish east window, but it has an unusual seventeenth-century brass on the south wall commemorating the births of James and Amy Strode.

It was the quarries of Doulting that supplied the stone for the building of Wells Cathedral and Glastonbury Abbey. When freshly quarried Doulting stone has a beautiful light cream colour, but it has the disadvantage of being rather soft and friable, so that there is a ceaseless round of repairs at the cathedral and a continual accumulation of light dust inside. The village of Doulting has an impressive tithe-barn and a much restored church with an interesting octagonal tower crowned with a spire. By the north porch is an ancient churchyard cross with panels showing the various instruments of the Crucifixion. The porch itself has suffered at the inexpert hands of the restorers, who have quite literally turned a Norman doorway inside out, but ample amends have been made in the skilful reconstruction of the south porch, which is said to be an exact copy of the original fifteenth-century work. The interior of the church is spacious and attractive, and somehow the central portion of its tower gives it something of a Continental appearance. There are some early English features in the building but most of the church has been rebuilt. There are some dainty blue tiles around the sanctuary. A careful search near the vestry door will reveal an interesting old brass to Robert Maiver with crude drawings of old Father Time, Death hurling his dart, a pickaxe and shovel, a skull, crossbones, and underneath it all the terse sentence, *Reader, imitate vertue.*

The dedication of the church and the holy well in the vicarage garden recall the association of this little village with Saint Aldhelm who died here over a thousand years ago. Bishop of Sherborne and Abbot of Malmesbury, this versatile Saxon ecclesiastic was a profound scholar, a wise administrator, a skilful musician, a practising architect, a writer of Latin riddles, and with it all a very human and attractive personality who was not above turning his gifts to practical use. It is said that on market days he would often stand in a town and sing comic songs to the people so that after he had attracted a crowd he could then preach a sermon to them.

The town of Shepton Mallet, like Frome, has seen the rise and decline of a flourishing cloth industry. Its very name "Sheeptown" recalls the days when large flocks were reared on the slopes of the Mendip Hills; the suffix Mallet is merely the name of the Norman family which owned the manor in the twelfth century. Even as late as the end of the eighteenth century Collinson described the town as still populous and busy and as having been "for many years famous for its manufacture of woollen cloth in which at present about four thousand hands are daily employed, and this, with a considerable manufacture of knit stockings, affords a sufficient object of industry to the indigent part of its inhabitants". By the beginning of the nineteenth century Shepton Mallet's population of about nine thousand had fallen to five thousand, but it was still the fourth largest town in the county, Bath being the largest,

Frome second, and Taunton third with only a few hundred more than Shepton Mallet.

When the industrial crisis came Shepton was unable to weather the storm like Frome. An attempt to introduce machines led to ugly riots and a contemporary magazine reported:

> "A riotous mob of weavers assembled at Shepton Malet to destroy some machines called the Spinning Jenny lately erected there for expediting their work. They had scarce accomplished their purpose when a party of soldiers appeared and some of the ringleaders were apprehended whom the mob endeavoured to rescue by attacking the soldiers. This brought on a serious action in which seven persons were either killed or wounded."

It is hardly surprising that the cloth factories closed down after this demonstration.

There is another interesting description of the disorderly elements in Shepton Mallet's eighteenth-century population written in John Wesley's Journal, where he relates with typically shrewd coolness that when he arrived in the town to preach he found his followers in a state of great apprehension for

> "a mob, they said, was hired, prepared, and made sufficiently drunk to do all manner of mischief. This mob followed us throwing dirt, stones and clods in abundance but they could not hurt us. After we were gone into the house they began throwing great stones in order to break the door, but perceiving this would require some time they dropped that design for the present. One of their captains in his great zeal had followed us into the house and was now shut in with us. He did not like this and would fain have got out but it was not possible, so he kept as close to me as he could, thinking himself safe when he was near me; but staying a little behind a large stone struck him on the forehead and the blood spurted out like a stream. He cried out, 'Oh sir, are we to die to-night? What must I do? What must I do?' I said, 'Pray to God.' He took my advice and began praying in such a manner as he had scarce done ever since he was born.
>
> I walked straight through the room and down the stairs, and not another stone came in till we were at the bottom. The mob had just broke open the door when we came into the lower room and exactly while they burst in at one door we walked out at the other. Nor did one man take any notice of us though we were within five yards of each other. They filled the house at once and proposed setting it on fire, but one of them happening to remember that his own house was next with much ado persuaded them not to do it. Hearing one

of them cry out, 'They are gone over the grounds', I thought the advice was good, so we went over the grounds to the further end of the town and in less than an hour we came to Oakhill."

There is a faint air of shabby gentility lingering in Shepton Mallet, as if it still regretted its palmy days, but it is still proud to show off its antiquity and picturesque interest. Much more than most towns of its size the market-place is literally a meeting-place and however much motorists and pedestrians may hate each other in the narrow streets no one would wish the Market Cross removed. When beyond repair the original cross was demolished and the present one was set up on the old site, reproducing many of the features of the original. Nearby a small portion of the mediæval shambles which once lined the market-place has been preserved. Most of the town's life is still centred round this cross just as in the old days.

"Queer scenes have been enacted in this old forum [wrote the town's historian, Farbrother]. Rebels have been hanged, drawn and quartered here; it has been the arena of rioting, of political harangues and open-air preaching; and the chosen place for trials of skill in wrestling and single stick. It has been the meeting place for strolling players, acrobats and conjurers. Sales of so unnatural a character as knocking down your wife to the highest bidder have on several occasions been transacted here. At the last of these, which was accidentally witnessed by a lady whose authority I cite, the wife was coolly handed over for a crown with a halter round her neck."

The church is so hemmed in by houses and narrow lanes that it is difficult to get a satisfactory view of the building as a whole. The tower has an unfinished spire base, and the fine combination of sturdiness and grace obtained without a spire may well have encouraged the building of the later great spireless towers of Somerset. Inside the finest thing is the magnificent oak ceiling with 350 panels and 350 bosses, all of different design and making an intricate whole quite dazzling to the eye. An elaborately carved stone pulpit is another treasure of this church, which needs only the removal of its ugly galleries to make it a very handsome building. The ordinary plain glass in the east window is seen to be a very welcome change whenever the morning sun streams into the chancel. Ignominiously stowed away on two window sills are the stone effigies of two knights, probably Mallets who added their name to Shepton in the reign of Henry I.

On the south side of the church are the Strode Almshouses, founded in the seventeenth century and added to two centuries later. When I last looked at them I found the white-haired occupant of one of these tiny cottages had just completed a journey of something like 10,000 miles. She had travelled all the way to the east coast of the United States, only to find she was so homesick for her native Shepton Mallet that she had to return. On the other side of the church is the building which originally housed the seventeenth-century grammar school of the town, which was also founded by a member of the Strode family. After moving into modern buildings at the beginning of the century it was finally closed in 1929, and this sudden end of their ancient school still rankles in the town.

It is impossible to walk round Shepton Mallet without seeing the grim walls of its old prison, which has a history dating back to the reign of James I. Farbrother's description of the building gives us a glimpse of life behind its walls in the nineteenth century. There were then 166 cells in the men's prison and 49 in the women's block. Separate apartments were set aside for sick prisoners, and there were three large yards for compulsory exercise. There were also work-rooms and sheds in which the prisoners were employed breaking stones, picking oakum, making mats, weaving "dowlas", and walking the treadmill which ground the corn. And his account ends with the cryptic remark, "The system pursued in the prison is the *Silent System*." The last civilian execution at this prison took place as late as 1926 and then a certain stir was created and a question was asked in Parliament because at the official inquest the Prison Governor had protested against the presence of a local pressman on the jury, since "in consequence of his position as a juryman he would be able to go over the prison and visit parts which the authorities did not think it advisable that a pressman should visit". The prison was closed in 1930 as a civil establishment and in 1939 it was opened as a Military Corrective Establishment and for a time during the war was used by the United States Military forces. In 1966 it reverted once again to the Home Office and today it deals with special classes of prisoners with inadequate personalities under Rule 43.

Perhaps the most picturesque part of Shepton Mallet is to be found round about Longbridge, where there are several old houses dating back to the prosperous days of the town's woollen industry. Nearby in Cowl Street there is an interesting Unitarian Chapel founded in 1692. Inside there are two things worth seeing: an enormous and elaborately carved pulpit with canopy, and on the wall a plain tablet to a native of Shepton Mallet which commemorates the story of a strange eighteenth-century personality. Simon Browne had already made his mark as a theologian when his mind "became unhinged by the sudden loss of his wife and only son, coupled with his accidental slaying of a highwayman who tried to rob him". Modern psychologists would doubtless have a word for it, but his contemporaries could not understand why this brilliant scholar and preacher would insist on trying to persuade them that he was "a mere beast and that God had annihilated in him the thinking substance so that his words had no more sense than a parrot's". Browne's delusion made him give up his ministry and retire to his native town, where he spent his time translating classics, writing some amusing books for children, and composing a dictionary. All this, he maintained, was performed in a mechanical way—"I am doing nothing that requires a reasonable soul although I am making a dictionary"—and when he dedicated a book to Queen Caroline he did it in these words (which his friends tactfully suppressed): "I ask for your Majesty's prayers in my singular case. I was once a man, but my thinking substance has for more than seven years been continually wasting away till it is wholly perished out of me." The monument in this little chapel tells us that although "nature was opprest by so strange a disorder that he thought himself less than man he attacked the boldest infidels of the age".

Shepton Mallet was the scene of two unsolved mysteries, both of them involving a sudden disappearance. The first story is told as a kind of local legend, although some Shepton inhabitants maintain that it is authentic. Nancy Camel was an ugly old hag who wandered about Shepton Mallet with a donkey and cart, shunned by everybody as a witch and ridiculed for her hideous appearance. At night she would drive away into the dark seclusion of a nearby wood and she was supposed to hold communion with the Devil. One sultry evening after the old woman had left the town and driven away to her hiding-place dark clouds gathered and closed over the setting sun, making the gloom still thicker. There was a sudden great rumble of thunder, a vivid flash of lightning, and above it all a loud, piercing shriek, the cracking of a whip and the rumble of wheels. Nancy Camel was never seen again; only the trace of wheels and the impression of cloven hoofs imprinted in the hard rock of her cave dwelling showed the searchers how horrible her fate had been.

The other story is more authentic, for it is set down in the parish records and quoted at length in Collinson's History, which says:

> "In the year 1763 one Owen Parfitt, an old man by trade a tailor but who had in his younger years served as a soldier in America, was living in this parish in the turnpike road to Wells. By long illness and a melancholy turn of mind he was reduced to such extreme weakness

as to be obliged to keep his bed and was emaciated almost to a skeleton. He depended on his neighbours for support and was taken care of by an aged sister. By his own desire he had several times been brought downstairs in an elbow chair and placed in the passage of the house for the benefit of the air. In this situation he was left one evening for a few minutes but on his attendant's return (strange to tell!) this helpless man was missing and nowhere to be found; nor has he ever since been heard of."

The road from Shepton Mallet runs through a beautiful valley at the foot of the Mendips, past Bowlish and Darshill with their ruined mills which once manufactured silk, and into the narrow, winding village street of Croscombe. At the corner of the steep lane leading up to the church stands a cross around which a battle was once fought; not a battle of history but an armed defence by a party of Croscombe villagers who were determined to save their old cross from destruction when it was proposed to remove it as an obstruction to main-road traffic.

The church stands halfway up the side of the hill and its spire dominates the little village. You enter by the south porch, a graceful example of Early English work, with two faces of rustic simplicity carved on either side of it. Inside there is an elaborate show of woodwork bewildering in its splendour. Roof, screen, pulpit, and pews are all carved with an almost pagan richness. Behind the organ there is a small two-storeyed vestry where the Seven Guilds of Croscombe used to meet in the village's more prosperous days—the Guilds of the Wives, the Young Men, the Maidens, the Webbers, the Archers, the Fullers, and the Hogglers (or labourers). The ancient building close to the church wedged against some cottages and now used as a Baptist chapel was once part of the Fortescues' Croscombe manor-house.

The very name Dinder conjures up a vision of rural beauty but the village itself surpasses even the promise of its name. To come into this drowsy little place on a summer evening when cattle are straying past the bow-windowed post-office and drinking from the stream which tumbles over its tiny weirs alongside the road is to feel that this place must be the English equivalent of Innisfree where "peace comes dropping slow". It would be difficult to find a lovelier picture than its church standing close by the fine grey-stoned Dinder House. Leading into the churchyard is a lych-gate built in memory of a Somerville, the family long associated with this village. The church has a rare stone pulpit of the Jacobean period bearing the date 1621; above it is a small window filled with fragments of ancient stained glass. The font is a fine example of Perpendicular work, with a beautifully carved bowl and stem. Outside on the south wall the old consecration crosses can still be clearly seen, and nearby there is the famous yew-tree which by measuring its enormous girth the experts consider to be something like 1,200 years old. In the graveyard among other memorials to members of the family is one to Admiral Sir James Somerville, who during his distinguished career of the last war was charged with "one of the most difficult and disagreeable tasks that a British admiral has ever been faced with"—the destruction of part of the French fleet at Oran. But in this peaceful village it is not so much "the Admiral of the Fleet" who is remembered, but "the Squire of Dinder", the man they all knew and who knew them all.

The view of Wells Cathedral from the Dulcote road is unique in the real meaning of that much abused word. It comes into view set in an olive-green bowl of the Mendip foothills, substantial in its proportions and yet pinnacled with such fragile beauty that in certain lights it seems almost transparent. Wells never fails to create an overwhelming impression on a visitor. Henry James confessed that although he knew in a general way that this little town had a great Cathedral to produce he was far from suspecting the intensity of the impression that awaited him. Another writer has stressed that it is easier to suggest the character of Wells than to describe it, to dream about it than to think clearly of it. "It is a place for halfway seasons and half-lights, for early spring and late autumn, for dawn and nightfall."

The car-park ticket of the Corporation of Wells bears these words: "Welcome to Wells. You should not fail to see the Cathedral, the Vicar's Close, the Museum, the Palace Moat, St Cuthbert's Church." This gives five focal points of interest, but perhaps one of the loveliest features of Wells is the series of ancient gateways, each a perfect unit in itself and at the same time a harmonious part of this mediæval cathedral city, shutting off the ecclesiastical quarter from the secular township. This unique group of ecclesiastical buildings has been described as the best example to be found in the whole world of a non-monastic church with its subordinate buildings still standing and still put to their own use. And there could be no better way of getting something of the atmosphere of the city than by viewing the pictures framed in each of these ancient gateways— the "Dean's Eye", leading from Sadler Street to the Cathedral Green; the "Chain Gate", north of the Cathedral on the way to the Vicars' Close, which is itself approached by yet another arched gateway; the smaller "Penniless Porch", leading from the Cathedral Green into the Market Place; and the "Bishop's Eye" between the Market Place and the Bishop's Palace.

It is the West Front which perhaps more than anything else has made Wells Cathedral famous, and the fine open space of the Cathedral Green gives a magnificent approach to this "sermon in stone and poor man's Bible", the earliest of all the great European Gothic façades. In spite of the defacement of time and man this sculptured representation of a great company of angels, saints, monarchs, and bishops is still a superb work of art. It has been shrewdly pointed out that the design of this West Front is subtly enhanced by the eight boldly projecting buttresses which are the great secret of the outstanding and beautiful effects produced; for "although themselves completely loaded with rich figures and abounding in the most luxuriant and minute architectural foliage and deeply cut mouldings, yet by their great projection, they so separate the extraordinary mass of workmanship as to relieve the eye and give the required breadth to the work that would otherwise become confused".

Although the details of this great façade have been greatly praised there has been a good deal of criticism levelled against it as an architectural whole. The historian Freeman, in spite of his enthusiasm for everything else in Wells, roundly condemns the West Front as a fraud because it is not really a screen for the nave and aisles—it includes also the two western towers outside the body of the church and so becomes a mere mask designed in order to gain greater room for the display of statues. Havelock Ellis, in a characteristic passage, voiced the same opinion. For him it was "a meaningless façade put up in a hurry by ambitious builders reckless of the fact that what they were putting up had no organic relation to the church behind it, and was therefore quite false". And yet anyone who looks at the West Front once again in the evening when the setting sun brings ethereal lights and shadows to its intricate sculptured architecture will undoubtedly feel that judged on its own merits it still superbly overrides all technical criticism, for it is more than a work of art—it is a confession of faith.

It is unfortunate that the magnificence of the West Front often distracts attention from the north porch, which is in some respects the most interesting part of the whole cathedral, showing as it does, with a fine blend of dignity and grace, the gradual evolution of the Early English style from the Norman. The Cathedral of Wells, like those of York and Lichfield, has no trace of pure Norman work, although it stands on the site of an earlier Norman building, but it is quite a museum of architectural styles. There is, for example, the early Transitional of the north porch, the pure Early English of the West Front, the

Decorated work in the Chapter House, and the Perpendicular style in the western towers.

Any detailed examination of the Cathedral would be impossible in this book and only a few outstanding features can be mentioned. The great inverted arches spanning the nave and transepts arrest the attention immediately on entry by the west door; they are the skilful engineering contrivance adopted in the fourteenth century to prevent the collapse of the central tower. In the nave and transepts the capitals of the pillars have fascinating carvings which show mediæval craftsmen giving full rein to their skill and humour. Those of the south transept are the most popular and include one series which represents two men stealing fruit, the farmer in pursuit, the capture of one of the thieves, and his chastisement. The carvers of the *misereres* * in the choir stalls vied with their fellow-craftsmen in stone to produce quaint and original figures such as a cat and a fiddle and two dragons biting each other's tail.

The famous and much photographed stairway leading to the Chapter House has been described as a frozen cascade in stone. It is so remarkably constructed that its division into two parts (one leading straight over the Chain Gate and the other curving gracefully into the Chapter House) seems to be blended imperceptibly into one harmonious whole. The Chapter House itself is a magnificently proportioned octagonal building with a gracefully vaulted roof supported by one central pier of sixteen delicately clustered shafts.

One of the great attractions to the sightseers in the Cathedral is the ingenious old clock in the north transept. The outer circle of the dial marks the hours from one to twenty-four; the gilt star travelling round the inner circle shows the minutes; and the central circle registers the days of the month and the phases of the moon. The quarters are sounded by the figure on the right of the clock, John Blandiver, who kicks two bells with his heels. When the hour is sounded four knights revolve around a little castle turret above the clock, and as they charge each other one horseman is noisily unseated at each revolution, mounting again only to be knocked off once more.

A stone in the middle of the floor of the nave near the pulpit inscribed with the words INA REX recalls the association of this great Saxon King of Wessex with the beginnings of Christianity in Wells, but it is the magnificent collection of effigies in the aisles north and south of the

* These were spared by the nineteenth-century restorers, who, as the historian Freeman expressed it, "rammed, jammed and crammed the new seats into the choir."

choir which provides the real historical portrait gallery for the Cathedral. The elaborate tomb of Bishop Beckynton with its skeleton as a *memento mori* was built by himself some years before his death. This fifteenth-century prelate's name crops up everywhere in Wells: one of the gateways bears his name; he built the Chain Gate Bridge; and he left instructions in his will for the rebuilding of the Vicar's Close as it is today. The tomb of Bishop Bytton is reputedly the most ancient incised slab in England. To touch this tomb was once regarded as a specific for toothache, and the carver of one grotesque figure on a south transept capital has perpetuated the agonised expression of one suffering pilgrim. During the restoration work of the nineteenth century the tomb was opened and an eyewitness has described the finding of a skeleton laid out in proper order with every bone in its right place and with all its teeth undecayed and absolutely perfect in shape and colour. This preservation of sound teeth would doubtless have been regarded as miraculous in the thirteenth century and it is a likely explanation of the superstitious veneration of the Bishop's tomb.

A small brass in the wall of the south choir aisle transept is worth looking for. Its Latin inscription bewails the loss of a husband, but two lines have been slyly added by the attractive young widow's cousin and admirer:

'Tis thus a disconsolate widow sings,
T. P. her cousin hopes for better things.

There is a marble effigy of Bishop Creghton in the small chapel of the north choir aisle. The Bishop was abroad with Charles II during the Commonwealth and the Cathedral's great brass lectern commemorates his return from this fifteen years' exile. Near the steps leading to the Chapter House is the elaborate monument to Bishop Kidder and his wife, who were both killed by the fall of a chimney stack through the roof of the Palace during the night of the terrible hurricane which struck England on November 26th, 1703, sweeping away the first Eddystone Lighthouse and destroying hundreds of ships around the coasts. Bishop Kidder had succeeded the deprived Thomas Ken and the townsfolk of Wells regarded this sudden calamity as a sure sign of divine displeasure at the unjust treatment of their rightful bishop.

A stone in the retro-choir just behind the High Altar bears the inscription CLAVER MORRIS M.D. 1726 and marks the grave of a Wells doctor whose recently published diary has made him something of a celebrity as a local Samuel Pepys. *The Diary of a Country Physician* gives many interesting sidelights on everyday life in eighteenth-century Wells and describes this busy doctor's friends, patients, work, and recreation. The musical activities of the city are reported in detail, for to Dr Morris music was not so much a hobby as a passion. Besides being a passable singer he played the harpsichord, violin, double-bass, bassoon, oboe, and flute. He founded a Wells Music Club which met weekly in the Vicars' Hall and performed works by a wide variety of composers. He was also something of an authority on the organ and in 1709 was asked to go to Shepton Mallet and give his opinion on the new instrument in the church.

One of the most dramatic incidents reported in the diary is the marriage of his daughter to an impecunious suitor. Morris had done his utmost to prevent this match, but a Rev. Samuel Hill performed the ceremony secretly in the Cathedral and the Sacrist gave the bride away. For their part in this clandestine marriage the Rev. Hill was "prohibited from serving in the Cathedral again on any pretext" and the Sacrist was suspended for a year.

After the ceremony Dr Morris turned his daughter out of the house and refused to see her for nine months, and then the womenfolk of his household effected a reconciliation which is amusingly related by the diarist:

> "October 23, 1719. My daughter Betty with my wife, Mrs Evans, and all the maidservants came into my chamber while I was putting on my clothes. I refused to see her and ordered her to be had down, and going into my closet I shut the door. But she opened it and with abundance of begging and crying she forced me to beg God Almighty to bless her. And so my wife kept my daughter to dinner."

An elaborate memorial tablet and bust which was originally near Claver Morris's burial-place has now been moved to the east wall of the cloister. On the same wall is a monument to Thomas Linley and his daughter Elizabeth, the famous eighteenth-century singer and beauty who married Sheridan. The penitent dramatist had taken his much-neglected wife to Clifton in a vain attempt to save her life, and after her death she was brought to Wells to be buried. It was an amazing funeral, with hundreds of people lining the road all the way from Bristol, and inside the Cathedral there was such a crush that dozens of people fainted.

For anyone who can face the climb it is well worth while to go up the central tower for the fine view of the layout of the city and its places of interest. To the south the impressive Bishop's Palace can be seen with all the detail of an aerial photograph; the walls, moat, gateway, drawbridge, and ruined Banqueting Hall stand out clearly. The Palace gateway is a favourite place for visitors, who flock there to see the swans pull at a small bell at feeding time. The original swan which was taught this trick by a nineteenth-century bishop's daughter can be seen stuffed in the Wells Museum. The Museum also possesses a remarkable collection of "Club Brasses", the emblems of the first Friendly Societies, many of them bearing the dates of the eighteenth century and some of them belonging to clubs which were in existence four hundred years ago.

Looking westward from the tower we see St Cuthbert's, a handsome parish church with proportions of a young cathedral, and close by the church a collection of ancient almshouses. To the north we look down on that unique little street the Vicars' Close, a double row of lovely mediæval houses with a tiny chapel at the end.

For the most part Wells has been a placid little backwater undisturbed by the main stream of national history. Occasionally a King has arrived in the city—Edward IV in pursuit of the Earl of Warwick; Henry VII chasing the impostor Perkin Warbeck—but it was only during the Civil War and Monmouth's Rebellion that Wells became closely involved in stirring events. The city was mostly pro-Royalist during the Civil War, but the county as a whole favoured Parliament, and so Wells suffered from the lawlessness of troops on both sides as they moved in and out of the city. Soldiers smashed windows and statues in the Cathedral, plundered the Bishop's Palace, and on one occasion in a drunken frenzy they "rusht into the cathedral, broke down the organ, font, seats in the quire and the bishop's throne beside many other villainies". On July 1st, 1685, Monmouth's rebel army passed through the city and once again the Cathedral was attacked by brutal, ignorant soldiery who defaced statues on the West Front, almost destroyed the organ, and stabled their horses in the nave. In Conan Doyle's novel *Micah Clarke* there is a vivid chapter, "The Fight in Wells Cathedral", based on a traditional story that the rebels broached a barrel of beer on the High Altar. It is not certain that this story is true, but the Cathedral records do state that the Sacrist was later presented with ten pounds as a reward for his courage in preserving the church vestments and plate from the depredations of Monmouth's soldiers.

The village of Wookey is composed of two separate groups of houses. The one on the slopes of the hills is built around the famous Wookey Hole Cave described in Chapter III. The school in this part of the village once had on its staff a young teacher named H. G. Wells who at the time nursed the secret ambition of taking a degree in science and had no idea of becoming a famous writer. Wookey's church, on the other side of the main road, is an interesting building with a tall spirelet on its stair turret. The church still preserves souvenirs of May 13th, 1906, when during evening service a great thunderstorm broke out with dramatic suddenness and a flash of lightning shattered the stair turret, which crashed through part of the roof. The congregation miraculously escaped injury and the only victim was a small bird which can still be seen in a glass case in the church. It is hardly surprising that the congregation could never forget that the rector had read in the first lesson just before the storm the significant words in Deuteronomy: "Did ever people hear the voice of God speaking out of the midst of the fire, as thou hast heard, and live?"

In this village of Wookey was born the famous journalist Cyril Arthur Pearson, founder of the *Daily Express* and other well-known papers. When in later life he lost his sight Sir Arthur Pearson devoted his chief energies to promoting the welfare of the blind, and in 1915 he started the great St Dunstan's Charity for sailors and soldiers blinded in the war.

After Wookey the main road follows the lower slopes of the hills fairly closely and gives some fine views of characteristic Mendip scenery, with Ebbor Gorge showing as a grey rocky cleft in the hills. This pocket edition of its great neighbour Cheddar Gorge offers an attractive scrambling walk up a wild tree-shaded steep path.

Beyond Easton the main road rises slightly up the side of the hills and there is an extensive view of the level moorland country to the south-west until we reach Westbury-sub-Mendip with houses straggling along a winding village street. The church has an interesting Norman arch supporting the Perpendicular tower and on the outside of the north wall there are the remains of a blocked-up Norman doorway.

An amusing personal memory of Westbury is provided by the story of a small boy who whispered to my wife when she was visiting the village during the last war: "Do you see that man there? He has a lovely stamp-collection and he's the cleverest man in Westbury". Enquiry revealed that this elderly grey-haired stamp-collector very probably was the cleverest man in Westbury, for he was none other than Sir James Jeans, the famous mathematician, who at that time was living at Lodge Hill House.

The next village, Rodney Stoke, has a beautiful setting right below a finely wooded slope of the hills. In King John's reign the village was known as Stoke Giffard, but when the last heiress of the Giffard family

The Bishop's Eye, Wells

married a Rodney the name was changed to Rodney Stoke. The church is particularly attractive and is full of interesting things to see. In its small north chapel there is a complete collection of memorials to members of the Rodney family, including one stone effigy of the last of the direct male line representing the young man rising out of his coffin and casting aside his shroud.

The Norman font has an unusual twisted effect reminiscent of the pillar in Compton Martin church, but perhaps the outstanding feature of the church is the magnificent collection of bench-ends, all carved by local amateur craftsmen at the beginning of the century.

The road continues through Draycott, a village of strawberry beds and fine views over the countryside stretching out from the base of the hills, and then there is the first glimpse of Cheddar—a glimpse of a slender, graceful church tower framed in trees, and provided with a background of the Mendips which curve westwards behind the village. For most people Cheddar means the three C's: Caves, Cliffs, and Cheese. To these might be added Church and Cross. The caves have been dealt with in Chapters II and III; as to Cheddar cheese, the genuine article seems now to be almost unobtainable by the ordinary consumer, who is fobbed off with a not very convincing imitation. As long ago as 1886 that stalwart champion of Harvest Home and the Harvest Feast, Archdeacon Denison, fulminated against "so-called Cheddar cheese made in America". In his opinion the only thing in its favour was its cheapness and its capacity for concealing for about six weeks at the most "its native characteristics of unpleasant smell and taste"; English people, he was convinced, would never buy sham Cheddar twice. As in so many other things we have retrogressed since those days; now there are very few, of the younger generation at least, who have ever tasted genuine Cheddar cheese, and as a sign of the times there is no longer that fascinating cheese shop in Cheddar which in the days of my youth sent delicious Cheddar cheeses of every size and weight all over England and all over the world.

To approach Cheddar Cliffs from the village end is to sacrifice more than half the impressiveness of this towering rock-walled ravine, and in any case the commercialised atmosphere surrounding the caves, the shops, and the "Cave Man Restaurant" with its skeleton sign picked out in neon lights would daunt any but the most hardened sightseer. The gorge should be approached from the top of the Mendips and then gradually as you descend the winding road the towering vertical faces of rock, some of them 450 feet high, increase in height and ruggedness until you reach Wind Rock with its fretted pinnacles, its festoons of

Priddy Green

creepers, and its trees growing out of precarious crannies in the craggy face of the limestone. This extraordinary impression of grandeur does not, of course, depend on size: I have known Americans compare it quite seriously with their mighty Colorado. There was even one Frenchman who admitted that it was finer than anything his country could offer in the Tarn. It is partly, I suppose, a question of proportion—"the mind sets the scale", as Stevenson says, "one can enjoy a Niagara falls of thirty inches"—partly, it is the perpendicular face of the cliffs which gives such a feeling of immensity, and partly the narrowness of the defile adding to the general effect. Some years ago a summer picnic at midnight gave me an opportunity of seeing the gorge by moonlight, an unforgettable sight with the clear light of a full moon picking out the jagged crags with a strange silvery distinctness and throwing dark blue shadows in unexpected places.

In the village itself there is little to see except the Market Cross and the church. Recollection of the elaborate cross at Shepton Mallet might encourage a feeling of disappointment at Cheddar's smaller, plainer hexagonal market shelter built around its ancient shaft, but it is just this simplicity and its perfect proportions which make it a particularly attractive example of a small market cross. The interior of the church recalls the Middle Ages with its brightly coloured fifteenth-century stone pulpit, its painted roof, and the whimsical carving of some of its bench-ends. There are three in the north aisle representing the deadly sins of the tongue—Deceit, Gossip, and Evil speaking.

Cheddar will always be closely associated with Hannah More, for it was here that she set up her first Sunday School in the circumstances which have already been described. An interesting proof of the influence her school exercised in the village can be found in the old parish registers, which show that whereas prior to 1806 most of the couples married in Cheddar church were illiterate and had to make a mark for their signature, after that date Hannah More's work was bearing fruit and all brides and bridegrooms could write their names.

The ancient town of Axbridge (now by-passed by heavy traffic) is perhaps the most fascinating of all the smaller places of Mendip land. Its long, narrow winding street lined on either side with attractive old houses with bulging storeys, its wide square, and its fine flight of steps leading up to the church suggest an atmosphere of the Middle Ages which is more often felt in an unspoilt French provincial town than in this country. Axbridge was once a borough town of great antiquity with a mayor and corporation and it still preserves a remarkable set of documents and deeds illustrating its civic and social life and customs, including the various charters of its former corporation from the reign of Edward the Confessor to the reign of Queen Elizabeth I. Queen Elizabeth's charter which regulated the government of the town until 1886 named as the town's first mayor "our beloved John By-the-sea", whose curious name, according to Rutter, was derived from an ancestor who had been picked up as a child on the beach near Weston-super-Mare. Many years later descendants of this first mayor were still living in the town and one of them, Thomas Bythesea, left a small sum of money to the parish church. Axbridge surrendered another of its privileges as far back as the fourteenth century: during the reigns of the first three Edwards the town had sent two members to Parliament, but in 1344 it petitioned successfully to be relieved of this honour on the score of expense.

The town's importance in the royal hunting forest of Mendip has already been mentioned in Chapter VII. After Bishop Ralph of Shrewsbury had secured its disafforestation by 1337 there must have been very little of the Mendips where the forest laws were effective and so the hills carried still larger flocks of sheep. The cloth industry thus became the basis of Axbridge's prosperity. When the woollen trade declined the sheltered position of a town protected on the north by the heights of the Mendips and open to the sun on the south was found particularly favourable for the cultivation of early fruit and vegetables, and this is still an important industry of Axbridge.

In spite of its deep roots in the distant past Axbridge has little exciting history to record since Mendip Forest days, although during the scare of the Spanish Armada the town was one of the six meeting-places where "captains were ordered to muster their men in full numbers and then in orderly sort to lead them to the coast to all likely places of the enemy's descent". And during the ill-fated Monmouth's Rebellion drivers of the Duke's ammunition wagons, panic-stricken at the flight of the rebel cavalry, unharnessed their horses and themselves fled at full gallop to Axbridge thirteen miles away from the battlefield. Six Axbridge men were afterwards convicted as rebels and were sentenced to death by Judge Jeffreys.

The town's prosperous independence encouraged in the old days a certain amount of boorish truculence which sometimes degenerated into downright barbarity. In the Town Hall there is still preserved a "bull-anchor" which was used for the annual bull-baiting on November 5th. A nineteenth-century manuscript shows how long this brutal custom survived and describes the procedure. Mayor and Corporation attended a special service in the church and then the whole populace assembled in the square, where a bull was released from an inn yard and hounded through the town up High Street and West Street, followed by yelping dogs and a yelling mob of men armed with cudgels. When the wretched animal, maddened by the blows and noise, reached the hills outside the town it was lashed to the bull-anchor and then stunned by clubs and worried to death by the dogs. As a variation on this savage theme a badger was sometimes placed in a barrel and the dogs set on to attack it and drag it from its shelter.

It will be remembered that Axbridge proved a very formidable task for Hannah More's energy and enthusiasm. "A wretched beggarly town", she called it, and although the people of Cheddar were just ignorant and stupid, here they were in addition self-satisfied and aggressive and ruled by an "unfeeling hard-hearted Corporation given to fine clothes and luxury". The rector, the Rev. Gould, was a hard-drinking cleric, often appearing in church on a Sunday morning with a black eye received during a Saturday-night brawl. Yet even he was sufficiently impressed by Hannah More's earnestness to be civil when she called on him.

> "He took us to several of the Corporation who were of his party [added Hannah More], for the town was all anarchy and malice, and pretty equally divided in enmity. However our cause compelled us to be equally civil and attentive to each party. Axbridge is a very poor place indeed, yet the luxury of this body corporate is so great that at their annual festivities they never admit to their table a vulgar joint of meat. In September we opened our school with upwards of a hundred poor little dirty, wretched-looking creatures, half-starved amidst the voluptuous eating of this *ancient corporation*, as they style themselves."

For a time there seemed to be some progress; the rector actually visited the school on one occasion and stood by while the children were taught the catechism; and once he allowed them to sing together in the church. By joint subscription the Corporation twice raised enough money to give the children a present of ginger-bread—"Our wildest heights of imagination never soared so high", confessed Hannah More. Evening readings were started in the town and were attended at first by nearly a hundred illiterate but smartly dressed young men and women, but later on the town lost interest in both the reading society and the school and "a disagreeable clergyman in sullen opposition, the heads of the town alike adverse and the Methodists officious and meddling" caused Hannah More to abandon her work in Axbridge.

There is one native of Axbridge famous enough to figure in the

Dictionary of National Biography—William Naish, who showed such talent as a young man that he was sent to study under Sir Joshua Reynolds. Later he became a fashionable miniaturist and practised in London with great success, exhibiting at the Royal Academy almost continuously from 1783 until his death in 1800.

The handsome parish church of St John the Baptist gains in dignity from its fine position overlooking the town. Its central tower adds to the beauty of its proportions and the interior has a magnificent plaster ceiling to the nave. This bears the date 1636 and it is the work of a local craftsman named George Drayton, who according to the church accounts received ten guineas in payment.

The church has many other interesting treasures, including a good Perpendicular font, a curious fourteenth-century representation of Christ painted on oak, and two elaborate monuments to members of the Prowse family at the east end of the north and south aisles. In front of the demure figure of Anne Prowse kneeling in the south aisle there is a charming tapestry altar-cloth worked in the eighteenth century by Abigail Prowse. In the floor of the vestry behind the organ will be found a good fifteenth-century brass showing the figures of an Axbridge merchant, Roger Harper, and his wife.

The church registers are all well preserved and as they go back to 1562 they form one of the oldest and most complete parish records in the Mendip district. On the first page of one of these volumes there is a reminder of the plagues which periodically swept over the town, for the rector has copied out a prescription to prevent the spread of infection. His mixture was made of various herbs such as rue, sage, lavender, and rosemary compounded with camphor and it was given the name of "thieves's vinegar, having been made use of by some abandoned wretches who plundered the dying and the dead in one of the great plagues abroad, and it was acknowledged to their confessor before their execution". In 1646 the register shows no fewer than ninety-seven deaths in three months, after a former average of five for a similar period. Twenty years later another epidemic was threatened and the population of Axbridge was forbidden to visit Bristol or receive any visitors or goods from that city.

On the south wall of the church there is a list of rectors since 1328, and among them is the name of Elias Rebotier. This French Protestant refugee who held the living for forty-five years until his death in 1765 must often have told his parishioners the astounding story of his escape from France—a story he afterwards set down in detail in his *Autobiography*. Rebotier was born in the south of France in the district of the Cevennes mountains, which has always been famous for its rigid, zealous Protestants. From his earliest youth he had decided to go to Geneva and study for the Protestant ministry, but edicts were issued by Louis XIV making it impossible to travel out of France without official passes, and these were rigorously withheld from all Huguenots. To avoid active persecution Rebotier's father sent his son to a Jesuit college, where he was wretchedly unhappy and planned to escape to Geneva in spite of the grim accounts he had heard of those who had been murdered or taken prisoner as they tried to get out of the country. With a single companion Rebotier, now a young man of twenty-two, set off one January evening, choosing this bleak time of year when the mountains would be covered with snow because he knew the passes were more strictly guarded in the summer months. The journey was beset with difficulties and dangers; hungry and exhausted the two friends pushed on over the mountainous country, often up to their knees in snow. At last they came to the frontier and after avoiding the guards by swimming across an icy river they reached Geneva.

Rebotier spent a short time in Switzerland and Germany and then, armed with several letters of recommendation from his father, he set off for England. Here he was not welcomed very warmly; various people who had received many favours from the elder Rebotier in France told him pointedly that his wisest course would be to return to Holland or Germany and settle there. In desperation he accepted an offer to become tutor to two youths of a rich family living in Barbados. After a short stay in this island he became seriously ill and was given a free passage back to England in a ship which had to run the gauntlet of several French privateers, for the two countries were now at war.

Shortly after landing at Plymouth Rebotier was appointed tutor in the family of John Strachey of Sutton Court near West Harptree, and this remarkable Frenchman's wandering and worries came to an end. "I had a considerable time of rest after so many fatigues," he noted in his *Autobiography*, "and I began to taste the pleasures of life. At Sutton Court my time was divided between the care of my pupils and my studies, the former by day and the latter generally by night, allowing myself one day in the week for exercise, either in hunting, shooting or fishing." Three years later Rebotier presented himself to Bishop Hooper of Bath and Wells and was ordained deacon on May 19th, 1706.

The bishop must obviously have been greatly impressed by this young foreigner who had suffered so much for conscience' sake; he offered him a position in his household at Wells in the capacity of secretary rather than chaplain, so as not to excite the jealousy of the other clergy of the diocese.

"In 1713 [wrote Rebotier in the concluding pages of his *Autobiography*], I married Margaret Bisse of Dinder and all this time I continued at the Palace as before (a favour seldom if ever granted), having a house in Wells where I retired every night after the service of the day was over, till I had a rectory at Axbridge where Thomas Prowse Esq. (grandson to the bishop) has a pleasant seat; he was sometime under my care at the Palace. This falling into the bishop's hands, I had the offer of it. I can safely say I never asked this or any other preferment of his lordship; whatever I had before and now enjoy came to me unexpectedly.

"Now Axbridge, being a corporate town, required my presence and I removed from Wells and settled in Axbridge in June 1720. In the following year I had the misfortune to lose my wife and in 1728 my son Elias also departed this life, reducing my family to my daughter Katherine and myself. This affliction was certainly great and my condition was dismal till, falling into the company of Elizabeth Chorley, my losses were happily repaired by my marriage with her."

The last stage of this journey along the southern slopes passes over the Bristol to Bridgwater road at Cross, an important posting station in the old coaching days, but since the making of the new section of the main road it has become an isolated backwater along the former winding highway which leads right into the heart of the last barren hills of the western Mendips, coming to a halt at Compton Bishop. This village is a mere sprinkling of houses sheltered in a little hollow under the shadow of Crook's Peak. Its church is attractively situated in this green valley and it has a fine churchyard cross with a beautifully restored head; a graceful Early English archway to the south porch; and a sturdy Norman font with an oak cover bearing the date 1617. But the loveliest piece of workmanship inside is the delicately carved stone pulpit, with a regrettable extra panel added to the original and a still more incongruous modern rail of wood set beside its stone steps.

Although the rocky horned summit of Crook's Peak is only some 620 feet high, it is a conspicuous landmark of the western Mendips. Its distinctive shape makes it a convenient direction point for navigation in the Bristol Channel, and it is the one Mendip outline that is immediately recognisable from almost any part of the great Somerset plain. In the anxious days before the attempted Spanish invasion culminated in the fiasco of the Armada, Crook's Peak was one of the chief Somerset beacon hills. The churchwardens' account book at Banwell contains the following entry for the year 1580: "Pd. The firste daye of July for one lood of wood for the beaken and for carrynge of the same to Croke peke. 0.5.0." In the following year there is a further note: "Recd. backe of oure money for the beakon at Crokes peacke. 0.2.0." The erratic spelling of these records does nothing to settle the old argument about the proper form of the name—Crook Peak or Crook's Peak. Those who favour the former variation base their preference on a very doubtful tradition that "Crook" is a corruption of "crux" and refers to a crucifix that was once set up on the hilltop.

Compton Bishop might seem an ideal starting point for climbing Crook's Peak, but a much finer though more gradual approach is from Shute Shelf, the well-known rocky ridge at the head of the beautifully wooded road from Sidcot to Axbridge. Shute Shelf, as it is always called locally in spite of the Ordnance Survey's "Shute Shelve", used to be a picturesque landmark crowned with a cluster of gaunt weather-beaten Scotch firs, but successive road improvements have now reduced it to a somewhat insignificant rocky bluff overlooking the road. In the seventeenth century it appears to have been a favourite place for executions and travellers along the main Bristol to Exeter highway must often have heard the mournful clank of chains as the grisly remains of malefactors twirled on the gibbet in the wind. There is a note in the parish records of Worle for 1609 which suggests some grim village drama: "Edward Bustle cruelly murthered by consent of his owne wyfe who with one Humfry Hawkins and one other of theyre associates were executed for the same murther and hanged in irons at place called Shutt Shelfe neere Axbridge. A good president for wicked people."

CHAPTER XIV

FARMING ON MENDIP

THE village of Priddy lies some 800 feet above sea-level in a shallow depression on the Mendip plateau. It is remote from main roads and is seldom visited by strangers. The homes of those who live there are widely scattered, though a few groups of cottages and farmsteads huddle close to the focus of the village, which is dominated by the eminence of Nine Barrows and by the stocky, grey stone church. Here five narrow roads with wide grass verges converge on the open sward of Priddy Green, on which stands a dark, weathered stack with a decaying straw thatch which can no longer be wholly proof against the rainstorms which drive across the hills. From a distance it looks dark and bristly like an old bean-rick, but a close view shows it to be a stack of grey sheep hurdles. There is a local belief, probably without legal foundation, that as long as this stack remains on the village green the people of Priddy will have the right to use this land for their annual Sheep Fair which has been held there for over six hundred years.

Priddy Sheep Fair is said to have owed its origin to the ravages of the Black Death at Wells which stopped the Charter Fair held annually on the Cathedral Green. Those who still had business to do were forced to find a place on the healthier heights away from the city and chose the village of Priddy, where the Fair continued. In the fourteenth century the Mendips produced a great deal of wool, and the spinning and weaving were done in the homes of the peasantry; Priddy Fair was not only a mart for the sheep and for cattle, but for merchandise of all kinds, especially woollen cloth. It came to be of such importance that it was chosen in 1352 as the first place in Somerset for the publication of a new Weights and Measures Act which forced all traders to discard their private yardsticks and to submit their fabrics to a uniform standard of measurement. The Fair has always been primarily a market for sheep, but in the eighteenth and nineteenth centuries it also served as a centre where the lead miners could equip themselves with working clothes and boots. Horse dealing has been carried on by gipsies even within living memory, and cattle have often been sold in large numbers. Despite a steady decline in sheep rearing over a long period of years the main purpose of the Fair has persisted. Now, happily, the number of sheep appears to be increasing again, due mainly to an improvement in the prices for wool and mutton, and to the fact that many dairy-farmers in surrounding districts have adopted a policy of running grassland ewes on their farms as a sideline, a practice which is being widely encouraged in the south-west of England. If you go to Priddy Fair today—it is held on the nearest Wednesday to August 21st—you will probably see nearly two thousand sheep, mainly healthy hill stores, penned on either side of the road which runs along the east side of the Green. On the south side, near one of Priddy's old inns, lies a temporary paddock holding thirty or forty store cattle. Nearby are the stalls, and although the gipsies may not be there, you can usually buy equipment for the farm, a fish-and-chip lunch from a travelling van, and certainly ice-cream, coffee, and sandwiches. On the triangular green itself the stock lorries are parked in front of Manor Farm—many of them from thirty or forty miles away.

For generations Priddy Fair has been run by Priddy people; a local committee of sixteen shareholders, mainly from Priddy families, organises the sale and at one time the shareholders used to pitch the hurdles for the sheep themselves from the stack on the Green, rebuilding and rethatching the stack afterwards to await next year's Fair. But today hurdles are brought by a firm of auctioneers from Farrington Gurney which has had connections with Priddy Fair since the turn of the century. (This firm, which conducts the actual sale, holds a single share which entitles it to a representative on the Fair Committee.) But the old hurdle stack on Priddy Green remains untouched—a symbol of the ancient wool trade which built so many of the fine Mendip churches and a symbol, too, of the continuity of Mendip farming.

Sheep rearing was undoubtedly the chief occupation on the Mendip uplands until the end of the eighteenth century, contributing raw material for the vigorous woollen industry which was already well established in the small valleys of the eastern Mendips and in western Wiltshire by the eleventh century. The money from wool built many of the churches with fine towers for which Somerset is so famous, and the cathedral at Wells. For more than six hundred years the lives of the people in this part of England were very largely determined by the state of agriculture and the state of the wool trade, which were closely dovetailed.

In the reign of Henry III the Carthusian monks of Witham Priory set up a cell at Charterhouse and farmed an estate which extended at least from Rowberrow Warren and Black Down to the village of

Priddy. They had no need to fear interference from the royal game-wardens, for the *Patent Rolls* for the year 1251 set down the following privilege:

> "Notification to foresters, verderers and other bailiffs and ministers of the forest that, whereas it appears by inquisition that the land of the prior and brethren of the new Carthusian house in Menedep is without the regard, though within the metes of the forest, they are to be quit for ever of regard."

The Carthusians kept large flocks of sheep on Mendip and no doubt established a tradition of good farming there; they may also have been responsible for establishing the distinctive Mendip breed of sheep.

As the woollen industry developed, the towns and villages of the Eastern Mendips became famous for making high-quality "broadcloth" (which included Kersey meres and livery cloth), and the towns on the southern fringe for knitted goods. Expansion was particularly rapid in the seventeenth and early eighteenth centuries, when many solid farms and manor-houses were built. Everything possible was being done at this time to stimulate the industry. A law was made in 1678 which required that all burials were to be in woollen fabric, under penalty of five pounds. There is an entry in the church records of Christon, for example, which reads: "John Combe was interred ye 4th of May, 1707, in Woollen according to ye act." According to Daniel Defoe, who visited this part of Somerset in 1724, the prosperous town of Frome made fine Spanish medley cloths "with which all the gentlemen and persons of any fashion in England are cloth'd, and vast quantities of which are exported to all parts of Europe." Wells and Shepton Mallet were noted for the knitting of stockings, principally for the Spanish trade. The spinning of the wool was done by women and children in Frome itself, in the villages of Mells, Laverton, and Nunney, and in the smaller hamlets and scattered cottages of the surrounding countryside, the master clothiers distributing the wool each week and collecting the yarn. The towns, especially Frome, grew very rapidly at this period as a result of the flourishing wool trade. Daniel Defoe wrote of Frome:

> "It is so prodigiously increased within these last twenty or thirty years that they have built a new church * and so many new streets of houses, and those houses are so full of inhabitants, that Frome is now reckoned to have more people in it than the city of Bath, and some say, than even Salisbury itself, and if their trade continues to increase for a few years more, as it has done for those past, it is very likely to be one of the greatest and wealthiest inland towns in England."

* This refers to the church at Woodlands.

The Eastern Mendips area provided excellent conditions for the making of broadcloth. There were good supplies of water and the damp atmosphere favoured the easy working of the wool. Fine-quality Fuller's earth, used for scouring the wool, was dug within a few miles and was regarded as so valuable that at one time export was illegal. On the northern flanks of the Mendips around Ubley, Blagdon, and Harptree the strong soils were well suited for growing the teazels needed for dressing the woven fabric. Woad for making the indigo blue used in dyeing was also cultivated locally. The fine wool needed for making broadcloth was provided by the small Mendip sheep. "These will thrive on the poorest soil", wrote John Billingsley, "and fatten on such land as will scarcely keep other sorts alive. Pasturage ever so dry and exposed will feed this kind. They are very hardy, and the wool fine. The mutton is also excellent for the table, being full of gravy and of a rich flavour." Perhaps these excellent qualities attracted the sheep-stealers, against whom strong measures were taken. An inn sign near Shepton Mallet shows a man hanging from the gallows with a sheep nearby. This is known as Cannard's Grave after a highwayman—some say the landlord of the inn—who lived there about 200 years ago. It is said that he was arrested for stealing sheep, tried, condemned, and was then hanged on the village green and later buried in the porch (outside what is now the smoke-room window). Despite the considerable numbers of Mendip sheep, the woollen industry in Somerset grew to such an extent that wool had to be brought in to supplement local supplies.

We know very little about the arable crops on and around the Mendips before the middle of the eighteenth century, but grain, hemp, flax, teazels and woad were certainly grown, and it is probable that sheep were folded on fodder crops in arable enclosures.

The teazels grown for the woollen industry in the Blagdon–Harptree area were a very valuable crop. Many were sent away for use in the woollen mills of Yorkshire. The seed was sown in April and during the summer the land was worked over several times with long, narrow spades to destroy weeds. In November the teazel plants were thinned and earthed up, some of the thinnings being transplanted to fill gaps or to extend the area of the crop. In the following spring the land was worked again several times, and in July the plants flowered and the heads ripened. The ripe heads were cut by hand and tied together in bundles and then, for a period, were exposed on fine days to the sun and air until they were quite dry. The harvest depended very much on the season and in a wet year might be poor. The heads were graded into three qualities—"kings", "middlings", and "scrub". A pack of nine thousand "kings" fetched forty shillings and in a good year, when the yield might be fifteen or sixteen packs an acre, the crop was most profitable. One Blagdon record dated 1772 refers to a certain Robert Clark who "acquired a handsome Fortune by speculating in Teasils, buying them at a guinea and keeping them till they sold for five guineas a pack".

Woad took less time to mature. When the land had been ploughed and harrowed the seed was sown, often in drills, and after a few weeks the young plants were hand-weeded and thinned by women and children. The leaves of the plants were later cut by hand and taken to a mill, where they were chopped and bruised to a pulp, matured, and after being moulded into oval balls were dried ready for sale to the dyer.

Towards the end of the eighteenth century a revolution came to Mendip farming. Much of the land which had provided grazing for sheep and for a few young cattle was enclosed and methods of farming were drastically changed. We owe our knowledge of Mendip farming at this period largely to John Billingsley, a wool manufacturer who gave up industry to devote his time and thought to farming. Billingsley lived at Ashwick Grove, near Oakhill, and became a Vice-President of the Bath and West of England Society. He carried out many carefully controlled experiments on growing crops and animals before urging new methods on the local farmers, whom he regarded as extremely backward. His costings for farm operations were worked out in great detail. In 1795 he published a *General View of the Agriculture of the County of Sômerset* which was reprinted two years later as a Report to the Board of Agriculture. In this book he states that a great portion of the Mendip Hills was enclosed, divided, and cultivated "in the course of the last 40 years, nearly an equal portion still remaining in its open uncultivated state". The acreage of pasture land in Somerset was roughly twice that of the arable lands, and the average annual value of enclosed land was less than twenty-five shillings per acre.

The pattern of the Mendip countryside as we know it today was laid down, in the main, between 150 and 200 years ago. The eastern and western parts contrast sharply.The western ridges have a shallow, brashy soil and are of little use except as rough pasture. East of the Bridgwater road the Old Red Sandstone breaks down to a rather poor loam; the limestone areas have a richer, rather acid soil, which has probably only been derived in part from the actual limestone rock. Here the fields are large and are separated mainly by stone walls made from irregular blocks of grey limestone. Roads are few and relatively straight with wide grass verges. Many of the farms have been built in slight depressions in the plateau to protect them from the full force of the winds. To the east of the main Bristol–Wells road the fields are smaller, and there are more thorn hedges. Where stone walls are found, they are usually built of slabs of cream or grey lias limestone, seldom more than 6 inches in thickness, and more frequently only 2 or 3 inches thick; the walls must have been much easier to build than those on the Western Mendips. The countryside here is laced with a close network of winding second-class roads serving the farms and villages; they are used mainly by farm tractors, contractors repairing farm machinery, and tradesmen delivering household necessities. There is very little through traffic except on the Fosseway and on the Bath to Wells road.

The choice of wall or hedge to enclose the fields depended to some extent on local conditions. On some of the shallow soils, where the limestone rock often lies close to the surface, quickset hedges would not have grown well. Elsewhere, on the deeper soils, stone may not have been readily available. The question of relative cost may well have weighed heavily, since the stone walls cost roughly twice as much as the thorn hedges. Billingsley gives interesting information about the methods used at the end of the eighteen century to provide fencing, and the comparative costs. Walls were of two types, the list-wall in which cement was used, and the dry wall. Dry walls were usually built where it was possible to use a flat bed of stone as a foundation. In general the walls were five feet 6 inches high, and 2½ feet wide at the base, tapering to fifteen inches at the top, which was covered with 6 inches of turf. The cost of a "rope" (20 feet) of list-wall was as follows:

	£	s.	d.
To quarrying or digging eight loads of stone (25 cwt each) at 3*d*.		2	0
To hauling the stone (say half a mile) at 6*d*.		4	0
To building wall		3	6
To seven baskets of lime at 3*d*.		1	9
To covering with turf (if done very well)			3
		11	6

The cost of building 20 feet of dry wall was only 8*s*. 3*d*. Billingsley considered a stone wall better than a hedge on poor, exposed land. "It covers less ground; it does less injury to the crops; if part by accident fall, it is easily repaired, cattle are kept more secure, sportsmen are excluded." On the other hand, he considered a quickset hedge a better long-term proposition on the better soils and in less exposed places. "They afford good shelter for the cattle, and they furnish fuel and 'writh', or dead fence, for the necessary purposes of the occupier."

Before a quickset hedge could be established a ditch was dug and the material was thrown up to form a bank. A trench was made along the top of the bank and four- or five-year-old sets were planted in this trench, which was then filled with compost or rotted dung. Two dead hedges were then made, one on either side, to protect the young quicks from stock. The banks had then to be hoed and weeded twice a year for three years. Billingsley gives the cost per "rope" as follows:

	£	*s.*	*d.*
Making the bank			9
Quicksets (eighty in a rope)			9
Planting and dunging			2
Two dead hedges		2	5
Making two dead hedges			5
Weeding plants for three years			3
		4	9

Sometimes a wall was built in place of one of the dead hedges to provide better shelter for the young growing quick. After a few years the wall was then removed and the stone used for roadmaking or for making lime.

Another type of hedge which cost only 3*s.* 3*d.* per rope to make consisted of fully grown blackthorn with some hazel or withy stocks and briars planted on a rather higher bank. "The sloe will throw out so many shoots from its root, and the briar will so entwine its branches with the hedge, as to make it in a few years impervious to cattle of any kind". All these types of fencing can be identified on Mendip today, though many of the old stone walls are in a very poor state of repair; the gaps where they have fallen down are often stopped with sheep hurdles, or fenced with post and wire.

The enclosures created an entirely new situation: a few—but very few—appear to have been made with the unanimous consent of all parties claiming rights over the land, power being delegated to commissioners to carry through the agreed plans. But most of the Mendip enclosures were the result of Acts of Parliament. Opposition was often vigorous and many objections were raised. The enclosures were regarded by many as an invasion of the rights and interests of the cottagers. It was feared that they would upset the breeding system and lessen the number of sheep, lowering the quality of the wool and doing injury to the woollen industry. Some doubted whether the expense involved in fencing and in constructing farmhouses, stables, and drinking pools would be justified by the improved value of the holdings.

But opposition was overcome, and cottages and farm buildings were built. They were mainly of stone and were originally thatched, though today they are roofed with tiles (which were taxed when the enclosures were made) or with slates. Stalls for oxen were built round an open yard, and these can usually be recognised by their rows of arches which are now often built up to make cow stalls or loose boxes. The great problem, however, was to provide water for stock—a problem which has not been satisfactorily solved in some parts of the Mendips to this day. The common method was to construct pools to collect rainwater which served stock grazing on anything up to 100 acres.

Much of the land was ploughed for crops, especially cereals. Wheat, barley, and black oats were grown; indeed, Billingsley deplores the fact that three or four corn crops were taken from the land in successive years without a fallow or fallow crop—"Nor is the land sown with artificial grasses." It is interesting to know that the value of the short-period ley, so frequently urged today as an essential part of good rotational farming, should have been recognised over 150 years ago. Cabbages, turnips, potatoes, carrots, parsnips, vetches, flax, and clover were all grown, and in the journals of the Bath and West Society there is a record dated 1779 of the rotation used in a single Mendip field over a period of four years. In the first year it was given five hundredweight of lime to the acre and sown with turnips. In the second year it grew a crop of barley. In the third year it was manured with fifteen cartloads of horse-dung to the acre and planted with large Scotch cabbage which yielded over thirty tons an acre for feeding sheep and horned cattle. (The report stresses the advantage of cabbage in winter which is accessible in snow and frost when turnips are not.) In the fourth year the land was ploughed and harrowed for carrots, which yielded eight tons to the acre and were used for fattening pigs.

John Billingsley was responsible for introducing the double-furrow plough to Mendip farmers.

> "Formerly [he writes], the ploughs used here were the most awkward, and ill contrived, that could be conceived, but they have in a great measure given place to the double furrowed plough, which was introduced to this neighbourhood by a speculative man who turned farmer * on these lands, disregarded and despised by all

* I have seen a copy of John Billingsley's book in which this passage has the words "J. B. himself" written in the margin in faded ink.

Cheddar Gorge

> practical husbandmen. Though common farmers are for the most part backward in adopting new plans, yet I never knew any *valuable* discovery that they did not sooner or later fall into. So it happened with the double ploughs. For ten years, did the person above alluded to use this instrument, and was constant in season, and out of season, in recommending it to others . . . but all in vain, the more warm he was in enforcing its utility, the more reluctant were the common renters in adopting the use of it; and in all probability it would have remained to the present day, undistinguished for its superiority, has not the fame been manifested at the different trials of ploughs exhibited under the direction of the Bath Agricultural Society."

Great strides in all branches of farming were made in the enclosure period, though the improved methods of husbandry produced coarser wools which were not so suitable for the woollen industry, so that finer merino wool was imported from Spain. In some places the character of the country was completely changed. The creation of Ammerdown Park is a good example. This dignified house was built in 1788 by the wealthy Thomas Samuel Jolliffe among the sheep walks in the open down country between Radstock and Frome. He turned the land around it into a beautiful home park which came right up to the house, so that it was possible to feed the deer from the dining-room windows. The walled garden and orangery were set a little way away. The strip of formal garden edged by a low stone parapet which now separates the house from the park was added later.

Towards the very end of the eighteenth century and early in the nineteenth century the woollen industry in the Eastern Mendips began to decline; by this time the West Riding of Yorkshire had become the main manufacturing centre and the rise of the cotton industry was providing further competition. Machinery was being introduced, but unfortunately most of the clothiers in the Frome area were too conservative to adopt new methods. In many cases the hand-made cloth failed to compete with the machine-made material from the cloth-mills of Yorkshire and only the makers of better-class goods survived. In 1838 there were four factories working at Frome, one at Nunney, one at Whatley, and two at Great Elm. The poverty in Frome increased rapidly, yet the industry survived on a small scale. It is reported that in 1857 "superior cloth" was made for Alexander, Emperor of Russia, and kerseymere for "The Harem of the Grand Sultan of Constantinople". It is interesting to find that about this time an energetic young man named Joseph Tanner, who was anxious to apply up-to-date methods to industry, left the Frome cloth firm of Messrs Sheppard

Strawberry fields at Cheddar

after having failed to induce his employers to instal machinery. He went into the Steam Printing Works of W. T. Butler, later becoming a partner in the Selwood Printing Works (Butler and Tanner), which provided employment for many workers from the declining wool trade.

Meanwhile farming had reacted to the changes in industry. By 1870 the characteristic Mendip breed of sheep was all but extinct. The import of cheap grain, cheese, and meat at the turn of the century accelerated the decline in all branches of farming. At the same time methods of transport slowly improved and most of the village grist mills disappeared. Cider making on the farm declined and factories at Shepton Mallet and elsewhere absorbed the apple crops to make cider in bulk for bottling. Mendip farming prospered again for a short period during the first world war, but between the wars continued mainly as grass farming. Those farms which had a water-supply produced liquid milk which was taken to bottling plants or factories at Bristol, Frome, Trowbridge, and Highbridge.

The village craftsmen have changed with the changes in farming. The number of blacksmiths steadily decreases. The forge near the inn at Farrington Gurney stopped working in 1962. Workers in wood are fewer, though one or two traditional craftsmen remain. Sheep hurdles are made near Blagdon. There is also a small timber-mill at Leigh-on-Mendip, which you can find by looking for two old chimneys behind the cottages on the south side of the village street. One of these belongs to the mill and you will see ash poles stacked in the yard ready for making pick handles and draw-bars for agricultural implements. Brush heads are made and sent to Wells, where there is a small brush factory not far from the Cathedral. But if the old-type craftsmen are few, craftsmen with new skills now serve the farming community. Most villages have a builder who can instal water-supplies or build a concrete cowstall, and a garage mechanic who can repair tractors and modern agricultural machinery. And there are modern timber-yards and saw-mills at Chilcompton and at Ubley.

Most of these changes have come slowly but have been accelerated since the beginning of the second world war in 1939. Before the war much of the surface of the western plateau of Mendip was covered with rough grass, gorse, heather, and bracken and was useful only for rough grazing. The only cultivated areas were, as a rule, close to the farms, most of which extend over about 200 acres.

During the war much of this plateau land was ploughed and planted, usually with a potato crop, followed by oats or wheat. I have seen excellent crops of oats close to Priddy Nine Barrows some 900 feet above sea-level. The War Agricultural Executive Committee took over some 2,000 acres of Mendip land to grow crops and later reseeded it with good strains of pasture grasses. But since this land has gone back to private management, relatively little ploughing and reseeding has been done and some of the ley pastures are already beginning to deteriorate as the coarser grasses establish themselves again. This is understandable enough. It is seldom possible to sow early and the growing season is short. The chances are that harvest will be delayed by driving rain and heavy mists which so often come with autumn. I have seen corn standing in stook on Mendip in November. And in a severe winter snow may persist for long periods. During the winter of 1947 Tyning's Farm, near Black Down, had to be dug out seven or eight times by large gangs of council workmen who were given the job of clearing a roadway. Hay and oats were taken to the cattle on sheets of corrugated iron dragged over the surface of the snow. There are labour difficulties too. The uplands, especially in the Charterhouse area, are short of houses for farm-workers and those who live on the fringe prefer to avoid the daily climb and take jobs, if they can, near the villages.

In some places, especially near many of the old lead mines, there are other difficulties. Much of the land is rough for cultivation. There are sometimes tumuli which may not be levelled because of their historic interest, and sometimes "gruffy ground" which is usually not worth levelling. I have heard farms without gruffy ground described on Mendip as "clean farms". Around Shipham and Rowberrow and in one or two other places, waste from the old calamine workings, known locally as "Mendip mineral", poisons the soil with zinc compounds. The cottagers are able to grow very little in their gardens and most crops fail.

The lead ores do not appear to affect growing crops; indeed, certain wild plants flourish particularly well on the gruffy ground, especially alpine penny-cress and spring sandwort. But stock which are allowed to graze over gruffy ground sometimes show signs of lead poisoning, especially in very dry periods. This may well be due to fine dust from the old workings settling on the herbage, so that the cattle take the lead in mineral form rather than through vegetation which has absorbed it from the soil.

East of the market gardens of the Cheddar Valley the fringe farms have their farmhouses and buildings in the villages and the farmland extends on to the hills behind and out across the low moors to the south. This usually gives the farmer land of three types. The hill lands often have no water and are used only for winter stocking, using pond water. The land around the farm consists of a good red loam which is excellent for both arable crops and pasture. But it "poaches" badly and cattle are usually kept off it during the winter months for this reason. The low, level land to the south lies on alluvial silt, often badly drained and suitable only for summer grazing.

Where it has been possible to provide field water on the hill land, young cattle and sheep can also be grazed there in spring and summer, and this has led to an overall increase in stock on many farms. The Church Commissioners on their 1,200-acre Westbury-sub-Mendip Estate, and elsewhere, have gone a long way in this direction. Many of their farms have been provided not only with good water-supplies but also with new buildings, or alternatively old ones have been reconditioned. I have seen the improvements at a number of these farms. On one Westbury farm a cattle-yard on the moors has been provided which can be used for a milking bail in summer and for wintering heifers during the wet season, using hay and straw from a large hay-shed erected nearby. In winter the cows are milked in a new cowstall at the farm where there are food stores and a grass-drying plant.

Another farm of 200 acres uses a skid-bail on the moors in summer and the same equipment is moved in winter to a covered yard adjoining the farm buildings where the cows can lie on straw. When this farm was first let in 1899 there were eight acres of arable; today 100 acres have been ploughed to grow wheat, forage crops, and leys. Much of the grass is dried or converted into silage for winter feeding.

The dairy farms on Mendip differ very little from the lowland farms to north and south except that they are more exposed. On the dissected plateau land east of the Bristol to Wells Road I have watched expensive improvements on a farm near Ston Easton—originally built in 1613. A new cowshed was erected with an adjoining Dutch barn protected from stock by a cattle grid. The old yards were then concreted and the old stalls around them converted into an extensive series of loose-boxes. A concrete road approached from the public road across a cattle grid provided direct access.

These newly appointed farms are the exception, but in many places you can see the results of a change of practice in recent years. New concrete buildings and the curved corrugated iron of Dutch barns contrast sharply with old weathered sheds; you see a gruff hole is being used as a silage pit, and temporary lambing pens built of baled straw.

What does emerge from a study of Mendip farming is that it shows no sign of decadence. There has been a considerable infusion of new life in the last few decades. Some of the newcomers have failed and sold out. But those who have remained have brought new ideas and have been ready to experiment.

This chapter started with Priddy, the oldest farming village on Mendip. Today Priddy is a live and flourishing community, roughly 250 strong, despite its isolation and the fact that the bus to Wells runs only twice a week. The school bus brings in the children from the scattered homesteads to a two-teacher village school by the church. The housing record since the war is quite remarkable. A number of council houses have been built, a former Land Army hostel has been converted into flats, and other houses have been privately built. One of these was put up single-handed by a retired quarryman using local stone. But the most recent achievement of Priddy, which expresses the lively spirit of the villagers, is the village hall close to the church. The site was given by a local farmer and was cleared by voluntary labour. Money was raised to buy a large old hen-battery house with a sound wooden floor. It had been found near Glastonbury and had to be dismantled and brought to the hills by tractor and trailer. The walls were little over 6 feet high, so it was decided to raise them by building a 2-foot concrete wall. I called to see the hall on a Saturday afternoon just before it was officially opened. The inside was being covered with fibreboard, fixed to the walls by oak laths, a stage had just been built at one end, the village women had made curtains for it and were cleaning out the sawdust and shavings: others were waxing the floor. Much of the earlier work had been done in the winter evenings by the light of hurricane lamps.

This hall, which holds 200 people, was put up without grant of any kind, and entirely by free local labour, at a total cost of less than £500. It is managed by a committee of twelve: six representatives appointed by the Parish Meeting, and one from each of the village organisations—the Women's Institute, the Church Council, the Mothers' Union, the Boy Scouts, the Priddy Friendly Society, and the School. And the hall is well used. I have described this example of local enterprise in order to dispel any idea that those who live "on Mendip" are in any way sorry for themselves. They are still mainly landworkers and quarrymen, with a proud and independent spirit—some would say a stubborn streak—born of the grim struggle against natural forces over many generations, and they are content to live the hard way.

CHAPTER XV

CHEESE AND STRAWBERRIES

CHEESE and strawberries form an unholy alliance. The only real link between them is that one small area of fertile soil south of the Mendips has made both famous—Cheddar cheese and Cheddar strawberries. But whereas Cheddar cheese has been known for nearly eight centuries, Cheddar strawberries have been grown there for little more than one hundred years.

Cheese making must have been restricted in the early days to a very narrow belt of reasonably dry land between the limestone hills to the north and the marshy lands to the south—an area now generally known as the Cheddar Valley. It is certain that cheese has been made in Somerset for nearly 800 years and Cheddar early gave its name to the largest and most sought-after varieties. Camden, in 1586, wrote: "West of *Wells*, just under the *Mendippe hills*, lies *Cheddar*, famous for the excellent and prodigious great cheeses made there, some of which require more than a man's strength to set them on the table. . . ." In the seventeenth century they were in great demand in Court circles and cheeses were ordered for London markets before they were made. Farming in the area was organised on a communal basis, and Daniel Defoe, who visited Cheddar in 1722, gives us a vivid picture of this early co-operative diarying:

> "Before the village is a large green, or common, a piece of ground, in which the whole herd of the cows, belonging to the town, do feed; the ground is exceeding rich, and as the whole village are cowkeepers, they take care to keep up the goodness of the soil, by agreeing to lay on large quantities of dung for manuring, and inriching the land.
>
> "The milk of all the town cows, is brought together every day into a common room, where the persons appointed, or trusted for the management, measure every man's quantity, and set it down in a book; when the quantities are adjusted, the milk is all put together, and every meal's milk makes one cheese, and no more; so that the cheese is bigger, or less, as the cows yield more, or less, milk. By this method the goodness of the cheese is preserved, and, without all dispute, it is the best cheese that England affords, if not, that the whole world affords.

> "As the cheeses are, by this means, very large, for they often weigh a hundred weight, sometimes much more, so that poorer inhabitants, who have put few cows, are obliged to stay the longer for the return of their milk; for no man has any such return, 'till his share comes to a whole cheese, and then he has it; and if the quantity of his milk deliver'd in, comes to above a cheese, the over plus rests in account to his credit, 'till another cheese comes to his share; and thus every man has equal justice, and though he should have but one cow, he shall, in time, have one whole cheese. This cheese is often sold for sixpence to eight pence per pound, when the Cheshire cheese is sold but for two pence to two pence halfpenny."

Not long after Defoe's visit to Cheddar there must have been considerable changes in the organisation of farm work, for in the latter half of the eighteenth century much of the common land in Somerset was enclosed.

But farmhouse cheese was still made after the land had been enclosed and continued to be made on a considerable scale throughout the nineteenth century. Billingsley gives the traditional recipe:

> "When the milk is brought home, it is strained into a tub, and about three table-spoonfuls of good rennet put therein, (supposing the quantity of milk sufficient to make a cheese of twenty-eight pounds) which remains undisturbed about two hours, then it becomes curd, and is properly broken: when done, three parts of the whey is taken therefrom and warmed, and then put into the tub again; where it remains about twenty minutes; the whey is again put over the fire, made nearly scald hot, and put into the tub to scald the curd about half an hour, and then part of the whey is taken away, and the remainder remains with the curd till it is nearly cold; the whey is then poured off, the curd broken very small, put into the vat and pressed, where it remains nearly an hour; and then is taken out, turned, and put in again and pressed till the evening, when it is taken out again, turned, and pressed till the next morning. It is then taken out of the vat, salted, put into it again with a clean dry cloth round it, and remains in the press till the next evening, when it is taken out again, salted, put into the vat without a cloth, and pressed till the next morning; and then it finally leaves the press, and is salted once a day for twelve days."

Cheese making went on from March to December each year and the whey was used to fatten pigs and to rear calves for veal. The cows were mainly shorthorns, and calving was normally in February and March. By May they were turned out on grass to shift for themselves. The numbers were immense. As many as 400 fat calves were sold in

Shepton Mallet market in one day. They were bought by butchers from Bristol and Bath, slaughtered, and the carcases were then taken away in one-horse carts. Billingsley describes the veal as "delicately white—small in size, from sixteen to twenty four pounds per quarter". The veal from Batcombe was particularly prized. Its excellency was attributed to the fact that the calves were given small doses of metheglin—a kind of mead—in the milk, and that they were kept in the dark.

In later years Cheddar cheese was not restricted to the southern fringe of the Western Mendips. The enclosed lands to the east took to diary-farming and this area maintained a large output. Cheddar cheese has always been exhibited at the annual show of the Mid-Somerset Agricultural Society, which has been held annually at or near Shepton Mallet since about 1862, and also at Frome Cheese Show, which started in 1878. At one time the exhibits often totalled thirty or forty tons; today a three- or four-ton exhibit is more usual, including the classes for factory-made cheese.

The methods used today for making Cheddar cheese differ a little from those described by Billingsley as in use over 150 years ago, though the essentials are the same. The only cheese-maker I found living close to Cheddar village told me that she mixes the evening and morning milk in a tub, adds the starter, and then, after a period of two hours, heats it to about 85° F. and adds rennet. When the curd has become quite firm she cuts it into small pieces with a knife. The curd is then slowly heated, stirring very gently, until it will leave the hand freely "like boiled rice". The whey is then drawn off and the curd is cut and turned. After a while when the curd will pull out into threads about an inch long on a red-hot poker, it is ground up, moulded, and pressed. Next day she turns and presses it again, and the cheese is finally greased and wrapped in muslin. The maturing process takes four to six months. A very full account of the method of making Cheddar cheese recommended by the Ministry of Agriculture is given in an Advisory Leaflet (No. 156), in which acidity percentages at the various stages are given in detail.

Many of the old Mendip farmhouses still have their special "cheese-room" where the cheeses were stored to mature. I have even seen small rope-operated lifts by which the cheeses were taken to and from a cheese-room in an upper storey, and if you rummage around in the corners of Mendip farmyards and buildings you will often see the rusting remains of old cheese-presses. On the local buses and in the shopping centres of such towns as Wells, Midsomer Norton, and Frome you can meet middle-aged married women who can recall their girlhood days when they were dairymaids on local farms, sometimes employed just for the cheese-making season from April to September during the summer flush of milk. For years small cheeses were made weighing about 10 lb., known in the trade as "loaves", but locally as "trucles", which were collected by factors from a wide district and sent from Cheddar by road in considerable quantities, and after 1869 by the Cheddar Valley Railway. Quite small cheeses were made, weighing little more than a pound, for sale to tourists visiting Cheddar in the summer months. I often saw these myself in Cheddar shops about twenty-five years ago. The making of farmhouse cheese declined almost to the point of extinction with the 1939–45 war. In 1939 there were 1,120 makers of farmhouse cheese in Britain; in 1952 there were only 120, and of these 47 were makers of Cheddar cheese. Ten years later, in 1962, there were 66 farmers in the south-west of England making Cheddar cheese. In 1970 the number had dropped to 37 cheese-making farms, 30 of which worked on a co-operative basis using milk from two hundred farms altogether.

As the making of farmhouse Cheddar cheese began to decline a new industry was springing up in the Cheddar area—the growing of strawberries. Between Draycott and Axbridge a narrow belt of rich red loam three miles long and seldom more than a quarter of a mile wide lies against the southern slopes of the Mendips, between fifty and a hundred feet above sea-level. The hills to the north shelter it from cold winds and there is relatively little risk of early and late frost because the cold air tends to flow out over the low-lying moors to the south. There is a heavy rainfall and the soil warms up quickly, providing ideal conditions for early market-garden crops of all kinds, particularly strawberries.

The first strawberries were grown at Axbridge about 1870 and plantings were made in Cheddar a few years later by a Mr Spencer. I talked to his son, now retired, about the early days and he showed me old photographs of luxuriant plants of the "Black Prince" variety which was first grown there, but he told me of the trouble they had with juice running through the baskets if the berries were not picked before they were warmed by the sun. They did not travel well and the acreage under strawberries did not expand very greatly until the "Royal Sovereign" was introduced at the turn of the century. At this time strawberries were already being sent to Bristol in 6-lb. wicker baskets stacked on market carts which used the Axbridge–Bristol road to avoid the toll bar at Shipham. But with the coming of the "Royal Sovereign", which travelled well, consignments were sent away from

Cheddar by special strawberry trains for sale in South Wales, Birmingham, Manchester, Edinburgh, and Glasgow. Chip baskets were soon imported from Sweden and later were made locally.

At this period most of the work was done by hand, and animal dung was applied liberally to keep the land in good heart. Manure from cattle-boats could be bought at Avonmouth docks for 1*s.* a ton, and sheep manure at 1*s.* 6*d.* a ton. Unfortunately for Cheddar growers the supplies dried up after the 1914–18 war, partly owing to the greater use of refrigerator ships and partly because of stricter foot-and-mouth disease precautions.

The peak period for the Cheddar strawberry industry was between 1900 and the beginning of the first world war. After the war—in the 1920's—virus diseases began to affect strawberry crops in all parts of the country, and profits were less certain. Attempts were made to produce new varieties, many of which were not entirely satisfactory, but the Axbridge Early, introduced in 1929, is still the first strawberry to be marketed. The Royal Sovereign, once the leading variety, has been replaced entirely, mainly by varieties bred at Cambridge, especially Cambridge Vigour and Cambridge Favourite. Gauntlet is also popular. Long Ashton Research Station near Bristol, is working to produce still earlier and later varieties.

There are about 300 holdings growing strawberries on a commercial scale in the Cheddar Valley. They are mostly quite small, varying from less than an acre to about twenty acres. Indeed, a man, by hard work, can make a reasonable living from one acre of Cheddar land. And it is true that many of the growers—or "croppers", as I've heard them called by the hill farmers—employ no regular labour. Their little fields are scattered about on the southern slopes of the hills and you can still see a few cultivated plots and strips devoted mainly to strawberries among the houses in the village of Cheddar itself. The price of the best land in the district is high: it may fetch as much as £1,000 an acre, and very little is rented. The land is so valuable that it is difficult to find sites for new houses, despite a big demand.

The strawberry crop requires attention right through the year. If the soil is moist enough, the runners are planted out in July or August. Weeds are kept down by mechanical cultivation and the use of selective herbicides. Soon after Christmas the rows of plants are enclosed in polythene tunnels until cropping begins. Artificial fertilisers are applied, mainly to provide potash, and precautions are taken against botrytis. April is a month when troubles arise. After a few warm days aphis eggs hatch out and the aphis may "sting" the strawberry plants and make them vulnerable to various virus diseases such as severe crinkle, mild crinkle, and yellow edge. Fortunately the dreaded red-core disease, which has affected the Tamar Valley area in Cornwall so badly, has not been a real problem in the Cheddar Valley. To keep down the aphis crops are regularly sprayed and any plants severely attacked by virus disease are rooted out and burned. Eelworm is a serious pest and so is cutworm in the autumn. Control is costly and time-taking.

In April, when the fruit is beginning to set, there is a final clean-up of the ground between the rows of plants and straw is then put down to keep the berries off the soil. A few early strawberries are picked at the end of the month, but May is the main picking period and the growers and their families work very long hours to get the crop picked and packed. A grower told me that he had kept a note one picking season of the hours he had worked and it added up to an average of 110 hours a week. Picking is a skilled job and some growers prefer to over-work themselves than employ unskilled pickers who may tread on the plants and leave many of the best berries behind.

Yields are about three tons of strawberries per acre. At one time Birmingham was the main market but Liverpool, Bradford, Leeds, Manchester and Newcastle now take considerable quantities, though the local markets at Bristol and Cardiff (since the opening of the Severn Bridge) are the most valuable. Although rail transport is used, increasing quantities are travelling by road at night. This is often quicker and avoids double handling.

At one time Cheddar growers had profitable sidelines producing lettuce, cabbages and anemones. Today, the concentration on straw-berries is almost complete and the trend is away from the small hilly fields to the flatter land where water is available for irrigation and mechanical cultivation is easier. The flowers are now restricted to the delightful cottage gardens where even in January it is possible to see purple and scarlet anemones glowing vividly in the winter sunlight.

Chapter XVI

MENDIP WATER

Walking over the short turf on the limestone ridges of the Western Mendips, it is difficult to believe that the land receives a relatively heavy rainfall. The surface is dry, even where there is a reasonable depth of soil; the porous rock takes up the water, which percolates through joints and fissures deep into the hills, to reappear along the foothills as hard-water springs or as steady streams flowing from water-worn caves.

The River Yeo rises on the northern slopes of the Mendips where a small spring flows into a pond just below the church at Compton Martin. It flows westward, supplying most of the water for the Yeo Reservoir at Blagdon, and then—much depleted—crosses the low-lying land to the north-west as a sluggish stream which passes close to the village of Congresbury to the sea at Woodspring Bay. At one time these flats were ill-drained and often flooded, especially when high tides slowed down the flow of fresh water from the mouth of the Yeo. The River Chew also flows north from Chewton Mendip through a wide shallow valley past the villages of Chew Stoke and Chew Magna to the River Avon at Keynsham. The Chew Valley has also been dammed to make a reservoir.

Two main streams rise in the southern fringe of the Mendips and flow together to the sea north of Brean Down. The River Axe flows from Wookey Hole, near Wells, and a second River Yeo flows from underground caves in Cheddar Gorge, joining the Axe south of Crook Peak. Within half a mile the Axe is also joined by the Lox Yeo tributary which drains the meadows of the Winscombe Valley below Christon and Loxton. The Axe may once have been navigable as far inland as Axbridge and it is believed that Roman barges may have used the river to take lead from Mendip mines to a small tidal harbour at Uphill.

On the hills, especially on the Old Red Sandstone core, there is often a covering of acid, peaty soil which holds the water and provides a gathering ground for small surface streams which flow off the wetter slopes and then disappear down swallet holes in the mountain limestone. The twin streams which rise on the slopes of Black Down are good examples. They flow towards Burrington Combe, but disappear before they reach it. On the slopes of North Hill, south of Priddy Nine Barrows, a number of springs rise on the Old Red Sandstone, to disappear again in the nearby limestone; one of these flows into Swildon's Hole.

Throughout the Western Mendips the provision of water for human needs and for farm stock has always been a problem, but along the flanks and foothills water-supplies from springs are abundant. This accounts for the relatively small population of the limestone plateau and the strings of villages, now linked by roads, which form the northern and southern fringes. These villages have seldom had to worry about drought. Theodore Compton, writing in 1892 about the village of Winscombe, points out that during the long droughts of 1864, 1865, and 1871, when many parts of the country suffered severely, the spring at Winscombe Ford never failed and was able to supply the whole neighbourhood.

The springs and streams from the limestone, wherever the flow was strong enough, were used from very early times to provide power for mills. A water-mill at Rickford and Max Mill near Winscombe by a spring in the valley of the Lox Yeo are mentioned in Domesday Book. The Manor of Winscombe is described as comprising "a mill of five shillings rent, sixty acres of meadow, with one mile of pasture in length and breadth and a wood two miles long and one mile broad". At Cheddar, in the eighteenth century, a succession of mills must have used the water from the gorge. Collinson writes in 1791 of nine small springs, which "burst from the foot of the cliffs, all within the space of about thirty feet, and joining together within forty yards of their source, form a broad rapid river of the clearest and finest water in the world. This river . . . a few years ago turned thirteen mills within half a mile of its source. The number is now reduced to seven, three of which are paper mills, the others grist mills."

The pure Mendip water is particularly suitable for paper making. In most cases the flow is steadier than in the average surface stream. Heavy rains do not cause a sudden rise in level and the water usually continues to flow even in times of drought. There is, in fact, a delayed action: a dry summer is likely to be reflected in a drop in level of the Axe or Cheddar waters in October. But sometimes the flow is inadequate to use for water-power. There were paper-mills at one time at Rickford, near Blagdon, and at Dulcote, near Wells. The workmen would divide their time between these mills in the summer according to the flow of water. Records show that in the Western Mendips in the late eighteenth and early nineteenth centuries there were three paper-mills at Cheddar, four on the River Axe at Wookey and below, two at Dulcote, and single mills at Banwell, Rickford, Compton Martin, West Harptree, and Litton. This concentration may well have been partly due to the arrival in the area of Huguenot refugees already skilled in the trade.

The first paper-mill at Cheddar, which was built near the cliffs, was opened in 1765 and two more mills were established with more up-to-date equipment in the early 1800's. All these have now gone. The last—the Valley Paper Mills—was purchased by the Bristol Water Works Company in 1910 and is now owned by a concrete company. The mill at Banwell made good-quality writing-paper and banknote paper until 1850, when it became a brewhouse.

At one time, soon after the repeal of the Paper Duties in 1861, there was a fierce conflict between the lead-mining interests on the hills and the paper-making interests below. The mines polluted the water used by the paper-mills and eventually the issue was decided by a lawsuit in favour of the paper interests.

Only two paper-mills are still working in the Mendip area, both on the River Axe at Wookey. The older mill—Hodgkinson's—which lies near the entrance to the caves, dates from 1610 and is one of the oldest paper-mills in Britain. It employs about fifty people and still specialises in hand-made paper, including paper for banknotes.

St Cuthbert's Mill, half a mile downstream, stands by the railway line and has a siding of its own to which coal and raw materials are brought. It probably dates back to the end of the eighteenth century, when it was known as Lower Wookey Mill, or sometimes the Mendip Mills. But the present building is little more than a hundred years old, and some of the extensions are more recent. It was one of the earliest mills in Britain to use esparto grass from North Africa and in good times this still forms the bulk of its raw material. But during the last war, wheat and oat straw from local farms was used, and even since then the mill has been forced to use it again as an alternative raw material, though it is not so suitable and provides serious processing problems and a smaller output of paper per ton. There is also some trouble, at times, over pollution of the Axe—or so it is alleged by those who live in the lower reaches. Other raw materials include wood pulp, mostly from Scandinavia, and rags, mainly waste from Lancashire cotton-mills. St Cuthbert's Mill is larger than Hodgkinson's, employing some 300 workers drawn from Wells and nearby villages. Most of the employees are men, though girls sort, count, and pack the finished paper, much of which is used for making the finer grades of notepaper and envelopes. There is a good export trade to Australia and other Commonwealth countries.

Mendip limestone is used to reclaim the caustic soda from the liquid which digests the pulp, and a large dump of some half a million tons of waste with a high lime content has accumulated alongside the works over a long period. An enterprising local firm sold much of it to farmers for spreading on the lime-deficient soils of the Somerset flats.

For many years the coal for fuel was brought from the Radstock area, but in the modern furnaces which heat the boilers it has a tendency to cake into large irregular masses and does not burn well. Coal is therefore brought all the way from the Midlands or South Wales.

On the uplands west of the main Bristol to Wells road most of the farms and hamlets were at one time dependent on rainwater. Near Priddy Green an iron pipe delivers water to a trough above which a metal plate bears the following inscription:

MANOR OF PRIDDY

This the first supply of pure water to Priddy was brought here by James Green Esq. Lord of the Manor. October 1865.

Priddy was fortunate to secure running water, but in other areas there were no springs to be tapped. When the enclosures were made, mainly during the eighteenth century, pools were constructed to collect rainwater. They were usually about 40 feet long, 16 feet wide, and 6 feet deep in the middle. The masons who did the work used about 300 bushels of lime, ten loads of clay, and eight loads of ashes to make a surface which would hold in the water. They had to be repaired regularly and most of them have now either been lined with concrete or have deteriorated so they are mostly dry for long periods in summer and become a mere muddy patch in winter. Nevertheless a few are still used where the hard paths made by the hooves of cattle direct the water from heavy thunderstorms into the ponds. But it is an unreliable source at best and many Mendip farmers can recall the days when stock had to be driven to the foothills to drink and then driven back again to the upland pastures. I met one farmer who, as a boy, used to mount a pony and drive the stock to water each day when he came home from school. Even today steps are taken to conserve rainwater on Mendip. On the road which slopes north towards Priddy Hill Farm, for example, the rainwater from the road is drained off into little concrete channels which run parallel with the boundary walls, and these feed a walled-in pond in an adjoining field from which water is pumped into tanks for the stock to drink. Water is also collected in yard-ponds from the roofs of farm buildings.

Recently attempts have been made to bring piped water to many of the farms. Tyning's Farm which, together with other Mendip farms, was taken over by the Somerset War Agricultural Committee during the war, now has its own piped supply with a water trough in each field. At Priddy, water from the Old Red Sandstone springs and from an 80-foot borehole made during the first world war is now pumped to a 30,000-gallon concrete reservoir to feed the village and outlying farms to the south and east with a good piped supply. The Rifle Range and Camp at Yoxter, which is used at week-ends, is fed by pipe from the Axbridge water-supply to the south.

In the Eastern Mendips water-supply problems have never been very serious. Here the older rocks are overlaid by lias clays which trap the surface water and give rise to many springs and surface streams. The Mendip country between the main Bristol to Wells road and the town of Frome has always been much more thickly peopled than the western areas. This is where the woollen industry flourished, using water-power from the streams. The springs also provided good-quality water for brewing beer and gave rise to many breweries which supplied the heavy demand of the mining and quarrying villages around. Just over fifty years ago, at the turn of the century, there were breweries at Oakhill, Holcombe, Kilmersdon, Radstock, Shepton Mallet, and Midsomer Norton. W. H. Hudson refers to the Anglo-Bavarian Brewery at Shepton Mallet (now converted into a trading estate) as a "gigantic brewery which looks bigger than all the other buildings together, the church and a dozen or twenty public-houses included". In those days transport was usually by two-horse wagon, which limited the area of distribution. When motor transport came in many of the smaller breweries closed down.

Oakhill Brewery was undoubtedly the most famous of those on the Mendip plateau. It was started there as a major concern by Jillard and Spencer in 1767, using the water from nearby springs. In 1882 the Jillard interest in the firm was relinquished, and for the next seventeen years it was run by two brothers—John and Frederick Spencer. This was a period of expansion when most of the houses now seen at Oakhill were built as houses for the brewery workers.

In 1889, when it was made a limited liability company, a celebration dinner for twenty-five people was held in a 500-barrel vat, though exactly how the dinner was served has not been recorded. At this time

The Yeo reservoir or Blagdon Lake

the company owned sixty-three licensed houses in Somerset, Wiltshire, and Bristol.

A year later a malthouse was established. The workers spent the winter in the malthouse and the summer as quarry-workers at Gurney Slade or elsewhere, an arrangement which suited all concerned. At this time Oakhill "Invalid Stout" was becoming famous all over the country. Beer and stout were taken to Binegar Station by traction engine which made ruts two feet deep in the roads. In 1904 a private narrow-gauge railway was constructed between Oakhill Brewery and Binegar Station on the Somerset and Dorset line. Deliveries were then made by rail to distribution depots in London, Manchester, and Cardiff. This railway operated until the first world war, when the stout trade contracted owing to wartime restrictions on the use of grain, and it never recovered. Soon after the war the rolling stock and equipment were sold to the contractors who built the Barry Docks in South Wales. The railway from Oakhill turned west and passed over the main Bristol to Shepton Mallet road (A37) by a level-crossing just south of the Mendip Inn. It then swung away to the north-west to Binegar Station, where it ended in a well-built shed still to be seen in the siding. The stone-built piers of a bridge by which the railway crossed the minor road half a mile to the south of the station are also still to be seen.

In 1925 Oakhill Brewery was destroyed by fire during the night. How the fire started has never been decided; possibly a gas-jet had been left burning. It started in the offices and spread rapidly to the rooms above where hops and sugar were stored. The Frome and Shepton Mallet fire brigades were called, but by the time the flames had been brought under control the main buildings had been gutted and all the firm's records had been burnt.

At this time the brewery employed about one hundred men. Some of these left the firm, taking the capital value of their pensions, and started small farms or smallholdings. The business was sold to a large Bristol firm and most of the remaining staff stayed on. Although brewing ceased, most of the malt for the large Bristol brewery and for a brewery at Shepton Mallet was made at Oakhill from barley grown on Salisbury Plain, in the Exeter and Totnes districts of Devon, and from the Cotswolds. About sixty-five men were employed mainly from Oakhill village. Some 170 licensed houses were linked with the name of Oakhill. Since then the Oakhill Brewery has been taken over by a still larger firm and the name has disappeared.

The Mendips have always provided the larger centres of population

Somerset's last colliery at Kilmersdon

close to the hills—Axbridge, Shepton Mallet, Wells, and Frome, for example—with water for domestic and, in some cases, for industrial purposes. But perhaps the most striking development has been the provision of a water-supply for the expanding needs of the more distant city of Bristol. Early in the nineteenth century the water-supply of the city, which came mainly from draw-wells and pumps, began to prove inadequate. In 1845 a group of far-sighted citizens became so concerned that they formed the Bristol Waterworks Company with the object of bringing pure water by pipe-line from some of the nearer springs in the country to the south of the city. The Bill which was placed before Parliament received the royal assent in the following year, and work began on plans to draw water from the Mendips and elsewhere, a process which has gone on steadily ever since and which is still expanding. The first water to come to Bristol from these hills was drawn from springs at Harptree Combe and at Watery Combe, Chewton Mendip. A culvert from the latter source took the water south of the present Litton–West Harptree road to Harptree Combe, where it joined with a second culvert. The water was then carried in 30-inch pipes to Winford and thence to Barrow Gurney, where several million gallons a day flowed into a large reservoir. In order to compensate for loss of water in the Chew Valley, small additional reservoirs had to be constructed and cash payments had to be made to mill owners.

In the years that followed the company faced many difficulties. Early in 1854 a leakage in the Barrow Reservoir made it necessary to drain the water away, and this was followed by a serious drought. Ten years later there was another drought. F. C. Jones writes that "some of the Mendip springs dried to a trickle; cattle wandered disconsolately about the fields; miles of pasture land lay parched beneath a glassy sky; the noise of the babbling of water became a fancy for poets. Chaises, phaetons, wagons, pulled by thirsty horses, roamed far afield searching for the smallest trickle". The rainfall in Bristol from April to August was less than seven inches and in most parts of the city it was only possible to supply water for two hours a day; in some parts the supply had to be cut altogether.

As the suburbs of Bristol spread new sources in the Mendips were tapped. A large pipe was laid from Sherborne Springs at Litton, near Chewton Mendip. Plans were also made to impound the water of the River Yeo, which rises in springs near Compton Martin. For several miles its course kept close to the northern slopes of the Mendips, after which it flowed slowly across the alluvial flats around Congresbury to

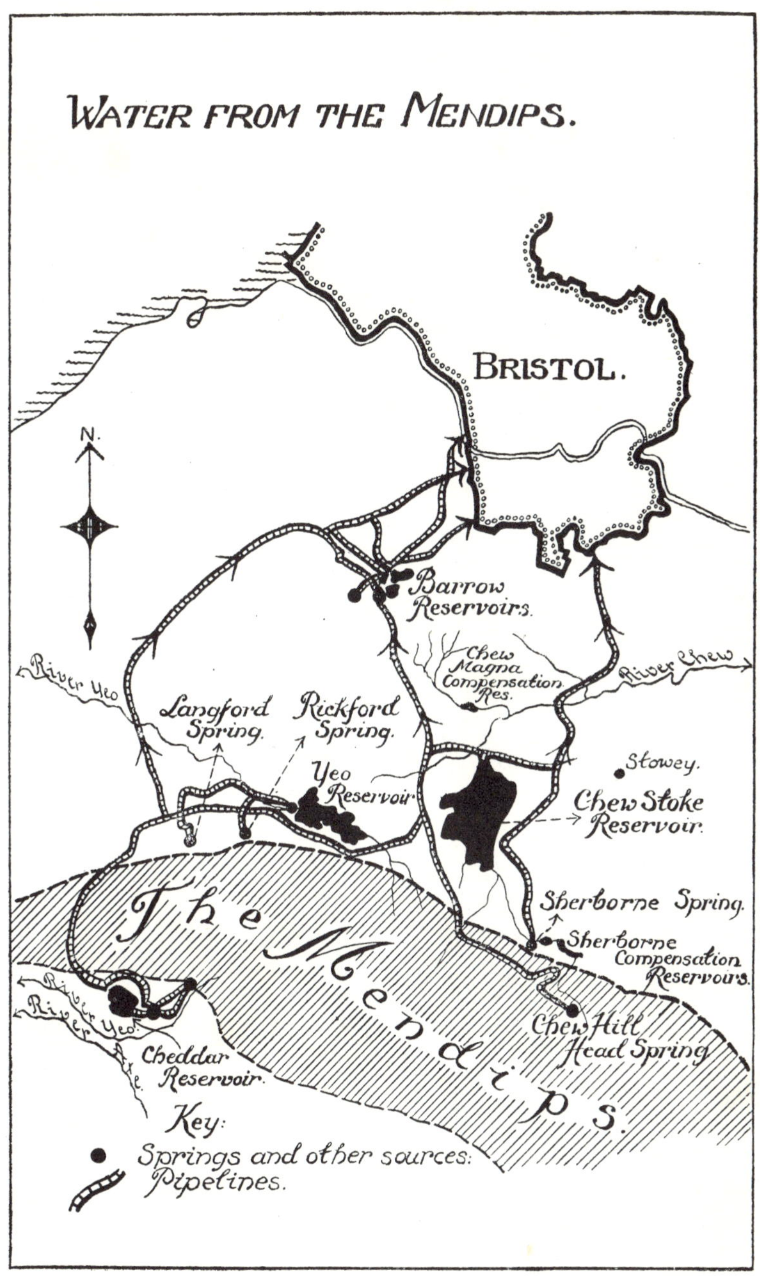

Water from the Mendips

reach the sea north of Weston-super-Mare. In 1899 an earthen embankment nearly 700 yards long was made across the shallow valley below the village of Blagdon to impound the water. An area of some 450 acres of farmland over a mile in length and three-quarters of a mile across at its widest point was drowned to form the Yeo Reservoir—more usually spoken of as Blagdon Lake. It draws its water mainly from the River Yeo, but water from springs at Rickford is also piped to the reservoir, which was completed in 1901 to hold 1,700 million gallons of water. Another spring at Langford is piped to the pumping station which forces the water to the large storage reservoirs at Barrow Gurney on the south-western outskirts of Bristol, where it is filtered and cleansed before use. To safeguard the purity of the water, the villages of Butcombe, Compton Martin, and Blagdon had all to be provided with sewers and sewage-disposal works, and many nearby farms had also to have similar means for sewage disposal, in some cases maintained by the company. Plantations of conifers were made to improve the appearance of the lake, often alongside tributary streams so that the roots may prevent scouring in times of heavy rainfall and thus reduce the silt carried into the reservoir. This is important, since the water is everywhere quite shallow: the average depth is only 14 feet. Blagdon Lake adds greatly to the beauty of the valley. My own favourite view of the lake is from Prospect Stile at Hinton Blewitt, looking towards the west.

Between the two world wars when the housing estates around Bristol were expanding at a great rate, more and more water was needed both for domestic purposes and for industry. This demand led to the construction of a large new storage reservoir, circular in shape, between Axbridge and Cheddar on the southern side of the Mendips. The catchment area extends roughly from Black Down to Priddy and water is drawn from springs at Cheddar and is then piped to Barrow or Blagdon. The Cheddar storage reservoir was finished in 1937. Even before the Cheddar Reservoir was complete, there was already need for still more water. The Chew Valley was surveyed between the Mendips and the village of Chew Stoke and the construction of a new reservoir to cover 1,200 acres was authorised by Parliament in 1939. Work was delayed by the war, but this latest and largest of all the schemes launched by the Bristol Waterworks Company was inaugurated in 1956 and a new reservoir slowly formed behind a dam across the valley of the River Chew at Chew Stoke, inundating a considerable area of land north of Bishop Sutton.

At an early stage the course of the River Chew was diverted so that a cut-off trench could be made right across the valley. This trench was filled with concrete to prevent any possibility of water seepage through the red marls beneath the dam, which is nearly a quarter of a mile long with a road along the top. The lake behind it extends for well over two miles along the valley and is one of the six largest reservoirs in the country, with a capacity of between four and five million gallons. The main catchment area lies between the Castle of Comfort Inn and Chewton Mendip and extends as far south as Stock Hill and Emborough. Water is now also drawn from the Winford and Norton Malreward areas to the north, and from the Chew Stoke area to the west. The Chew Valley Lake, as it is called, provides not only for some of the needs of Bristol, but also sends water from a large pumping works at Stowey to many other areas, including the city of Bath, the rural district of Clutton, Norton-Radstock, and to south and west Gloucestershire—a remarkable achievement of private planning and enterprise in the service of the public.

Very great care was taken in constructing the Chew Reservoir to preserve everything possible of historic interest. In order that a record might be kept of interesting features of the valley, the whole area was very carefully photographed; detailed records of the old farmhouses have been preserved, and in some cases special features were removed to museums. One of the most interesting problems was that of Stratford Mill at West Harptree, a fine old corn-grinding mill which once used a 12-foot undershot waterwheel for motive power with which to drive apple-wood machinery, constructed towards the end of the eighteenth century. Although it had been out of action for many years it was used again in the 1940s to grind dredge corn from the newly ploughed land on local farms. Every effort was made to preserve the building. Thanks to the Waterworks Company and a generous private gift, it was made possible to dismantle Stratford Mill and to re-erect it in the grounds of Blaise Castle, where a Folk Museum was established by the Bristol City Council. The mill now stands on the bank of a stream which flows through a small wooded limestone gorge and is still in working condition with its original machinery.

Much thought was also given to local scenery. Around the reservoir and on Denny Island which now stands out above the water level, many types of tree have been planted—chestnut, beech, sycamore, birch, maple, oak, willow, Corsican pine, Scots pine, and red cedar. A similar policy was adopted at Blagdon and today you can see how naturally the Lakes blend with the surroundings. There is no suggestion of the artificial about it. The reservoirs are not only a pleasant addition to the landscape: they provide active enjoyment for fishermen, yachtsmen, and bird-watchers.

Blagdon Lake has long been famous for both brown and rainbow trout. They reach a considerable size—far larger than trout from the average trout stream. This is probably due to the fact that the shallow waters with a high average temperature have an abundant food supply, so that the fish feed for a longer period than trout in many other parts. Only fly fishing and spinning are allowed, but brown trout over 10 lb. in weight have been caught and rainbows of over 8 lb., though the average is normally just over 2 lb. The season usually extends from May to the middle of October. Catches are highest in May and tend to decline in July and August. Trout feed when the water is between 45° and 60° F. and take little or nothing when the water temperature is higher. In very warm periods they spend their time in the coolest and deepest water, which in reservoirs, unlike natural lakes, remains sweet and fresh because the water is continually drawn off. Over 2,000 trout have been caught in Blagdon Lake in a single season.

The spawning season for brown trout begins in late October or November, when the natural urge leads the mature fish to move from the lake up the River Yeo to find gravelly shallows where they can leave their eggs and bury them. The rainbow trout spawn later, usually in February, March, or April, but much depends on the flow of water. If it is not sufficient, the fish will spawn on the edge of the lake, though the eggs seldom incubate.

At Ubley, at the eastern end of the Lake, advantage has been taken of the run of trout to establish a hatchery which is now known all over the world. The fish are caught in an automatic fish trap, and are spawned artificially. The fish are placed in concrete-lined ponds, the eggs are stripped from them, and fertilised. The best come from fish three to four years old and an adult female yields about 800 eggs for every pound of her weight. The fertile eggs are taken to the hatchery house, where they are placed in specially designed woven baskets immersed in shallow troughs through which a continuous stream of water flows. The eggs are then kept in the dark until the tiny embryo fish can be seen through the transparent shell. At this stage the eggs can be packed in trays in damp moss and provided they are kept cool they can be sent on considerable journeys which may last several weeks. Ova from Blagdon have been exported all over the world and trout bred at Blagdon are now swimming in the rivers of Kenya, South Africa, Ceylon, South America, New Zealand, and the Far East.

Thousands of the eggs of both brown and rainbow trout are hatched at Ubley and the fry are fed on minced liver and dehydrated whale-meat. The young fish when about nine months old are used to restock Blagdon Lake, the Barrow Reservoirs, and Chew Valley Lake which are all popular with fishermen.

Cheddar Reservoir is a "coarse-fish" lake which attracts many anglers who enjoy spinning for pike. These fish sometimes reach between 20 and 30 lb. and a few years ago a 30-lb. pike was caught containing a complete teal. The pike have descended from fish which lived in the "rhines" or drainage channels on the moors when the land was inundated. They literally "took charge".

Young eels or elvers come up the River Yeo each year in the late summer as far as Blagdon Lake and would invade the reservoir and compete with the trout for food were it not for the fact that special precautions are taken to trap them. An inclined wooden chute, with a trickle of water running down it attracts the eels when they arrive at the dam across the valley. They ascend the chute and at the top tumble into a tank, where they can be collected and used to feed the trout fry at Ubley hatchery.

At week-ends the reservoirs attract bird-watchers as well as fishermen. A remarkably large number of birds, especially duck, can be seen at Blagdon and Cheddar. Coot, which start breeding in March, are probably the commonest birds at Cheddar, and many teal are found there. Unusual visitors have included northern divers and a shag.

At Blagdon a great variety can be seen on a favourable day. One observer on a December day recently counted over two thousand duck, which included over a thousand widgeon, large numbers of teal, mallard pochard and tufted duck, and small numbers of sheld-duck, gadwall, pintail, shoveler, scaup, goldeneye, and smew.

Common snipe and black-necked grebe are sometimes seen and the bittern has been recorded. August migrants include such birds as the ringed plover, dunlin, the common sandpiper, green sandpipers, red-shanks, ruffs, and the grey phalarope. Sea-birds often fly inland to the reservoirs. Gulls are common and occasionally gannets have been seen resting.

At Chew Valley Lake there is a bird-ringing station and a number of hides have been established from which keen naturalists can observe the wild life.

Dinghy sailing has been popular on the Cheddar Reservoir since 1947, where men and women of all ages take part and competitions are held most Saturdays. The Corinthian Sailing Club is responsible for seeing that the necessary regulations laid down by the Waterworks

Company are strictly enforced.

Sailing is also popular on Chew Valley Lake where the first boats were launched in 1967. At first the sport was carried on only during the winter. In 1970, however, sailing was also permitted over a more limited area in summer without interfering with the anglers. No sailing is done in the bays and inlets so that the birds are left in peace and quiet.

Dinghy racing has been restricted for a time lest salmon disease might be introduced, but open meetings will undoubtedly be held on both Cheddar and Chew Valley waters in the years to come.

Many car owners from Bristol come to the Chew Valley on Sundays to watch the dinghies, and to cater for them there is to be a large lakeside picnic area.

Chapter XVII

MENDIP COAL

"Allmost as good as the sea coale from New-Castle," wrote Celia Fiennes of Mendip coal in the diary of her journeys in 1697. Mendip coal was certainly well known at that time. Indeed, coal has been dug from this small Somerset coalfield for at least 650 years; the earliest record is dated 1305. The coalfield is closely linked with the Mendip Hills, though it extends beyond them. From Mells and Kilmersdon on the uplands the coal-bearing rocks stretch north-eastwards across undulating country to Camerton and Dunkerton, though they are often covered by lias clays and limestones which provide good dairying land. The district is essentially rural, with none of the ugliness one usually associates with coal mining. The mining centres are overgrown villages; each pit with its tips of waste is an island surrounded by farmland. Mining and agriculture are closely dovetailed, and in the local pubs mine-workers and farm-workers drink their beer together, play darts together, and discuss the prospects of their local football or cricket team.

The original Mendip Coalworks, as they were called, lie in the south of the coalfield. The coal outcrops along the Nettlebridge Valley and has been mined at Mells, Vobster, Babington, Kilmersdon, Holcombe, Nettlebridge, and Stratton-on-the-Fosse. To the north, beyond the foothills of Mendip, lies the Norton–Radstock area which takes in Midsomer Norton, Radstock, Camerton, Dunkerton, Timsbury, and Paulton. The earliest workings were probably on the hills. Today the only mines are in the Norton–Radstock area. But the twofold division has no great significance; the development of the coalfield must be considered as a whole. The only area which is not considered in this chapter is the isolated Pensford district.

The coal was first dug from shallow pits—small open-cast workings which were usually rented from the owner of the land. The first record in 1305 refers to the lord's rent for one of these pits as worth 2*s.* 4*d.* per annum. Many of the fields in the Coleford area are pitted with small depressions made by these early workings, spoiling them for easy cultivation or haymaking.

Coal must have been dug sporadically from surface workings for some 300 years, but in the seventeenth century underground mining began despite the difficulties involved in providing good ventilation. A manuscript by James Twyford in the Ammerdown Collection—*Observations on Coal Works*—gives an extremely detailed account of conditions at the close of the seventeenth century. Twyford set his face against the earlier system of granting leases to individual colliers and asserted that "the Coal-works should never be let, but wrought for the person in possession of the inheritance". And he advised any owners of coal-bearing land to adventure for coal on their own account and to get a skilled collier as manager.

The mines of these days appear to have been sloping adits, or lanes, cut into the coal-bearing rocks.

> "They usually or always sink one pit first; when the air is bad they sink another pit about six yards distant on the same course as near as can, and cut a lane of communication from one pit to another to give air, or else, when one pit is sinking, they put down trunks, and make a trunk-hole to let the air to the nose of the shides or pipes, and so carry the air into the lane. About Midsummer the air is usually bad when the hedges are full of leaves, then they sink an iron grate about ten yards into the pit with burning coals, which draws the stenched or stagnated air from the bottom and lane."

The "breakers" of coal, as the coal-face workers were called, worked by turns or tasks. They cut into the seams with a mattock and broke very large pieces of coal away with a wedge. This coal was loaded into carts, which were pulled by carters—usually boys. The carters kept a tally of the loads hewn by each of the breakers, who were paid according to their output. In most cases the coal was drawn up the lanes to the surface by using an engine operated by water-power from a mill. One of these was described as follows: "Paulton Wheel at Mr Brewers' works draws about 17 fathoms deep. The wheel, of 8 feet diameter, 3 feet broad with two cranks, water troughs 20 inches broad, 10 inches deep." We know that there was such a mill at Farrington, and four near Vobster. For one of the latter the water "was carried in shutes made of elm board stood upon trees about ten feet high as the ground was".

In the Mendip mines the workers were provided with "the coal they burn, and working coats and waistcoats, that is drawers or breeches, and also shirts whilst they are working, but not otherwise, but at Paulton the men find all".

We know relatively little about the mines in the eighteenth century except that, in general, horses were being used to raise the coal and to take it to nearby markets, though a water-wheel was still working at Welton at the end of this period. Before the turnpike roads came in, the coal was actually carried on horseback, each beast taking a load of about 2½ cwt. The new roads improved transport enormously: they made it possible for a single horse to draw a light cart carrying 10 cwt and much time was saved on the journeys.

At the end of the eighteenth century, mining on a fairly large scale was firmly established. Good-quality coal was being sent as far as Bath, the chief market, and also to the nearest parts of Wiltshire. Some 1,500 men and boys worked the seams of the Norton–Radstock area, raising up to 2,000 tons of coal a week, and another 600 men and boys raised about 1,000 tons a week from the Mendip mines. Billingsley describes the coal as "of prime quality; pure and durable in burning; firm, large and of a strong grain; which ensures its conveyance to almost any distance without injury to its appearance or quality, which cannot be exceeded in any part of the Kingdom". This was a period of rapid development. Steam-engines were introduced which made it possible to mine at greater depths; until then, none of the mines had been more than 500 feet deep.

The natural lines of communication in this coalfield are east and west—shallow valleys cut by the Cam Brook, the Wellow Brook, and the Mells River which flows through the Nettlebridge Valley. When the canal boom came at the end of the eighteenth century the possibility of constructing canals in these valleys to take the coal to Bath and to the River Avon was soon explored. Between 1795 and 1800 Acts were passed through Parliament to allow the building of three canals to serve the coalworks.

The Somerset Coal Canal was to have two branches: one was to start at Paulton, the other at Radstock. These canals were to join at Midford, from which point a single canal would run to the Kennet and Avon Canal between Bath and Bradford. The Dorset and Somerset Canal was to link the Mendip workings in the Nettlebridge Valley with the northern parts of Dorset, passing through Frome.

The Dorset and Somerset Canal was a failure. It began near Stratton-on-the-Fosse and several sections were dug between this point and Frome. Indeed, barges are said to have been used on the stretch between the village of Edford and the Greyhound Inn at Coleford. But the sections were never finally linked. Today, in some places, you can still see the bed of the old canal, sometimes dry, sometimes filled with stagnant water. In one stretch, at Coleford, a cutting and an aqueduct, sadly overgrown, remain as a remainder of over-optimistic planning. The old Greyhound Inn is now a private house—"Greyhound House"—on the south side of the road known as Bullock's Hill. At the bottom of the hill, just behind the High Street Methodist Church, is the aqueduct which was to have carried the canal over a tributary valley. It consists of two solidly built rounded stone arches almost smothered in ivy.

The Somerset Coal Canal was more successful. The main stretch from Camerton to the Kennet and Avon Canal was finished before the end of the century. The branch from Midford to Radstock, through Wellow, had to be abandoned when nearly complete because money ran out. The final link with the mines at Radstock was made by a horse-drawn railway. This was later replaced by a steam railway known as the Somerset Coal Canal Tramway, which was extended to replace the whole of the Radstock branch of the canal as far as Midford. An attempt was made on the Somerset coalfield to transfer railway wagons to rafts on the canal in order to avoid handling the coal, but it proved difficult to load the rafts and also to navigate them with the wagons on board, and the attempt was abandoned. The coal was therefore transferred at Midford to canal barges.

The gradient at one point on the main canal near Combe Hay was so steep that some method had to be found for raising and lowering the barges. In 1796 Robert Weldon devised a balance lock, or caisson lock, with a 45-foot lift, but it leaked water and proved a failure. (There is today a house in Combe Hay which carries the name "Caisson House".) An inclined plane was then constructed, but this also failed and was finally replaced by a series of twenty-two locks which can still be seen. This canal prospered and was used for passenger traffic as well as coal. In 1814 the Benedictine monks who came to Downside Abbey are said to have used the canal for the last stage of their journey. In 1828 it carried 113,422 tons of coal valued at £15,000.

We know a great deal about conditions in the coalfield in the early part of the nineteenth century from the journals of the Rev. John Skinner, who was Rector of Camerton—which must have been a fairly typical colliery village—from 1800 until he committed suicide in 1839. He left his journals together with many other manuscripts to the British Museum. Extracts from these papers which have made some of the more interesting material generally accessible were published in 1930 under the title *Journal of a Somerset Rector*. It is clear from Skinner's diary that the coal canals provided opportunities for recreation both sedate and adventurous: they were used for excursions, for private boating, and in winter, when the ice was thick enough, for skating. He describes a pleasure outing in the late summer of 1823:

> "Having engaged one of the coal barges, I had it fitted up for the ladies with an awning and matting against the sides, and tables and chairs from the public house, in which we proceeded about eleven o'clock to Combe Hay, where we visited the Mansion House, walked round the premises, and afterwards dined under the trees near the cascade."

Small boats were built by local enthusiasts for use on the canal. Skinner encouraged his son, Owen, to build a small craft in order to try to keep him amused at home. It was 10 feet long and 5 feet wide at the widest part. The ribs were hoops bought locally, and these were covered with oilcloth. The boat was kept in the cart-house "as the colliers would destroy it in one week if it were left in the canal".

Skinner's journals give a vivid picture of change and unrest. There was poverty, illness, and drunkenness. Ardent churchgoers resented the increasing influence of the followers of John Wesley. The colliers were beginning to organise themselves and frequently threatened strike action.

A marriage or the discovery of a new coal seam provided a ready excuse for a carousal in the ale-houses. Skinner describes such an occasion in 1822 when a marriage followed by the finding of fresh veins of coal, led to a breach with many of his parishioners:

> "As there was a great shouting at the Coal Works, music, playing, singing etc. . . . I imagined at first that the whole populace participated in the glad tidings which set the bells aringing; but . . . the Proprietors of the Works were present at the Bailiff's, and had distributed money on account of the discovery of a fresh vein of coal, which promises to be very advantageous. This, I think, is indeed good news for the parish as it regards the future prospects of so many who depend on the prosperity of the mines."

This happened on a Wednesday. Celebrations continued for the rest of the week. On Friday Skinner records a visit he paid to one of his parishioners:

> "On going to West's wife I found her much worse, and making heavy complaints of the revelling in the parish, and saying that both her husband and her father had been so intoxicated during the whole time that it made her quite miserable. She had understood Smallcombe's son—one of the ringers—had so beaten his wife, she was

quite a mummy; her husband never comes near her in his sober moments, and her father has not been upstairs, she says, since she kept her bed."

Of Sunday evening he writes:

> "During the evening service the Church was crowded; and the singers, who have been in a state of constant intoxication since yesterday, being offended because I would not suffer them to chaunt the service after the First Lesson, put on their hats and left the Church. This is the most open breach of all religious decorum I have ever witnessed."

From the church his parishioners went to the Red Post public-house and there they decided that in future they would sing at the Methodist Meeting House, where the gallery would be enlarged to accommodate them.

Bell-ringing was a favourite pastime, and even the anniversary of a coronation was sufficient excuse for the ringers to abandon work, ring for the whole morning, and then to spend the rest of the day at an ale-house.

Industrial unrest in the coalfield led slowly to a measure of organisation among the colliers, and from 1820 onwards there were from time to time strikes over wages and alleged unfair dismissals. Skinner describes an interesting case at Camerton in 1830 in which he attempted some private mediation:

> "As I heard during the morning that the colliers had it in contemplation to strike work on account of their wages being about to be lowered, I spoke to one of the colliers and said if they had any just ground for complaint how much better it would be to send two or three whom they might depend on to state their grievances, and if there was any foundation for them I had no doubt but they would be attended to; but if they struck work it would only be taking bread out of their own mouth and the mouths of their families. The man said he thought with me on the subject, and that they would get no good by opposition. It is now six or seven years ago that there was a combination among the colliers, and the Camerton people struck with the rest and did not work for several days. I then went to them and gave them the same advice, which they would not listen to then, but afterwards told me they wished they had done so, as they were influenced by other people, having nothing really to complain of themselves."

It seems that Skinner's efforts were of little use. The miners were intimidated by the fact that the proprietors of the colliery had determined to dismiss any miners who spoke out against their actions and it was difficult to find any of them to go on a negotiating mission. Moreover a certain Mrs Jarrett who lived at the Manor House had great influence with the proprietors and complete power over the colliers, since she owned most of the cottages in which they lived as weekly tenants. No one was willing to risk her displeasure.

Unrest at this period spread from one part of the coalfield to another and groups of disaffected miners would journey from one village to another trying to gain support.

> "While writing in my study [writes Skinner] I saw numbers of men, at least fifty, cross the Park in front of my study window to go down to the pits at Camerton. I had learnt that the colliers meant to make a rise. Soon after, I saw this mob proceeding to our pits. I then walked to Clan Down, having heard that there had been a mob of the colliers assembled there yesterday, and that the Riot Act was read by Mr James, accompanied by other magistrates; indeed, they told me that some of the Camerton people had joined them and meant to be there again today."

These spontaneous risings seldom produced any useful results; no organised association or trades union, as such, existed at this time.

The Somersetshire Coal Canal and the Coal Canal Tramway continued to provide the sole means of long-distance transport for over fifty years. It linked the collieries with Reading by way of the Kennet and Avon Canal, and with the farmlands of the White Horse Vale by way of the Wiltshire and Berkshire Canal which branched north from the Kennet and Avon at Semington. Coal was sold retail in Wiltshire at little more than 25*s.* a ton. In the lounge of the Lansdowne Arms Hotel at Calne hangs a coal bill sent to the proprietor in 1829. He was charged 26*s.* 8*d.* per ton delivered. The first serious threat of competition came in 1854, when a railway was completed to link Radstock with Frome, though this still left the canal as the chief outlet for the Cam Valley.

In 1859 the coalfield suffered one of its worst pit disasters. Twelve men and boys were killed at Well Way Coal Works and were buried in a single grave which may still be seen in the churchyard at Midsomer Norton. It is marked by a slab of weathering Pennant sandstone which lies beneath a tree where the raised pathway of Church Lane abuts on the churchyard wall. This gravestone is already several inches below the level of the surrounding turf which is beginning to encroach, and part of the inscription, including the date, has now been lost through the flaking of the stone. It is to be hoped that this tablet may be preserved, for it has a unique interest. Few epitaphs can have included an allegation against some person, or persons, unknown—as this one does. The victims of the disaster died, it states, "by the snapping of the rope as they were on the point of descending into the pit", and "the rope was generally supposed to have been maliciously cut". Then follows a list of those who lost their lives, with their ages. The first three are named Keewill, ages forty-five, fifteen, and thirteen; then follow three Langfords, ages forty-five, fifteen, and thirteen—presumably two fathers with their sons. The youngest victim was only twelve years old. In those days there was no cage for the miners descending the pit. The men sat in a loop in the rope, each with a boy on his lap. A batch of six men and six boys would go down together. The Vicar of Midsomer Norton tells me that he knows an old man who well remembers his father talking about the disaster. He did not believe the rope had been maliciously cut, but that it had got caught in the cog-wheels and damaged. Strangely, the burial books at the church do not record the deaths or refer to the incident in any way.

Although young boys were used in the mines I have been unable to find a single record of women or girls being used for underground work in Somerset as they were in the North Country coalfields.

Coal mining continued to expand. In 1868, despite railway competition, the Coal Canal carried 140,112 tons of coal—40,000 tons more than forty-years earlier. But tolls had been cut and revenue was down to less than 11*d*. per ton carried. The margin between receipts and the costs of maintenance yielded little profit and the shareholders soon became only too willing for the railways to take over the traffic. Several proposals had already been put forward for further railways to serve the coalfield. One was for a Somerset Coal Railway from Wincanton to Timsbury; another suggested a rail link between Farrington Gurney and the mines at Nettlebridge. But Parliamentary sanction for these was not forthcoming. In 1873, however, the Bristol and North Somerset Railway completed its line between Bristol and Radstock, and the Somerset and Dorset Railway was building a line across the Mendips from Evercreech to Bath via Shepton Mallet and Radstock. Between Radstock and Bath the line follows the route of the old Somerset Coal Canal Tramway to Midford and the Coal Canal itself from Midford to the Avon Valley, though in places it takes a slightly straighter course to avoid the sharper curves.

It is possible to follow the course of the original canal in many places. It shows as a shallow grass-covered depression which winds along the hillside, following the contours. One of the easiest ways to approach it is from Bath. Follow the road to Timsbury for about four miles and turn left down a short steep hill at Longhouse. The canal passed over this road on a freestone bridge and it is easy to park one's car for a moment and to climb up to see the old canal course.

The Somerset and Dorset line was finally opened on July 20th, 1874, but the financial resources of the company were by then nearly exhausted and there was insufficient money to provide good rolling stock and adequate siding facilities. D. S. Barrie and C. R. Clinker, who have written a most useful history, *The Somerset and Dorset Railway*, describe how

> "Under-engined trains crawled hesitantly up the gruelling Mendip grades and went bucketing down the reverse slopes at hell-for-leather speeds to make up time, with the rattle trap coaches cavorting on the primitive, ill-ballasted track in a manner that 'shook' (in more senses than one) even such a hardened railwayist as the late E. L. Ahrons. Long delays and complex shunts were the order of the day at the crossing stations, between which trains moved spasmodically on the telegraphed instructions of a functionary known as the 'Crossing Agent', who from his office in Bath endeavoured to play a nightmare game of blind man's chess—with an odd piece or two inexplicably missing ('Left Evercreech Village two hours ago, not yet showed up at Shepton')."

After two years of struggle against financial odds and protracted negotiations, with the larger railway companies the Somerset and Dorset Railway was eventually leased to the Midland and London and South Western Companies jointly, as equal partners. Within a month of the confirmation of the agreement by Parliament there was a serious accident on the line between Wellow and Radstock during the holiday season, when an excursion train from Dorset filled with passengers ran head-on into a goods train and twelve people were killed.

Slowly conditions on the railway improved and coal was sent south to Dorset and by branch lines across the alluvial plains south of the Mendips to Highbridge and Burnham. Developments were continuous and coal output climbed steadily. There were probably about sixty collieries working at this period, quite apart from surface workings, and the tonnage produced from Somerset mines rose from 525,000 tons in 1870 to 757,000 tons in 1880 and continued to rise until 1910, by which time it had reached over 1,200,000 tons. There were striking social changes too. The miners organised themselves and tested their strength. In 1874 the Radstock Branch of the Amalgamated Association of Miners were faced by the colliery owners with the threat of a considerable wage reduction. After discussion among themselves, the miners decided to strike. A few days later the dispute was settled by arbitration, when the Association was recognised as a representative body.

The railways made it possible for the miners and their families to move about more freely. Occasional excursions—the equivalent of the modern "works outing"—were organised from the collieries and more frequently various groups connected with the Wesleyan chapels arranged visits by rail to Bristol, Bournemouth, or Weymouth.

The steady expansion of the coal trade in Somerset depended not only on the railways but on a better understanding of the disposition of the coal-bearing rocks. The first comprehensive survey of the coal resources in the county was made by Prestwich in 1871. He pieced together and classified existing information and gave us a clear statement of the rock sequence which forms the basis for all later classifications. This was not an easy task, for the coal measures have been much folded and faulted and are almost everywhere steeply tilted. In some places they are vertical or even inverted. Moreover their upturned edges are concealed over much of the coalfield by newer beds of Jurassic rocks—mainly lias—lying more or less horizontally. The Coal Measures are probably about 7,000 feet in thickness and the actual coal-bearing rocks are separated by about 2,000 feet of almost barren Pennant sandstone, a greenish-grey rock, occasionally iron-stained, which has been widely used in Somerset for building purposes. In some places the rock quarries easily to yield the thin even slabs which form the stone floors of so many of the old Mendip farmhouses and cottages. They are also seen as gravestones in most of the Mendip churchyards. Thicker blocks have been used to fashion gateposts and kerbstones, and for building walls and sometimes houses.

The full sequence of Coal Measure rocks is as follows:

Upper Coal Series	Radstock Series Barren Measures Farrington Series
Pennant Series	Mainly sandstone
Lower Coal Series	New Rock or Newbury Group Moorewood or Vobster Group

The Lower Coal Series is about 3,000 feet in thickness and contains about twenty-six workable seams. These rocks outcrop in the Nettlebridge Valley of the Mendip area proper but elsewhere are concealed. There is much very valuable coal in this area, but the rocks are highly contorted and the seams are often dislocated, so that mining which has always been difficult has for some years been uneconomic. The last mine to produce coal from the Lower Coal Seams was the New Rock Colliery. At one time there were pits at Edford, Vobster, Moorewood, Newbury, Mackintosh, and Mells. The coal from Vobster and Moorewood was excellent for coking and supplied local ironworks. Much of the smaller coal which was not suitable for carrying long distances was used locally because it was "excellent for the forge".

Early in the nineteenth century a flourishing trade in edged tools was established by Fussell's of Mells as a result of a visit by the founder to ironworks in the North of England. The Mells ironworks was started between Mells Green and Finger Lodge on land belonging to Colonel Horner, the lord of the Manor. The landlord, however, did not like the prospect of belching chimneys spoiling his view, so he made available some land in the valley on the way to Great Elm where water-power was available from the Mells River, and two works were established there to make shovels, bill-hooks, axes, and breast-ploughs. Smaller centres were also established in two small tributary valleys—at Chantry and Railford by the stream which flows through Whatley Bottom to Great Elm, and at Nunney on the Nunney Brook. Another works at Great Elm itself was used for making scythes and reaphooks from bar iron with steel insertions. At Chantry there were furnaces and some grinding and plating were done. Skinner writes in his journals that he "rose before seven, and walked to the Iron Works at Nunney to purchase a scythe for mowing the garden, as the best in the county, perhaps in the Kingdom, are made by the Fussell's". This was, I am sure, no exaggeration. Tools from this firm were sent all over the world and in 1860 gold medals were awarded at an exhibition in Vienna to James and Thomas Fussell for their reaphooks and scythes.

Edward Tylee in the *Somerset Year Book* for 1934 reports his conversations with people who remembered the mills where the men who did the grinding lay straddled across a sort of "horse" or table, like a vaulting-horse in a gymnasium, and wore a large apron of woollen material. The grindstones revolved at terrific speed just under one end of the table, and the scythe or other tool was held against it with both hands, so that the sparks flew upward in a shower. A new grindstone was about 6 feet in diameter, but they gradually wore down until they were only about 18 inches across, after which they were discarded. Some of the old grindstones, cut in half, may be seen as topping stones on some of the old walls in the village of Chantry.

Unfortunately, when more up-to-date methods were introduced

and rolling-mills were built to do away with hand-forging, Fussell's began to decline. A manager had to be brought in from the Midlands, and eventually—soon after 1880—the whole business was taken over by a Yorkshire firm and was later moved to Sheffield, where it continued to trade under the same name. Both the coal mines and the ironworks in and around Mells are finished. Today the chief industry—apart from farming—is quarrying for limestone.

The Upper Coal Series, not quite so thick as the Lower Coal Series, contains only about fourteen seams and is mined in the Norton–Radstock area. Roughly three-quarters of the output of the coalfield comes from the Farrington Series (the lower beds of the Upper Coal Series), which contains several seams over two feet in thickness, including one excellent seam known as "Big Vein" which has long proved fruitful. The Radstock Series was mined at Camerton, but the closing of this pit in 1950 brought to an end a long history of mining along the Cam Brook. The site of the mine is marked by a great grassy mound of pit waste which rises above the silent, wooded valley. At its base the pithead buildings are crumbling and derelict. Ivy, bramble and elder trees grow from the cream coloured lias stone of which they were built. The old railway which served the pit winds like a wide grassy bridle track towards the Avon valley; the metal rails are now gone though in earlier days the track was used by film companies to shoot railway sequences undisturbed. In Camerton the line ends at the station where the road to Radstock passes over it. The bricks of the bridge parapet are still discoloured where they were charred by the smoke from the engines. By the bridge there is a Great Western Railway notice in iron which warns you—"Notice is hereby given that this is a PRIVATE ROAD". Today, it is no more than a rough track which runs along by the overgrown iron railings to the station platform. The whole place is tumbledown and decaying. It is hard to realise that this valley once fed the busy Somerset Coal Canal. The coal industry is now dead and the miners who live in Camerton and Timsbury must travel to the active pits to the south.

The closing of individual mines has gone on since the first world war, when coal production from the Somerset Coalfield was over a million tons a year. The most rapid decline was between 1920 and 1930, though even then many of the miners showed great enterprise and a stubborn tenacity. In 1924 a group of fifty unemployed men put up a £5 share each and bought permission to start a drift mine at Marsh Lane, near Farrington Gurney. A year later, after they had obtained the necessary equipment, the Government, through the Ministry of Labour, granted the men unemployment pay while they developed their mine. This small venture succeeded and in the best years the mine produced an average of about 120 tons of coal a week. In 1949 the drift was closed by the National Coal Board because working was uneconomic. The men found employment in neighbouring pits and the equipment was used elsewhere.

The decline of the Somerset Coalfield has been slow but continuous. In 1920 the pits employed 7,380 miners; in 1962 they employed 1,760 men, only 643 of whom were face workers. In 1970 the mines employed 635 men of whom about 120 were face workers.

Since 1960 five collieries have closed down. These include Braysdown (1963), Radstock (1964), Old Mills (1967), Norton Hill (1967) and New Rock (1968). Only two are left—Kilmersdon and Writhlington—and these are now worked as a single unit. The men use the Kilmersdon Shaft, but the Writhlington Shaft is still used to bring coal to the surface. The problems are great. Although the coal seams are thick enough for coal cutting machines to be used, they are distorted and seldom offer an economic length. New roads have continually to be driven. Moreover the present coal faces are in the Faringdon Series near the edge of the coal basin, 500 yards deep and two miles from the pit bottom. Although the large coal can be used locally for domestic purposes, 80 per cent of the output is untreated "raw small", suitable only for industrial purposes. Some goes to the zinc-smelting plant at Avonmouth, but four-fifths is absorbed by the power station at Portishead on the Severn. If this were to become an oil-burning station the last Somerset coal mine might well be doomed, together with the railway tracks which link the mines to the main railway from Frome and Bath to Bristol.

Fortunately, the decline of the coalfield was foreseen and the problems of redundancy and redeployment have been handled locally and with understanding. Today the average age of the colliery employees is about 54 and there is virtually no local recruitment or training. The workers who have left mining have been able to buy their houses and Norton Hill Colliery has been sold "for industrial purposes". Displaced labour has been absorbed by other industries. The enormous expansion of the printing works at Paulton and Midsomer Norton, where a great deal of colour printing is done for trade catalogues and newspaper supplements, has helped to some extent. So has a shoe factory at Midsomer Norton, though these industries depend largely on female labour. Fortunately there are other firms which demand male workers. Some serve the farming areas around, providing prefabricated buildings of many kinds. There are wagon works, engineering works and companies engaged in the foundry trade. Many workers travel as far as Bath by car to their employment. Although changes have been great, the area has nevertheless maintained a healthy balance between farming and industry.

BIBLIOGRAPHY

Great Church Towers of England, F. J. Allen, 1932.
Old Mendip, R. Atthill, 1964.
The Somerset and Dorset Railway, R. Atthill, 1967.
The Netherworld of Mendip, E. A. Baker and H. E. Balch.
The Mendip Caves, H. E. Balch.
The Somerset and Dorset Railway, D. S. Barrie and C. R. Clinker, 1948.
A General View of the Agriculture of the County of Somerset, John Billingsley, 1797.
Proceedings of the Bristol Naturalists' Society.
Proceedings of the University of Bristol Spelæological Society.
The Mesolithic Age in Britain, J. G. A. Clark, 1932.
Bristol and Somerset Coalfield, Regional Survey Report, 1946.
Plan for Coal: The National Coal Board's Proposals, 1950.
History of Somerset, J. Collinson, 1791.
A Mendip Valley, T. Compton, 1893.
Journal of a Somerset Rector: John Skinner, Antiquary, (ed.) H. Coombs and A. N. Bax, 1930.
The Royal Forests of England, J. C. Cox, 1905.
Sedgemoor and the Bloody Assizes, C. D. Curtis, 1930.
Wells, P. Dearmer, 1898.
The Archæology of Somerset, D. P. Dobson, 1931.
History of Shepton Mallet, J. E. Farbrother, 1859.
The Mines of Mendip, J. W. Gough, 1930.
Mendip Mining Laws and Forest Bounds, J. W. Gough, 1931.
The Preparations in Somerset against the Spanish Armada, E. Green, 1888.
The Diary of a West Country Physician, (ed.) E. Hobhouse, 1934.
Wells and Glastonbury, T. S. Holmes, 1908.
The History of the Parish and Manor of Wookey, T. S. Holmes.
Highways and Byways in Somerset, E. Hutton, 1919.
History of Kilmersdon, Lord Hylton
The Bristol Waterworks Company, F. C. Jones, 1946.
Hannah More, M. G. Jones, 1952.
A Corner of Arcady, F. A. Knight, 1904.
The Heart of Mendip, F. A. Knight, 1915.
A History of Sidcot School, F. A. Knight, 1908.
The Seaboard of Mendip, F. A. Knight, 1902.
Wild Flowers of the Chalk and Limestone, J. E. Lousley, 1950.
The Story of Wells Cathedral, R. Malden, 1934.
Somerset, A. Mee, 1948.

Old Stone Crosses of Somerset, Pooley, 1877.
Life and Correspondence of Hannah More, W. Roberts, 1834.
Mendip Annals (Journal of Martha More), (ed.) A. Roberts.
Two Men o' Mendip, W. Raymond.
A Geological Excursion Handbook for the Bristol District, S. H. Reynolds, 1912.
Delineations of the North-Western Division of the County of Somerset, J. Rutter, 1829.
Proceedings of the Somerset Archæological Society.
Somerset Year Books.
Life of Hannah More, H. Thompson, 1838.
History of the Somerset Carthusians, E. M. Thompson, 1895.
Victoria County History of Somerset.
Rambles in Somerset, G. W. and S. H. Wade, 1923.
The Bristol Flora, J. W. White, 1912.
Churches of Somerset, A. K. Wickham, 1952.
Journals and Correspondence of the Rev. T. S. Whalley, H. Wickham, 1863.

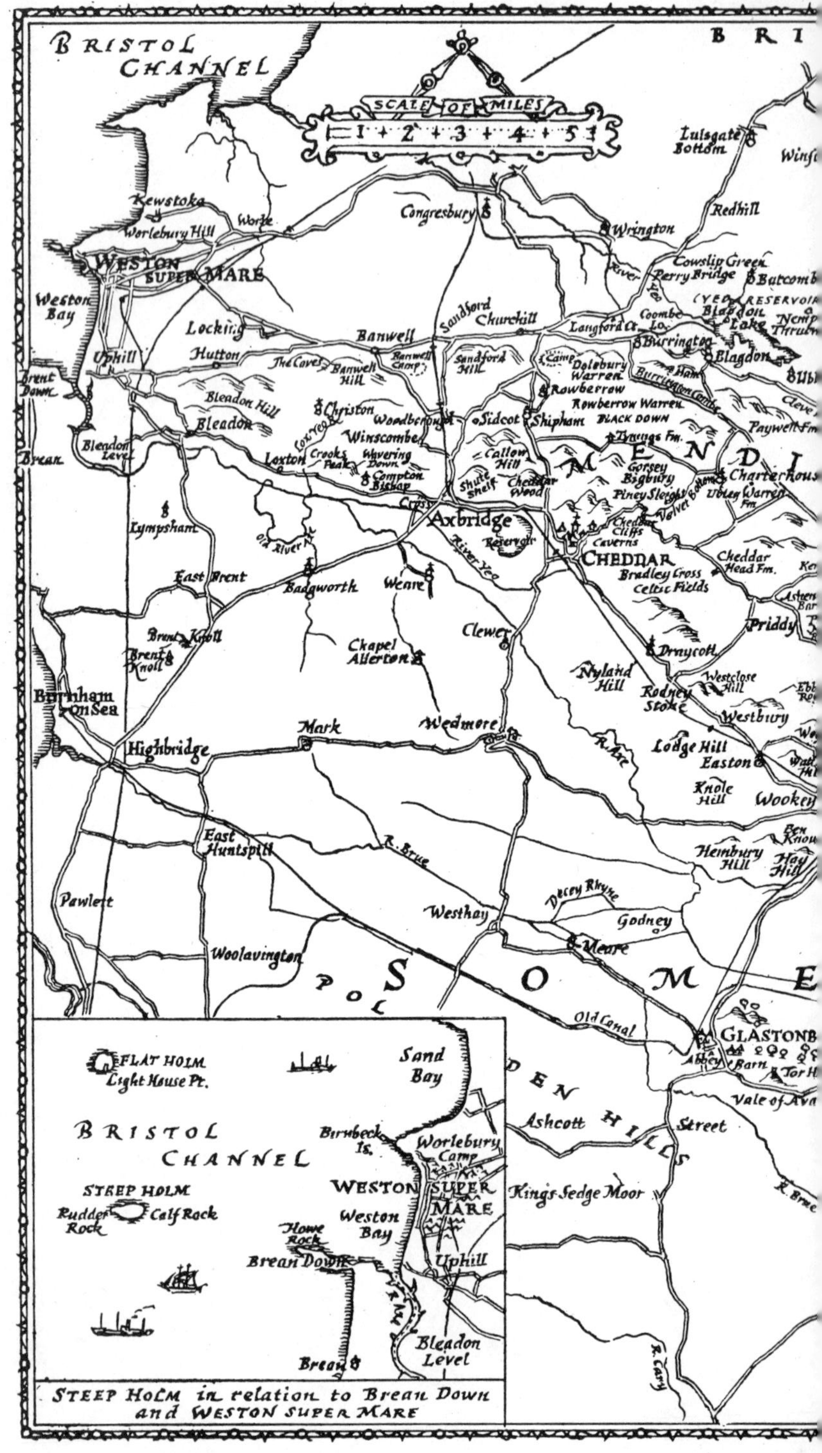

BRISTOL CHANNEL
SCALE OF MILES
1 2 3 4 5
Kewstoke
Worlebury Hill
Worle
WESTON SUPER MARE
Weston Bay
Locking
Hutton
Uphill
Brent Down
Brean
Bleadon Level
Bleadon Hill
Bleadon
Congresbury
Wrington
Banwell
Sandford
Churchill
Banwell Camp
Banwell Hill
The Caves
Sandford Hill
Christon
Woodborough
Winscombe
Loxton
Crooks Peak
Wavering Down
Compton Bishop
Cross
Axbridge
Reservoir
River Yeo
Old River Axe
Lympsham
East Brent
Badgworth
Weare
Brent Knoll
Chapel Allerton
Clewer
Burnham on Sea
Highbridge
Mark
Wedmore
East Huntspill
R. Brue
Pawlett
Westhay
Godney
Meare
Woolavington
Old Canal
Sidcot
Shipham
Callow Hill
Shute Shelf
Cheddar Wood
Camp
Dolebury Warren
Rowberrow
Rowberrow Warren
BLACK DOWN
Tynings Fm.
MENDI
Gorsey Bigbury
Piney Sleight
Velvet Bottom
Charterhouse
Ubley Warren Fm.
Cheddar Cliffs
Caverns
CHEDDAR
Bradley Cross
Celtic Fields
Cheddar Head Fm.
Priddy
Draycott
Nyland Hill
Rodney Stoke
Westclose Hill
Westbury
R. Axe
Lodge Hill
Easton
Knole Hill
Wookey
Ben Knoll
Hembury Hill
Hay Hill
Lulsgate Bottom
Redhill
Cowslip Green
Perry Bridge
Butcombe
River Yeo
YEO RESERVOIR
Blagdon Lake
Coombe Lo.
Langford
Burrington
Blagdon
Ham
Burrington Combe
Paywell Fm
Decoy Rhyne
SOME
GLASTONB
Abbey
Barn
Tor H
Vale of Ava
POL DEN HILLS
Ashcott
Street
King's Sedge Moor
R. Brue
R. Cary
FLAT HOLM
Light House Pt.
Sand Bay
BRISTOL CHANNEL
Birnbeck Is.
Worlebury Camp
WESTON SUPER MARE
STEEP HOLM
Rudder Rock
Calf Rock
Weston Bay
Howe Rock
Brean Down
Uphill
R. Axe
Bleadon Level
Brean
STEEP HOLM in relation to Brean Down and WESTON SUPER MARE

SKETCH MAP OF
THE
MENDIPS
BATH
R. Chew
Chew Magna
Chew Stoke
Marksbury
English Combe
Monkton Combe
Midford
Stowey
Timsbury
Cam Brook
Dunkerton
Radford
Camerton
Wellow
Wellow Brook
West Harptree
Paulton
Richmont Castle
East Harptree
Chew Reservoir
Farrington Gurney
Rush Hill
Litton
Smitham Hill
Colliery
Midsomer Norton
Radstock
Colliery
Writhlington
Norton St Philip
Park
Ston Easton
Norton Hill Colliery
Haydon Hill
Chewton Mendip
Celtic Fields
Eaker Hill
Kilmersdon
Ammerdown Park
Chilcompton
Old Down
Emborough
Downside Abbey
Babington
Buckland Dinham
Inn
Marchants Hill
Green Ore
Blackers Hill
Colliery
Stratton on the Fosse
Colliery
Vobster
Mells
FROME
Tedbury Camp
Binegar
Gurney Slade
Holcombe
Coleford
Whitnell Corner
Pen Hill
Ashwick
Nettlebridge
Mells R.
Mells Park
Whatley
West Horrington
Maesbury Ring
Oakhill
Leigh upon Mendip
Chantry
East Horrington
Stoke Lane
Vallis Vale
Lyatt
Burnthouse Fm
Beacon Hill
Downhead
Dinder Wood
Dinder
Croscombe
Cranmore Tower
Nunney
Marston Bigot
Dulcote Hill
Church Hill
Ham Wood
SHEPTON MALLET
Dean
East Cranmore
Leighton
Worminster Sleight
Knole Hill
Bowlish
Doulting
West Cranmore
Gannards Grave
Wanstrow
Witham Friary
R S E T
A. E. TAYLOR

INDEX

INDEX